VINTAGE STYLE

THIS IS A CARLTON BOOK

Published in 2011 by Carlton Books Limited
20 Mortimer Street
London W1T 3JW

10 9 8 7 6 5 4 3 2 1

A CIP catalogue record for this book is available from
the British Library.

ISBN  978 1 84732 776 5

Senior Executive Editor: Lisa Dyer
Managing Art Director: Lucy Coley
Designers: Penny Stock and Barbara Zuñiga
Copy Editors: Jane Donovan and Lara Maiklem
Picture Researcher: Jenny Meredith
Production Manager: Maria Petalidou

Printed in Dubai

OVERLEAF: Singer-songwriter Kate Bush, early
1980s, was known for her theatrical costume
changes and choreography as well as her
musical talents.

RIGHT: Twiggy (Lesley Hornby), 1967.
Her androgynous looks, skinny figure
and huge eyes made Twiggy an icon of
Swinging Sixties London.

# VINTAGE STYLE

ICONIC FASHION LOOKS AND HOW TO GET THEM

SARAH KENNEDY

**CARLTON**
BOOKS

# Contents

# Introduction

Vintage style is a constantly revolving door through which it is possible to peek back in time and luxuriate in the sheer glamour of the past. The power to captivate others comes from a combination of charisma and radiance, and on the following pages we feature women whose unique personal style has captured hearts and imaginations for decades. From Louise Brooks to Kate Bush, this is a celebration not simply of each icon, but also of the creative geniuses behind their classic looks.

Choosing the entries for this book was an inspirational experience. It is important to remember that behind the style and glamour, beat the hearts of some incredible and fascinating women. Audrey Hepburn, for example, was so much more than a fashion icon – for the last five years of her life she devoted her time to UNICEF and the Audrey Hepburn Children's Fund. Screen goddess Marilyn Monroe tragically failed to overcome the demons of a harsh upbringing, while Kate Bush, Diana Ross, Cindy Crawford and Debbie Harry continue to inspire today. Every woman in this book represents a moment in time for the female spirit, and each one is beloved for her talent and style.

Fashion has played a key part in creating some, but not all, of these iconic women. Hepburn's incredible Ingénue look would not have been possible without the magnificent designs of Hubert de Givenchy, but Jackie O's classic First Lady style was so cool it rendered the labels she wore almost meaningless. Marlene Dietrich's visual statement

FAR LEFT and LEFT: Audrey Hepburn, 1954 and Debbie Harry, 1978: two icons of their times who developed fun, gorgeous personal styles that have inspired millions. Hepburn's tidy yet playful look offered the perfect antidote to the 1950s va-va-voom silhouette. The star's boyish figure was cleverly enhanced by well-cut clothing emphasizing her wrists, shoulders and ankles. Harry brought edgy, New York riches to the dirty old rags of punk. An innate sexiness added a provocative element to Harry's sometimes-space-age looks.

came from drama and difference, while Wallis Simpson's signature was slender severity. Hair, make-up, the angle of a hat and the height of a heel can all help to create a sensational style, and this was an instinctive knowledge shared by both Dietrich and Simpson. Chic requires conviction; it cannot simply be worn.

Some style icons had professional help achieving the looks that made them great. Twiggy and Jean Shrimpton owe much to David Bailey and Barry Lategan, two of the greatest photographers of the 1960s, and Debbie Harry might not have made such an impact without the help of designer Stephen Sprouse. The inbuilt ability to define and accentuate nature's gifts is also undeniable. Brigitte Bardot enjoyed only

a modicum of success when she adhered to the 1950s beauty blueprint of artificial curls and red lips. But when she eventually grew out and bleached her hair and swapped ruby lips for a pale pout, everything changed for her, and the original "Bombshell" was born.

While it may seem odd to feature Kate Bush alongside Grace Kelly, her style influence is equally strong. Kate Bush is one of several vintage icons, including Jean Shrimpton, Talitha Getty and Grace Slick, whose most memorable moments in style are perennial, popping up on catwalks every few seasons. What pulls all of these women together, however, is the "it" factor, that special combination of style, substance and individuality from which true icons are born.

# *Making vintage work for you*

Imagine looking so good that the whole world is hanging on your every move. Through the clothes we choose, our personalities shine. Whether we are dressed by the world's most sought-after stylists or pick out our own clothes in front of a cramped bedroom mirror, the process is essentially the same. Women have been stealing style inspiration from each other for generations, and adapting fashions to suit their individual figures and tastes. We all admire a beautifully dressed runway model or star on the red carpet, and often forget that their glamour and style can be more easily achieved than we think. With the right knowledge and some easy planning, getting a gorgeous, individual look is simple.

LEFT: A classic T-shaped body gave Dietrich carte blanche when it came to adapting menswear with feminine touches. Shoulder pads enhanced her natural shape, adding drama to her look and emphasizing the 1930s most fashionable body silhouette. Soft fabrics and a narrow-belted waist ensure the look featured here was all woman.

OPPOSITE: The Duchess of Windsor capitalized on her boyish shape with slender dresses cut to enhance her elegant figure and show off a super-flat stomach. Indecently expensive, one-off jewellery pieces and the odd scarf were her only adornments. The effect was an understated sexiness designed to score points off every other woman in the room.

Captivating, cool and charismatic, we all dream our clothes will convey at least one of these magical qualities. To help you achieve a unique sense of personal style, this book guides you through the best vintage looks of the twentieth century, and includes essential shopping tips and beauty advice. From Louise Brooks to Audrey Hepburn, Molly Ringwald to Debbie Harry, there is a vintage look to suit just about everyone.

Vintage shopping – rummaging through gently used clothing, shoes and accessories – can give you the chance to explore not only your own personal fantasies, but also to create a unique day-to-day style. Knowing what looks good and pursuing items that suit you is a life-enhancing and positive process. This book will help you navigate the crammed rails, overflowing boxes and mountainous piles of clothes in shops and at clothing fairs to find the gems that are exactly right for you. One of the joys of shopping for vintage is the elusive element of surprise. Discovering a vintage evening dress that fits well always feels far more rewarding than walking into a conventional store and pulling something straight off the rail that is identical to the one next to it. The vintage shopping experience is even more rewarding when you have a vague idea of what you are looking for. Cementing a look in your head, with a rough idea of all the shapes, colours, fabrics, heel heights and accessories you might need, will improve buying decisions and enhance the fun of the hunt.

Some of fashion's most iconic looks can also be surprisingly versatile. Audrey Hepburn created an impeccable designer-inspired look, yet her signature style looks surprisingly good on all body shapes. Although she was petite, her covered-up sexiness revealed gorgeous wrists, calves, ankles, shoulders and neck, making Hepburn's look one of the most wearable. The same is true of the classic French style of Françoise Hardy – clean lines and classic pieces suit any woman looking for an easy, everyday look. Hardy's relaxed, sexy appeal came from its simplicity. A knee-length boot, a skirt at just the right length or a snugly fitting matelot sweater can look good on absolutely anyone.

Most twentieth-century fashions were designed with the real female physique in mind (as opposed to the model's figure). Style icons in the 1950s concentrated on enhancing an hourglass. Curvaceous figures suit the shaping of the Goddess, Ingénue, Ice Princess and American Classic looks. For a more contemporary take, curvy girls also look gorgeous in the flowing but fitted dresses and striking colours of Kate Bush's Free Spirit or the Boho Contessa.

Willowy figures suit the wistful shapes of the 1930s Tea Dancer and the masculine glamour of the Femuline look. The key to successfully sporting menswear lies in the cut of the garments and the right accessories. Each chapter explains the correct shaping, styling, cut and colour to best create an authentic look or simply to steal elements of the style of one of the great beauties of all time. The differences within each genre are isolated to make shopping, trying on and selecting key pieces a more fulfilling process. A wardrobe that segues seamlessly together is far easier and more fun to wear, compared with a hotchpotch of gorgeous but mismatched finds.

Lovers of more classical styling can feel inspired by the British Classic look of Jean Shrimpton or Grace Kelly's Ice Princess. Classic should never mean boring; instead it should signify an easy, quality way of dressing. Knowing the names and labels that are relevant in the history of fashion can greatly enhance your chances of creating an authentically glamorous look, so each chapter reveals the best vintage brands and the key labels to hunt for.

Many modern style icons, including Kate Moss, Chloë Sevigny and Lily Allen, express their quirky cool through a love of vintage clothing. It is not unusual to see the rich and famous clad in elements of Molly Ringwald's ubiquitous 1980s look or Diana Ross's diva-esque styling. Vintage looks offer the chance to pay tribute to an icon, while expressing a personal attitude and personality. Emulating Debbie Harry or Joan Jett might not work 24 hours a day, but what better way to address your inner punkette?

Celebrity vintage fans are great arbiters of cool and often use hair and make-up to create a successful look, giving vintage styling a modern twist. For example, the singer Duffy's slightly less-full bouffant is the perfect modern take on Bardot's long beehive. Deep, dark lips and full curls add modern flavour to Florence Welch's favourite 1930s looks, while Charlize Theron is still remembered for her 1920s-inspired, slicked-down bob and pin curls. Stealing beauty looks from back in time and combining them with modern products and styling makes for even more individual vintage looks. Short hair is also incredibly versatile for vintage styling – sleek it down into a Twiggy or Brooks-style crop, add waves for a Wallis Simpson mood or mess it up and go a bit Molly Ringwald.

Making vintage fashion work for you is all about finding the look that best suits you and your lifestyle. By devoting a bit of time and effort to the search, you can find a unique look of your own.

RIGHT: Grace Kelly in a still from *Rear Window*. Kelly demonstrates two styles her perfect, hourglass figure helped make famous. The deep "V" back flatters and elongates the neckline and led to girls wearing cardigans back to front in an effort to mimic Kelly's look. The dark-coloured, close-fitting top half of the dress gave the illusion of a very slender waist.

# What's your style?

Find your shape and your favourite style below, then match them up with the vintage look that best suits you in the chart opposite.

**SHAPES:**

Boyish – slender with narrow shoulders and hips.
T-shape – flat body with broad shoulders.
Curvy – well-rounded and shapely.
Hourglass – good proportioned body with a neat waist.
Pear-shaped – wide through the hips.
Apple – rounded in the middle.
Voluptuous – large breasts.

**STYLES:**

Fashionist – trendy and fashionable.
Classic – simple lines and shapes.
Casual – chic but comfortable.
Quirky – a sense of fashion fun.
Sexy – sensual with the body shape showing.
Feminine – womanly chic.

| VINTAGE ICON | YOUR SHAPE | YOUR STYLE |
|---|---|---|
| Louise Brooks | Boyish, hourglass, apple | Fashionist, classic |
| Jean Harlow | T-shape, boyish, voluptuous | Classic, feminine, fashionist |
| Marlene Dietrich | Hourglass, boyish, T-shape, pear | Masculine, classic |
| Wallis Simpson | Boyish, T-shape, hourglass | Feminine, sexy, classic |
| The Mitford Sisters | Pear, curvy, boyish, apple, pear | Quirky, fashionist |
| Marilyn Monroe | Voluptuous, curvy, pear | Feminine, sexy |
| Audrey Hepburn | T- shape, curvy, pear | Feminine, quirky, fashionist |
| Grace Kelly | Boyish, hourglass | Classic, feminine |
| Elizabeth Taylor | Voluptuous, curvy, pear, hourglass | Feminine, sexy, classic |
| Jackie O | Boyish, hourglass, pear, T- shape | Classic, casual |
| Brigitte Bardot | Curvy, pear, hourglass | Feminine, sexy, casual |
| Twiggy | Boyish, hourglass, T- shape | Quirky, classic |
| Jean Shrimpton | Boyish, pear, T-shape | Fashionist, classic |
| Marianne Faithfull | Boyish, apple, hourglass, pear | Fashionist |
| Talitha Getty | Apple, pear, curvy, voluptuous | Sexy, fashionist |
| Françoise Hardy | Boyish, T-shape, curvy, hourglass | Classic, fashionist |
| Bianca Jagger | Pear, hourglass, T-shape | Fashionist, quirky, sexy |
| Grace Slick | Hourglass, voluptuous, pear | Casual, fashionist |
| Joan Jett | Boyish, T-shape, hourglass | Quirky, casual |
| Debbie Harry | Pear, apple, hourglass | Quirky, fashionist, sexy |
| Lauren Hutton | Boyish, T-shape, curvy, pear | Classic, fashionist |
| Diana Ross | Hourglass, curvy, voluptuous, pear | Feminine, sexy |
| Kate Bush | Hourglass, voluptuous, T-shape | Quirky, sexy |
| Molly Ringwald | Apple, curvy, boyish, voluptuous | Fashionist, quirky, casual |
| Cindy Crawford | T-shape, boyish, hourglass, voluptuous | Sexy, fashionist, classic |

# Louise Brooks: Flapper

The most-copied party look of all time dates back to the Roaring Twenties. Flapper style is sleek, sexy and, most of all, easy to move in. F Scott Fitzgerald first coined the phrase in *Flappers and Philosophers*, a collection of short stories published in 1920. In 1926, American silent-movie star Louise Brooks starred as a jazz-age flapper in the comedy drama *A Social Celebrity* and also *Love 'Em and Leave 'Em*, a tale of two sisters set in a department store, where she made the look her own. The word "flapper" has several origins. In this context it is thought to have emerged from the trend among wealthy American college girls for wearing unfastened rubber galoshes over their shoes with the tops left "flapping" around on post-World War I university campuses.

Louise Brooks was a dancer at heart. Aged just 17, she travelled to London to perform at the Café De Paris and Europe fell in love with her. Thanks to her originality and fast, fluid grace she became a huge star in France. Brooks' trademark blunt bob was the decade's most coveted hairstyle even though she grew it out and wore her hair slicked to the side as her career progressed. Brooks' beauty was legendary yet somehow she never quite managed to make the right career or marriage choices. In between starring roles she worked as a sales assistant at Saks Fifth Avenue in New York and later in life, dreamt of becoming a respected writer.

Sadly, Flapper style has been watered down through the decades. All too often, it's heartbreaking to see fancy dressers clad in long, droopy, drop-waist dresses with low-heeled shoes, their hair a mess. Vintage fans understand the true nature of the

**Flapper Lookalikes**
Theda Bara
Clara Bow
Mary Astor
Erin O'Connor
Carey Mulligan

OPPOSITE: Louise Brooks pictured against a fashionable butterfly motif screen in 1928 by Paramount photographer Eugene Richee.

LEFT: British model Erin O'Connor re-vamps the classic Flapper bob with modern make-up in 2004.

ABOVE: Actress Carey Mulligan's dainty 1920s-style features make her a perfect Daisy Buchanan from *The Great Gatsby*.

> **"***A well-dressed woman, even though her purse is painfully empty, can conquer the world.***"**
>
> *Louise Brooks*

### Key Looks

- Shift dresses, on or above the knee
- High Mary Jane heels with button fastenings
- Light-coloured silk stockings held up with garters (visible when dancing!)
- Shimmering or shiny textured silk and rayon for evening
- Fringing, beading and heavy-edged weighted dresses (to make them hang straight)
- Shawl-collar, wraparound coats or velvet opera coats
- Narrow, sparkly scarves worn cravat-style or around the head, secured at the side
- Toques with huge faux flowers or beaded motifs attached
- Beaded headdresses
- Long ropes (*sautoires*) of pearls or glass beads
- Enormous tortoiseshell bangles, layered up each arm
- Close-fitting, pulled-down, bell-shaped cloche hats to keep hair in place
- Tennis sweater and knee-length white kilt for daywear
- Cigarette holders
- Large, sparkly chandelier-style earrings

look: dresses worn short with necklines daringly elongated by low-cut fronts and backs, heels high and hair sleek. Nothing was shapeless.

During World War I, Jeanne Lanvin designed a simple shift for eveningwear, a garment women loved for its easy-to-wear spirit and sobriety. When war ended in 1918, Lanvin's fashion house in Paris continued to produce the same style, adding beads and decorative details, and so the flapper dress was born. Meanwhile, Gabrielle "Coco" Chanel's obsession with skinny, boy-like figures formed the silhouette for the emerging Flapper trend. The "garçonne" shape, fundamental to Chanel and Jean Patou's sporty designs, was seized upon by the fashionable young elite. They loved the edgy, new style which required only simple, stretchy underwear after the constrictions of the corset.

Jean Patou designed sporting ensembles featuring his coveted logo for athletic females, including the brilliant Suzanne Lenglen. She won the coveted Wimbledon Women's title seven times clad in Patou's creations, including a knee-length silk pleated skirt and a sleeveless sweater with an orange headband. Young women everywhere adored and copied her look, particularly the headband. Flappers, meanwhile, wore the toque, a tight-fitting scarf or headband with a flower or Art Deco motif attached.

Flappers were essentially creatures of the night. Their stick-straight dresses were adorned with eye-catching fringing, sequins and rows of beads that jumped around as they danced. Sleeveless and also knee revealing, such garments were racy in the extreme, made even sexier with the addition of high heels.

The work of other great designers of the time such as the Parisian-based Brit Edward Molyneux was also highly influential. Captain Molyneux was a former army officer and a friend of the English playwright and director Noël Coward. His designs consisted of simple outlines in luxurious fabrics such as exotic but muted printed satins, and navy and black velvet. The evening slip dresses he created for society clientele in Paris between 1919–25 undoubtedly influenced Flapper style, but were longer in length and built for a decorous wearer rather than the one flinging herself around the dance floor. Molyneux's use of revealing necklines and backs, of satins covered in rickrack or expensive lace, and beaded detailing, was much-copied by high-street department stores on both sides of the Atlantic.

# Style Guide

**The Palette:** Black, beige, brown and white mixed with Art Deco brights in violet, jade and metallics.

**Key Designers:** Coco Chanel, Callot Soeurs, Jeanne Lanvin, Captain Edward Molyneux, Jean Patou, Paul Poiret

**Silhouette and Cut:** A vertical, narrow shape is crucial for an authentic Flapper look, with straight, up-and-down shift-style dresses, on or above the knee. Bare arms (but for a few clunky bangles or a mass of thin bracelets) balance the look. In contrast, coats were full and voluminous; ankle-length and wrap-over for evening, double-breasted for day.

## Dresses

Characterized by simple vest-shaped necklines dropping down into a shift. Variations included square necklines and layered fabrics. Fur, velvet and quilted satin evening looks contrasted with heavy wool and tweed for day.

*Shop vintage for:* Rayon, the new artificial silk at the time, with netting or lace overlaid on top. Other authentic Flapper details include lace or net panels across a deep, daring V-shaped back or scoop neckline and sheer chiffon panels over Dupion silk. Drop waists gradually arrived by the mid to late 1920s, with pleated, gathered or simply swingy skirts, but are not truly Flapper, so look for short versions or take up the hems; you will also find scallop and handkerchief hemlines. Quality-wise, there is something charming about an old dress, even if it has a few holes or mends. Nasty stains are harder to cover up, but fragile-looking sparkles can be extremely becoming.

### Style Tips

- The look relies on a small head shape with emphasis on the eyes and lips.

- Keep dresses short to avoid looking frumpy.

- A black crochet shawl works well as a wrap.

- Small, beaded bags are the perfect accompaniment.

- Bare arms and bangles make a sexy flapper look – cleavage does not!

RIGHT: Evening dresses from Jeanne Lanvin, depicted in a 1920 advertisement from *Le Bon Ton*. At the time Lanvin's creations were showing at Mercie McHardy in London's Oxford Street. Her loose chemise-style flapper dresses allowed for more curve in the body than other narrow, binding styles of the time.

## Coats and Wraps

The three-quarter-length jacket was big fashion news. Boxy, with slim-line lapels and single- or double-breasted, the jackets were worn by day with knee-length, stretchy-knit skirts or longer sporting kilts and thrown over evening dresses to hop from car to nightclub door. For evening, volume was crucial (big enough to keep a party girl warm), as were rich, luxurious fabrics and colours. Velvet and fur, including fox and mink, became fashionable. Coats were elongated for evening, for a rich, romantic look.

*Shop vintage for:* Opera coats and wraps in velvet. In 1922, the designer Jeanne Lanvin created a kimono-style coat for a French socialite fashioned from black taffeta with silver-grey silk embroidery and fur edging. Look for copies with large embroidered motifs mimicking Elsa Schiaparelli's famous Dalí "moon and stars" designs. Vintage dressing gowns will do nicely, too. A fur wrap was the height of style and luxury, and flappers loved fox and mink stoles complete with heads and eyes still attached. Fur wraps in the 1920s were longer and less boxy than later versions. A feather boa makes the perfect substitute; no flapper should be without one.

## Knitwear

Coco Chanel developed a new fabric of close-knitted yarn that stretched and clung to the body. First formulated to enable girls to flit around the beach and swim in comfort, the fabric quickly caught on for daywear. Chanel began making long, lean cardigans, twinsets, skirts and dresses in the same fabric for her boutiques in Deauville and Paris. Flappers borrowed sweaters from male friends and not for the last time did the large, man-size V-neck sweater or cardigan become fashionable.

## Accessories

Elaborate accessories such as chandelier earrings, huge cocktail rings and upper-arm bracelets were decorously arranged to accent the sleek Flapper silhouette. Around this time, costume jewellery became an end in itself instead of the only jewels you could afford. Paste or diamanté were fake versions of precious stones and diamonds, made from glass mounted on silver or gold plate. Sometimes foil-backed for extra sparkle, diamanté was much coveted during the nineteenth century and by 1920, it was perfectly acceptable to wear fake without being considered poor or cheap.

*Shop vintage for:* Paste earrings in chandelier styles – take time to source highly collectable silver versions. Also worth collecting are early examples of Bakelite plastic in the form of bangles and beads in typical 1920s blacks, creams and browns. Rare bone or horn was also used for bangles and hair accessories, including the precious "tortoiseshell". No longer allowed to be farmed, genuine tortoiseshell and horn accessories are highly collectable.

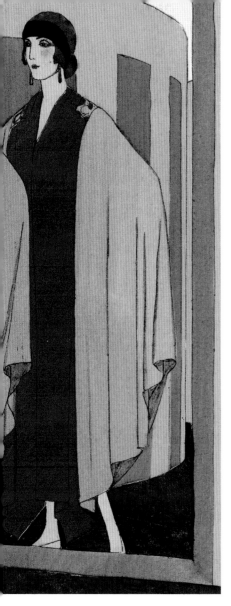

## Hosiery

Summer flappers shocked the world with their bare legs, but they generally wore highly visible sheer silk stockings, fastened just above the knee with a lace-adorned garter.

ABOVE: A 1920s opera-goer clad in full-length Paul Poiret cape with contrasting embroidery detail. Opera enjoyed a re-birth in popularity after the First World War as a glamorous form of evening entertainment.

ABOVE RIGHT: *Boardwalk Empire*, the 2010 television series based on 1920s Atlantic City and starring Steve Buscemi, is meticulously accurate in it's historic styling – beaded evening gowns and shawls, elaborate embroidery, ropes of pearls, floral toques and silk stockings.

RIGHT: A 1927 felt cloche hat with plenty of room on the long, domed crown for decoration. The shape emphasized the neat, rounded profile so fashionable in the 1920s.

## Hats

As well as knitted everyday versions of the cloche hat, close-fitting beaded caps were worn in the evening. A rounded head shape was key to balance out the simple dress style although toques with attached corsages or big, beaded butterflies were also popular. Butterfly imagery appeared on fabrics and in patterns; also as a beaded or embroidered motif. Louise Brooks was famously captured against a background of giant butterfly motifs (*see page* 12).

# Beauty Guide

One of Louise Brooks most iconic features was her short geometric bob with a fringe. The hairstyle started in 1915 with the debut of the Castle bob, named after the celebrated ballroom dancer Irene Castle. She cut her hair short, from just under the ear, for convenience, little knowing she would trigger a revolution in twentieth-century hair fashion. The bob would be the first indication of things to come – the rage for short hair. Bluntly cut, level with the bottom of the ears all around the head, bobs were worn with bangs or hair brushed off the forehead. It was a simple look but a drastic departure from the long-haired feminine looks created by Gibson and Marcel. The length just covered the ears to lie at the cheekbone and was a look that Vidal Sassoon revived in the 1960s. Then, and today, it has many variations and can be angled in any direction, worn straight or wavy, but the defining feature is the clear clean line at the ends of the hair.

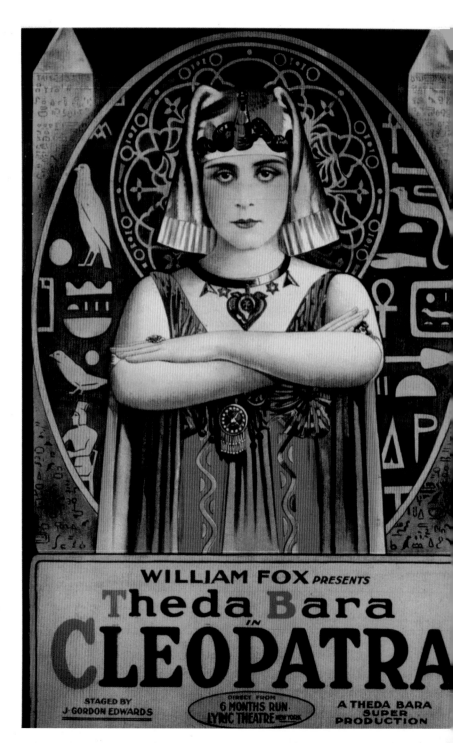

RIGHT: Theda Bara poses as Cleopatra in a publicity poster for the 1917 film. Known as the "Vamp" for her likeness to a vampire, the term soon became identified with a femme fatale, like many of the roles Theda played on film.

OPPOSITE: A model wearing a sequinned dress and chandelier earrings with a daring, asymmetric version of the Brooks bob hairstyle in 1925.

WILLIAM FOX PRESENTS
Theda Bara
IN
CLEOPATRA

STAGED BY
J·GORDON EDWARDS

DIRECT FROM
6 MONTHS RUN·
LYRIC THEATRE NEW YORK

A THEDA BARA
SUPER
PRODUCTION

By 1923 the bob, in the form of a pageboy style with some length, was seen everywhere on enlightened women. The razor-cut shingle style was introduced around 1924, featuring hair that tapered into a V-shape at the nape of the neck, with waves or spit curls at the sides. Long on top, with short sides and back, it was a more masculine look created by Antoine de Paris, which replaced the conventional bob. From mid-decade on, shaped-to-the-head cuts, featuring gentle waving from the Marcel to finger waves, became the norm. All of these new short haircuts enabled smaller closer-fitting hats, like the cloche, to be worn without ruining the hairstyle.

To modernize the sleek Louise Brooks bob, keep the fringe longer and side-swept. Alternatively, if you have long hair, try a blunt-cut fringe – the 1920s version ends just above the eyebrows. You can always create a "faux" bob by curling up longer hair and pinning it underneath to create a "helmet".

Until the 1920s, women wore little make-up other than a touch of rouge on the lips and cheeks. Very thin, downward-sloping eyebrows were also popular and women often shaved their entire brow and re-drew the line. The 1917 silent film *Cleopatra* starring Theda Bara as the fabulous Queen of Egypt inspired a big change, however. In those days, films lasted much longer at the box office and their influence was enormous. *Cleopatra* coincided with the exciting discoveries of the ancient tombs of the Pharoahs in Egypt's Valley of the Kings by Howard Carter and George Herbert, Earl of Caernarfon. Egyptomania brought a craze for shiny, jet-black hair, kohl-rimmed "panda" eyes, and dark crimson cupid's bow pursed lips.

## Cupid's Bow Lips

This style is traditionally achieved using a matt finish lipstick to ensure the colour to stays put and does not bleed into the natural lipline.

1 Blank out your lips with a thin application of concealer or foundation. Dust with powder.
2 Using a sharp lip pencil in a rich crimson colour, draw a V-shape over the upper centre lip, exaggerating the natural peaks.
3 Connect the line to the corners of the mouth using a sweeping, curving line that comes inside the natural corners of the mouth. The lines need to curve inward so keep the line rounded.
4 Next draw the bottom line in a sweeping curve, starting inside the corner of the mouth and reaching outside the natural bottom lip at the centre to create a pout.
5 Fill in with the lip pencil.
6 Using a lip brush and matt lipstick in the same crimson colour, layer more colour on top.

**You will need:**
Concealer or foundation
Translucent powder
Dark crimson lip pencil
Matt-finish crimson lipstick
Lip brush

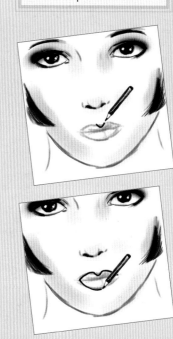

# Jean Harlow: Tea Dancer

Known as the "Blonde Bombshell" Jean Harlow ushered in a more streamlined, sexy look with her slinky bias-cut dresses and fluffy platinum hair. This is a look for romantics who adore the wistful mood of the early 1930s, when fragile dancers floated about in bias-cut dresses or simple panelled frocks with flared hems and button-front fastenings. Vintage fans can seek inspiration from the American HBO series *Carnival* and *Boardwalk Empire*. Both feature stunning Marcel-waved beauties sporting variations of this eternally elegant and easy-to-wear style. Accessorized with small hats perched atop wavy hairdos and gloves, the accent was on the collar and neckline, with shoulders accentuated by lace, voile, piecrust frills, bows, ribbons or "tippets" (little capes). The fitness fad of the 1920s had taken hold and silhouettes were still slim but more feminine with broad shoulders. Dresses had narrow waists and long, flared skirts (mid-calf for day, floor-length for eveningwear). The drop-waist of the late 1920s disappeared as enthusiasm for the straight up-and-down look waned and body accentuation became important to designers including Elsa Schiaparelli and Madeleine Vionnet. The bias cut was a great favourite of Harlow's, whose super-glamorous style inspired eveningwear design. This was the golden age of movies and although tea dances were chaste affairs, women flirted with a new glamour and sexiness, thanks to the firing up of their collective imagination by the fantasy world of cinema.

Dresses were adorned with lightweight chiffon and lace arranged in tiers or layers to create a floaty, drifting feel during movement. New fabrics included artificial silk (rayon), which made it possible to mass produce eveningwear for department stores and shops. Beading and embroidery could now be factory-made on new machines specially designed for the purpose and

## Key Looks

- Long satin gowns, cut on the bias
- Layers of delicate chiffon, lace and lightweight voile
- Square-cut or shawl collars edged with lace
- Scarves tied across the shoulders, shawl-style
- Voile or lace mini-capes worn across the shoulders
- Narrow, matching fabric belts on dresses
- Long, flared skirts reaching to mid-calf
- Low or Louis XIV heeled shoes
- Pale, coloured stockings
- Shirts with pin-tucking, button and lace-front details
- Light, semi-opaque fabrics offering a glimpse of camisole or lace
- Short puffed sleeves

### Tea Dancer Lookalikes
Ginger Rogers
Florence Welch
Charlize Theron
Keira Knightley in
*Atonement*

OPPOSITE: Jean Harlow in 1935. Called "Baby" by her family and "Blonde Bombshell" by the public, everything about her was white – from her platinum hair to her sequin dresses.

FAR LEFT: Keira Knightley captures the look of the 1930s with her wavy bob in *Atonement*.

LEFT: Florence Welch of Florence and the Machine: her statuesque figure perfectly suits her retro-inspired look, so reminiscent of 1930s and '40s glamour.

beautiful, shimmering gowns became widely affordable. While the Depression raged on both sides of the Atlantic, advances in technology allowed a wider range of styles to become available.

The look required a simple, slightly flattened and natural bustline achieved with the silk and cotton button-strapped vests of the day. Washable Lastex fabric made comfortable girdles for women who desired a little more control, though brassières as we know them had not yet made an appearance. Clothing remained easy to dance in, and the Tea Dancers relaxed in silk chemises, slips and pyjamas edged with delicate French lace and tied at the side in the fashionable wrap-over style.

## Style Guide

**The Palette:** Harlow stuck to dramatic monochrome shades but the Tea Dancer look can explore pretty pastels for floral prints in summer and deep ochres, rusts and greens to warm up pale winter colouring. Muted off-colours were also key, floating like dew over a mauve satin gown, while clouds of tulle, light netting, lace or chiffon in shades of palest cloud, creating an ethereal look. Pale, silvery-grey or barely-there blues and mauves in rayon fabrics shimmered and changed colour according to the light.

**Key Designers:** Madeleine Vionnet, Elsa Schiaparelli, Marcel Rochas, Adrian of Hollywood.

**Silhouette and Cut:** The "coathanger" silhouette had a square-shoulder and narrow waist above a flared-out skirt to mid-calf. Flat-front, wide-cut trousers copied the essential outline but were worn long enough to cover shoes. Evening dresses were in bias-cut foundation shapes, often masked in floating chiffon, feathers or tulle.

### Knitwear

Flamboyant Italian designer Elsa Schiaparelli created sweaters with designs such as her iconic bow motif. Her designs were quickly imitated and sassy, fitted sweaters became chic winter daywear teamed with neat-waisted skirts or flat-fronted trousers. Knitted suits had really taken off, inspired by Chanel's early designs. Peplum waists, part of Paul Poiret's legacy from the early twentieth century, enjoyed a popular renaissance on cardigans worn over long and stretchy, wide rib-knit skirts.

*"No one ever expects a great lay to pay all the bills."*
*Jean Harlow*

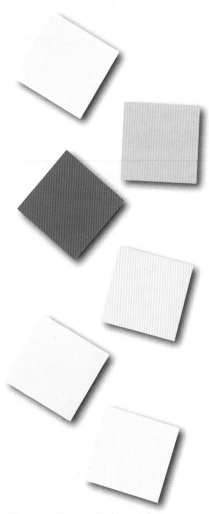

ABOVE: Two models wearing bias-cut designs by Madeleine Vionnet: on the left a sleeveless black velvet dress with a plunging V-neck and hem of white ermine; on the right a sleeveless white dress with crepe V-neck bodice and lustrous panne velvet skirt.

OPPOSITE: Dancers at the Dorchester Hotel, London, in 1931. By the 1930s, dancing had returned to being a couples-only sport; note the backless styles demonstrating that "racy" remained fashionable.

## Blouses

Tops emerged as a charming wardrobe essential, worn alone as a centrepiece to an outfit instead of buttoned up beneath a jacket or cardigan. The ruffled jabot collar was exceedingly popular on blouses and day dresses.

*Shop vintage for:* Fine cotton lawn versions gathered into pin-tucks or jabots at the front, with short, puffed or elbow-length sleeves. Keep an eye out for sheer fabrics. This pretty, slightly sensuous look benefits from delicate outlines and camisoles glimpsed beneath blouses.

## Dresses

Couturier Madeleine Vionnet discovered that cutting fabric crossways created a unique stretch and versatility not permitted by conventional tailoring. This enabled slender, swirling gowns to cling to the body without the need for straining seams. Delicate fabrics, including silk and crepe de Chine, hung beautifully on the bias and the bias-cut dress remains an opulent style that suits almost any shape and size of woman: the loose but shaped effect emphasizes femininity while length adds proportion. Gilbert Adrian, employed as a costume designer for MGM Studios before setting up his own Beverly Hills store in 1942, designed the bias-cut satin gowns that helped to launch Jean Harlow as a smouldering siren, plus show-stoppers for Greta Garbo, Joan Crawford and Bette Davis.

*Shop vintage for:* Bias-cut evening gowns are central to this glamorous image, although sadly few have survived. However, vintage stores have plenty of lingerie and nightwear dating back to the 1930s, so take that route to source your own slinky look. Look for black velvet or silk offset with elaborate embroidery and beading in sparkling rainbow shades; also pale, shimmering off-blues, greys and pinks. Washed-out silks and satins also work with this look.

## Jewellery and Adornments

Brooches, pins and sewn-on adornments in modern, geometric or floral shapes enhance Tea Dancer chic. Faux silk rose corsages might be carefully sewn onto a frock one day, then promptly snipped off and added to another garment. Silver and paste jewellery came in maze-like and angular Art Deco designs or platinum-and-diamond "white on white" set pieces. Inventiveness really came into play during these hard times: jewel-like fabric accessories added panache, while ribbons tied about the wrist and lengths of sequinned fabric knotted in a bow at the neck compensated for a lack of the real thing and contributed to the general prettiness of the moment.

*Shop vintage for:* Murano or Venetian glass beads, Art Deco brooches, diamanté chandelier earrings, costume sets by Joseff of Hollywood or Hobé and fake diamond-and-platinum pieces that imitate the real 1930s versions by Chanel and Harry Winston.

### Style Tips

- Mix patterns and plain fabrics in one look – try a plain, fitted jacket over a floral dress.

- Wear camisole-topped, long silk chemises as dresses with lacy knitted cardigans or shawls over the top.

- It's fine to break the rules occasionally and vamp it up with a high heel.

- Harlow reputedly never wore underwear – this kept her look soft and avoided lines under silky dresses.

- Keep jewellery small and complementary to the look.

- Harlow has said of the bias-cut dress: "They require more poise than any other kind of formal dress. You can't slouch in them or walk heavily in an ungainly manner. You have to hold yourself up and carry your head high to give them the right line."

## Hats, Bags and Shoes

During this era, hats increased a little in size. Cloche styles gained brims, with scarves wrapped around them or flower and feather adornments. Lower heels became popular after the teetering Flappers made heels a little too racy for polite society. "Louis XIV" heels shaped like a woman's hourglass figure came into style. Handbags were small and rounded, often made of heavy cotton as well as leather, with metal clips.

*Shop vintage for:* Leather or lace gloves in pale, creamy or grey colours. Small "tango" bags that wrap around the wrist for dancing, or metal mesh bags, particularly those by Whiting & Davis.

## Beauty Guide

In 1931 Depression-hit America was dazzled when Jean Harlow appeared in Frank Capra's movie, *Platinum Blonde.* Harlow had dyed her hair a whiter than white shade of blonde and, as she slunk her way languidly across the set in a brilliant white, ciré silk bias-cut gown – so tight she was unable to wear underwear – an erotic charge zapped through cinema audiences. Not only did the brilliance of her hair catch the movie lights, the luminous effect was also exaggerated by the black-and-white celluloid film. Harlow's blonde hair perfectly complemented the oyster and cream evening dresses of the time, while diamond and crystal hair decorations created a fantasy feeling.

The fashion for "going blonde" was not new, but the Tea Dancer was an entirely different creature to the Flapper. Heavily made up, with black-ringed eyes and scarlet lips offset with a pallid face and phosphorescent blonde hair, the Harlow look was blatantly artificial.

Actors such as Anny Ondra, Toby Wing and Marion Martin helped popularize the look in films like *Sinners in Paradise* (1938). Hollywood fan magazines of the 1930s including *Life & Look* disseminated the image with magnificent portraits of the stars, lit and arranged for maximum glamour and sex appeal. All over the United States Jean Harlow fan clubs sprang up and sales of hydrogen peroxide, invented by Louis Jacques Thénard in 1818, trebled during the 1930s. As more women took to the bottle, dyed blonde hair lost it's high-glamour status. By the middle

### Beauty Tips

- Gently waved hair, cut into a bob or long and drawn back into a loose chignon at the nape of the neck sets off the Tea Dancers look.

- Hair should not be perfectly set – in fact, wispy tendrils add romance and a slightly "undone" feel.

- Keep eye make-up smudgy in shades of grey or mauve lightly rubbed around the eye line, with lashings of mascara on curled lashes.

- Colour lips in fuchsia-pink stain, but keep the skin tone alabaster.

- Apply rosy pink blusher to the centre of cheeks for an apple blossom blush.

TOP: A Harlow-esque platinum blonde in a Tootal Robia voile dress in 1935. Frilled tiers and matching sleeve frills enhance the simple summer frock.

ABOVE RIGHT: Hot, narrow tongs are used to create Harlow's blonde Marcel waves before she goes on to the set in the Metro Goldwyn Mayer Film studios, Hollywood, June 1933.

of the decade, the look was so common that society hostesses and shop girls alike would be seen sporting a similarly luminous look as they walked down the street.

The Marcel Wave took off on both sides of the Atlantic and if you have the time to spare, this bewitching style sets off the Tea Dancer look to perfection. French coiffeur François Marcel perfected a technique for waving hair with iron curling tongs in 1872. Straight hair could be encouraged to ripple across the head in waves, and tongs to achieve the desired effect came in various sizes. In the early days, tongs were heated over a gas burner and first tested on paper: if they burned a hole, the tongs had to be cooled down before being applied to the hair. Electrical versions with heat controls were available by 1924, but were mainly used in professional salons. Thanks to François Marcel, hairdressing really took off as a trade and instead of home visits, stylists set themselves up in small shops and built up a clientele.

## The Finger Wave

Similar to the Marcel, except that you use a pinching action to mould the S-shaped undulations instead of tongs, the finger wave was used to create a softer variation on the sleek bob in the 1920s and 1930s. If your hair is super-straight, re-create this style using hot curling tongs which will have a longer-lasting effect. The waves should curl at an angle away from the face, toward the back of the head.

**You will need:**
Super-hold setting lotion or fixative spray
Hairdresser's clips
Rat-tail comb

1 Wet your hair thoroughly and apply a strong setting (waving) lotion.
2 Comb and part your hair, following the natural growth pattern.
3 Using the index finger as a guide, press the comb against the side of the finger, and in 1-inch(2.5cm) sections, drag the comb (teeth straight down) sideways along the finger until a ridge forms. Without lifting the comb, lay it flat against the scalp.
4 Pinch the ridge and secure with a clip.
5 Continue along the length, one or two finger-lengths apart, securing the waves as you go. Work section by section from the crown.
6 Allow to dry naturally, then remove the clips.

# Marlene Dietrich: Femuline

Unconventional fashion icon Marlene Dietrich shunned top name designerwear for her own androgynous style in her debut *The Blue Angel* in 1930. Ever since, the extraordinary German actress and singer has been a beacon for Femuline fans, inspiring females to borrow from the boys. The Femuline look is particularly fun to put together via the vintage market because so much good-quality menswear is still around.

Successful Femuline style depends on understanding your natural silhouette and finding good matches, shape- and fabric-wise. Marlene Dietrich recognized which cuts and fabrics suited her long legs and boyish T-shaped figure – she never looked mannish or butch. Even an army green wool uniform looked sensuous on Dietrich. When she visited American troops in Germany during 1944–45, she wore a short, boxy version of the standard-issue jacket, tailored to fit over Oxford "bag" trousers, which were pleated at the waist. This style of trouser is most flattering to women because it offers the chance to draw in the waist, hourglass style, while flattening the tummy.

Katharine Hepburn and Lauren Bacall took their cue from Dietrich and wore men's suit trousers with fitted sweaters, brogues and shirts for daywear in the late 1930s and '40s. Hepburn adored a tweed trouser suit or a golfing ensemble complete with Argyle checked sweater and shirt underneath, while Bacall was photographed in an open-neck shirt with a scarf arranged cravat-style and high-waisted men's-cut trousers. The Hepburn/Bacall look is a specifically 1940s take that works well for every day. Marlene Dietrich's masculine clothing choices translate well through the decades and often feature in designer collections by Sonia Rykiel and Giorgio Armani.

**Femuline Lookalikes**
Katharine Hepburn
Lauren Bacall
Diane Keaton
Grace Jones
Annie Lennox
Tilda Swinton

OPPOSITE: Dietrich in a 1933 grey men's suit with turn-ups on the Oxford "bags".

ABOVE: Katharine Hepburn casually elegant in a softly draped men's suit in 1938.

FAR LEFT: Diane Keaton in her 1977 *Annie Hall* look, created by Ralph Lauren.

LEFT: Annie Lennox accessorizes a trouser suit with trademark leather gloves and Ray-Ban shades in the 1980s.

Photographed in a white suit with shirt, tie and beret, Dietrich is the epitome of crisp, summer style. Diane Keaton reprised the look in 1977 as Annie Hall in Woody Allen's movie of the same name, adding a floppy hat and more laid-back 1970s styling, but it was Yves Saint Laurent who really made the Femuline style buzz for the second half of the twentieth century. Saint Laurent opened his ready-to-wear boutique, Rive Gauche, in 1966 and the store was stocked with the kind of clothes women could simply walk away in. Trouser suits were an ideal option and fitted well into the androgynous framework of 1960s fashion.

Saint Laurent played with the trouser shape, adding knickerbockers, culottes and even tailored shorts to wear beneath a tailored, double-breasted jacket. Then, in 1971, he was to surpass himself with his amazing women's tuxedo, "Le Smoking". Still available now, the sleek fitted jacket and long-line trouser suit makes the perfect evening ensemble for the kind of woman who does not wish to flounce in frills or play it safe in a little black dress. Marlene wore her suit with full men's accoutrements but you could try a simple white silk shirt or even a sparkly vest. Stiletto sandals or spiky courts add glamour.

During the early 1980s, the legendary performers Annie Lennox and Grace Jones rocked menswear styles to perfection. Jones sported a mohair suit with nothing underneath. Copyists beware: a gleaming, taut body is crucial for this look. Annie Lennox preferred a white shirt or T-shirt beneath her suit, coloured leather gloves and sparkling lapels or a monster brooch for added effect. Never one for heels, she wore Dr Marten boots and brogues onstage. Moving on, Madonna rocked a corset with a built-in conical bra beneath her Jean Paul Gaultier suit for the Blond Ambition World Tour of 1990. The corset beneath a man's suit became a big 1980s nightclubbing look. In fact, it's just about due for a rebirth, so why not be one of the first and put together your own version?

> **"I dress for the image. Not for myself, not for the public, not for fashion, not for men."**
>
> *Marlene Dietrich*

### Key Looks

- Black tuxedo
- White dress shirts
- Tie or long silk scarf worn as a belt or a men's tie worn around the neck
- Slinky vest with sequins or luxurious sheen
- Velvet suit with frilly shirt underneath
- Waistcoat
- Statement Art Deco jewellery
- Fedora or beret

# Style Guide

**The Palette:** This look relies on a combination of colour. Colours to avoid are lighter hues of grey, beige or cream as these can be unforgiving and are hard to blend with anything but black. The only exception would be a linen suit, which looks best in lighter colours. Monochrome dogtooth or Prince of Wales check fabrics go with anything, but be cautious of too-bulky fabrics. Tuxedos should be black, but seek out colour for daywear.

**Key Designers:** Yves Saint Laurent, Calvin Klein, Geoffrey Beene, Hugo Boss, Giorgio Armani, Ralph Lauren, Brooks Brothers.

**Silhouette and Cut:** A T-shape silhouette with wide or square shoulders and a narrow body: masculine shapes with feminine contours.

## Suits and Separates

Dietrich favoured men's separates as an easy way to dress smartly, quickly. She went on several morale-boosting trips to visit American troops in France during the Second World War and chose comfy Argyle knitted sweaters and soft woollen slacks for travelling in. She wore tweed jackets with belted waists over men's shirts and knitted waistcoats, too.

When shopping for men's clothes, always try them on before you buy to ensure previous wear and tear has not spoiled the shape of jackets or created irredeemable bagging on trouser knees. Also, form an idea of the look you are going for before shopping. It is helpful to keep, for instance, a loose *Annie Hall* or a 1940s Femuline blueprint in your mind to assist with in-store editing. If it's eveningwear, take along heels of a similar height to the ones you plan to wear with your outfit. Slightly long is better than short regarding trouser length. Men's suits come in a range of hues but the most versatile would be light wool fabric in a smallish cut, in granite grey or chocolate brown. If a whole suit is hard to find, try a jacket or trousers and mix with other items such as jeans or a plain white shirt.

*Shop vintage for:* You are unlikely to find an original YSL "Le Smoking" in a random vintage store. However, they can be tracked down online but expect to pay quite a lot for a good quality 1970s or 1980s original. You may well find men's versions, and don't forget to rummage through boys' rails for teenage sizes, too. For evening, black close-fitting tuxedos in lightweight wool or silk work best. When it comes to daywear, look for double-breasted suits (the jackets tend to have a more contoured shape) or small-cut three-button, single-lapel jackets.

LEFT: Yves Saint Laurent's "Le Smoking" trouser suit, 1967: ultra-neat and tailored to perfection, complete with waistcoat, shirt and tie. The jacket is double-breasted and trousers are flat-fronted for an extra-sleek shape.

RIGHT: A Katharine Hepburn-style ensemble from 1946. Men's-cut, loose-legged trousers fall away from a cinched-in waist and padded shouldered shirt. The lapel collar adds a smart, feminine touch.

### Style Tips

- Break men's rules: try a three-piece suit with no tie and wear a two-piece with a corset.

- Keep flat shoes clean and polished for a sharp, smart look.

- Add a man's big, shiny wristwatch – a Timex will do.

- Ties with shirts look good if there is something quirky elsewhere, such as stiletto heels or shorts instead of trousers. Avoid dressing exactly like a man, though!

- Approach bow-ties with extreme caution.

## Suit Styles

**Double-breasted** jackets feature a crossover front, generous lapels and four or six buttons. Buttons lowered with fashion trends in the 1970s, but since the 1990s they have risen again. Double-breasted suits often come with pleated-front trousers. Popular in the 1980s, too many pleats or gathers can be unflattering, so stick to a minimum of one or two pleats either side of the fly front.

**Single-breasted** suits usually have a three- or two-button fastening. Modern and pre-1980s styles have flat-fronted, straight-legged trousers whereas 1960s versions taper at the ankle.

**Three-piece** is the name for a suit with a matching jacket, trousers and waistcoat. Unless you are tall, a Prince of Wales check or tweed might look a little bulky. The look can work for evening when nothing else needs to be worn beneath a well-fitting waistcoat.

**Linen** suits are strictly for summer, and the white linen suit is a traditional classic. It looks gorgeous with a simple navy-and-white striped vest and deck shoes for day or a black silk shirt and stilettos in the evening.

**Tuxedos** come in black or white, usually single-breasted with one or two buttons and a long shawl collar in a contrasting fabric, such as satin. Usually worn with black trousers, white jackets can look chic worn over a sparkling black vest top or a corset. With a light-coloured shirt, you may look blousy or lumpy.

## Waistcoats and Extras

What do you wear with your suit? Fine-knit sweaters look good over a shirt, then tucked into Oxford Bags, Hepburn style. Well-fitting waistcoats are sexy and most come with adjustable back buckles to strengthen your silhouette.

*Shop vintage for:* Knitted or patterned silk waistcoats to break up the heavy fabric of a suit, fine-knit sweaters in light pastel shades, sheer or silk shirts for a sexy contrast beneath a jacket.

## Just a Jacket

A man's tuxedo jacket in black or white looks fabulous over jeans. If you're wearing it with flares or bootcuts, look for a shorter, more fitted style; with straight or skinny jeans, go for a broad-shouldered boxy jacket. Navy wool or linen blazers with brass buttons work for day and are especially good with white jeans.

## Accessories

The Femuline look is as much about accessories as the clothing: ties worn as belts, handkerchiefs tucked into top pockets, narrow leather belts, men's satchels, briefcases, cigarette cases to carry a credit card and lipstick, lace-up brogues, college loafers, ankle socks, Homburg hats and satin evening scarves. One thing does not go: braces (suspenders). Braces are for clowns, fancy dress and old men only – you read it here.

*Shop vintage for:* Mother-of-pearl cufflinks, Liberty handkerchiefs, Hermès ties.

ABOVE: Dietrich's perfect profile provided feminine balance to the masculine look.

OPPOSITE: Dietrich softens her masculine accessories with soft, wavy hair.

# Beauty Guide

The Femuline look depends upon feminine make-up to retain the glamour essential for the overall effect. Hair can be a dapper crop in the style of Annie Lennox or even a partially shaven Grace Jones but lips, eyes and cheeks should be enhanced.

Dietrich's God-given bone structure meant that she needed very little shading or highlighting on her skin but she used it anyway to enhance her ultra-pronounced cheekbones. Her beauty was popularized by the fashion for sophisticated, feminine beauty: streamlined but exaggerated body shapes, coloured-in eyebrows, enhanced lips and cheekbones. She plucked out her eyebrows and drew on a thin line with pencil, while other stars of the day simply shaved off their brows. This is not recommended by beauty experts, who claim the natural "line" of the brow can be lost permanently, resulting in a random growth of hair.

Heavy eyeliner and darkened lashes offer a simple but gorgeous eye make-up solution for Femuline fans. The look works on any eye shape, ditto the carefully painted-in lips. Not exactly a cupid's bow – considered too "girlish" and old-fashioned looking by the 1930s, Dietrich's mouth was wide but with fuller lips. Since then, times have changed and fuller lips are more fashionable but it's worth taking a look at the chic, simple face of Dietrich at her most beautiful for a reminder of the old adage that less, very often is more.

Her hair was a softly waved bob, a sure-fire look for adding a 1930s vibe to the Femuline wardrobe. She sometimes grew it longer so it hung in a mass of curls at the nape of her neck but a bare neck or hair neatly pinned up looks best with the Femuline look. According to Hollywood legend, it is said that Max Factor sprinkled real gold dust onto Marlene's hair and wigs so they would sparkle on film.

## Sculpted Cheekbones

The effect of high cheekbones can be achieved by contouring using two shades of bronzer, or alternatively two shades of powder foundation or blusher. You can use creams or liquids, but powders are easier to blend in and to correct if you've overloaded the shade. Before you begin, apply your foundation and concealer to create a blank canvas to work on.

1 Using the darker colour and a contouring brush, suck in your cheeks to find the hollow below your cheekbone. Brush the darker shade into the hollow and then toward your hairline and up toward your temple. You are using the dark colour to create the deepest shadow.
2 Blend well and repeat on the other side.
3 Sweep a little dark bronzer under the sides of the jawline.
4 Using the highlighter and the blusher brush, sweep the highlighter along the top of both cheekbones to add dimension.
5 Now add the lighter colour of bronzer or blusher to the apples of the cheeks only.

**You will need:**
Bronzer or blush powder
in two shades
Highlighter powder
Contouring brush
Brusher blush

# Wallis Simpson: Mistress

"A woman can never be too rich or too thin" summed up Wallis Simpson's attitude to life. Believing herself plain-looking, the American divorcée for whom Edward VIII relinquished his throne, scandalizing a nation in the process, decided to compensate for her appearance by being well dressed. "My husband gave up everything for me. I'm not a beautiful woman. I'm nothing to look at, so the only thing I can do is dress better than anyone else. If everyone looks at me when I enter a room, my husband can feel proud of me. That's my chief responsibility," she once wrote. The Duchess of Windsor was to succeed and her style formed part of the harder, yet sensuous and more womanly edge to late 1930s, early '40s dressing: the Mistress look is definitely for women, not girls.

Wallis Simpson's signature draped jersey dresses, knee-length, flippy skirts, fur necklines, luxurious jewellery and tummy flat as an ironing board inspired women to copy her style. Despite her reputation for being someone of not quite the right calibre for high society, she was admired for her chic appearance. When Mrs Simpson finally enticed her king away to the South of France in 1937, London flopped into wartime misery, missing the frisson of Wallis and her sheer hedonistic glamour.

Similarly, Ginger Rogers, the young Joan Crawford and Bette Davis brought a new, cinema-tastic sheen to Europe. Thousands flocked to see the stunning creatures starring as alluring sirens or heartbroken, dangerous women. Cheery Ginger Rogers danced her feet off in an effort to keep up with her highly critical partner Fred Astaire, but her tough, humorous style lent her a sexiness that good-girl stars such as Judy Garland and Deanna Durbin lacked: the Mistress look comes with a sophisticated attitude and an air of experience.

## Key Looks

- Knee-length, slightly flared A-line skirts
- Fitted jackets with peplum waists
- Detachable fur collars
- Fox-fur wraps
- Bias-cut, long evening gowns and cloaks with Art Deco motifs
- Hats angled to slightly mask one eye (in shadow or with netting)
- Long, tight sleeves slightly covering the wrists
- Nautical stripes
- Expensive-looking colourful jewels or big pearls
- Mid-height heels
- Fitted-waist, flat-fronted wide trousers
- Chanel suits
- Christian Dior-style crocodile handbags
- Louis Vuitton luggage and vanity cases

## Mistress Lookalikes
Bette Davis
Joan Crawford
Marion Cotillard in *Public Enemies*

OPPOSITE: Wallis Simpson in a short-sleeved Madeleine Vionnet dress and belt in 1945.

FAR LEFT: A young Bette Davis sports a chic, well-fitting woollen dress in 1937.

LEFT: In costume for her role in *Letty Lynton*, Joan Crawford wears a long, belted coat with a fur collar, a beret and gloves in 1932.

Mainbocher and Elsa Schiaparelli were favourites of Wallis Simpson. The Chicago-born Main Rousseau Bocher, who combined two of his names to create the famous couture label in 1930, began professional life as a fashion magazine illustrator. He went on to work on French *Vogue* before setting up his salon. Mainbocher had an inherent understanding of fashion and how to make a woman look good from every angle. In 1937, he designed Wallis Simpson's beautiful wedding dress, perhaps one of the most flattering garments ever. In beautiful silk crepe, with a high gathered neck, elegant buttoned bodice and long, slender skirt, the gown remains a blueprint for designers everywhere.

Elsa Schiaparelli, whose unique collaborations with Salvador Dalí and Jean Cocteau married the worlds of fashion and art, was Wallis's designer of choice for eveningwear. With Cocteau, she created embroidered satins with vase and floral motifs, while Dalí provided moon and star images and famously produced a hat shaped like a high-heeled shoe for the designer. It is highly likely any surviving Schiaparelli still resides in private collections but many copies were around at the time. With the sudden outbreak of World War II in Europe, Schiaparelli's designs and their imitators were promptly relegated to the back of everyone's wardrobes while they concentrated on the 1939 war effort, hence you may find pieces that are hardly worn.

After Mrs Simpson and the former king relocated to the South of France, Wallis's wardrobe took on a fresh, nautical theme. A navy blue fitted blazer with white edging over wide sailor-style trousers or matelot striped top beneath a white cardigan created a crisp, cool daywear ensemble that still works today. Throughout her life, Wallis Simpson made alluring skirt suits with short, fitted or peplum waisted jackets worn over flippy little skirts part of her signature style.

> "*Never explain, never complain.*"
> **Wallis Simpson**

RIGHT: Wallis Simpson in a photograph by Cecil Beaton wearing a jacket and skirt designed for her by Schiaparelli, circa 1937. The long-sleeved, fitted jacket is trimmed with white leather appliqué.

# *Style Guide*

**The Palette:** A powdery sky blue and vivid, clean cream were Wallis Simpson's two favourite colours for clothing. She chose the light blue shade for her wedding dress and it became known as "Wallis Blue".

**Key Designers:** Mainbocher, Elsa Schiaparelli, Gabrielle "Coco" Chanel, Hermès, Madame Grès, Lucien Lelong.

**Silhouette and Cut:** The Mistress outline accentuates the body, displaying curves around waist and derrière in a manner that is almost severe but far sexier than it first appears. Although cleavage is not a part of the look, legs are an important focus and skirts dramatically shortened by the end of the 1930s. Even when she wore long gowns, Wallis Simpson kept her dresses closely fitted. She was not known for dancing and liked to pose with a cigarette, her dresses outlining slender contours.

## Suits

The Mistress look is fabulous in skirt-suit form. Wallis Simpson's wardrobe staple came in all fabrics, from lightweight crepe de Chine to heavy tweeds for winter. Make this style more sensuous with a chiffon blouse bow-tied at the neck or a plain crew-neck sweater for everyday wear. Wallis preferred a slightly puffed sleeve on a closely fitting shoulder to give her an overall balanced silhouette.

*Shop vintage for:* Well-made suits in swingy crepe or wool fabrics. Original 1930s clothes are still prevalent in vintage stores, distinguishable from 1950s garments by their shorter skirt lengths. Thirties' fastenings include hooks and eyes, rows of tiny buttons and press-studs (snaps). Scour knitwear sections in vintage stores for home-knitted suits – the quality can be astounding.

RIGHT: A jacket and skirt by Victor Stiebel from 1940 displays typical Mistress style – a narrow-hipped, slightly severe, structured sihouette. The gloves, clutch bag and jauntily angled hat make perfect accessories.

## Eveningwear

Wallis Simpson crossed boundaries in eveningwear. A favourite outfit was a long black dress and jacket designed by Elsa Schiaparelli in 1937 (*see page* 34). This is a signature look, encapsulating Wallis's golden rules for simplicity with an opulent touch.

*Shop vintage for:* Good-quality, form-fitting evening dresses that resemble daywear, with added length. This is a small-silhouetted, colour-blocked look, so source dresses in dark velvets, crepes or even light wools.

## Accessories

Buttons of all sizes make their mark on the Mistress look. Large-scale buttons on small cardigans or fitted suits added a touch of chic fun and proved an eye-catching distraction. The Duchess of Windsor often clipped a brooch to a collar to add sparkle near her face, and hats were secured further back on her head with jewelled pins and clips. She enjoyed luxurious details, including a jewelled cigarette case, a fox-fur collar and even a fur muff.

*Shop vintage for:* Hair accessories, small, jewelled evening purses, silk or fine cotton lawn and lace handkerchiefs, cigarette cases and lighters, fox-fur collars, thick-framed tortoiseshell sunglasses. Fur muffs in leopardskin or mink doubled up as evening bags – look for examples containing a concealed compartment inside to store coins and make-up.

## Jewellery

The iconic Cartier panther bracelet created for Wallis Simpson has changed hands many times at auction. Legendary for her jewellery choices, it is rumoured she may have snaffled heirlooms from the Royal Collection and had the stones reset in new designs. Even her evening bags – or, as Cartier dubbed one design her "Necessaire du soir" – were crafted by

### Style Tips

- Wallis Simpson always carried an accessory such as sunglasses, a scarf or a hat so that she had something to do with her hands in photographs or to prevent herself from constantly smoking cigarettes.

- Matching statement earrings and necklaces add clout.

- A huge, jewelled brooch worn close to the neck is flattering – Wallis loved her diamond-encrusted brooches.

- Choose stud or cluster earrings, not dangling styles.

- Never deviate from the silhouette – avoid baggy, loose shapes.

- The Mistress look requires strict discipline – in dress, diet, grooming and manners.

- Society photographer Cecil Beaton called her "tiny, neat and immaculate" so remember to cultivate poise and a regal bearing (even if you never made it to the ranks of a royal family).

- Be "*soignée*, not *degage*" (polished but never casual), as *Harper's Bazaar* editor Diana Vreeland once said.

master jewellers including Van Cleef and Arpels. Edward enjoyed giving Wallis jewellery gifts including a bracelet of cross-shaped charms, each bearing an inscription regarding a special event in their life. Key features of jewellery at this time were angular, Art Deco designs, square-cut stones (which replaced romantic oval shapes) and coloured precious stones.

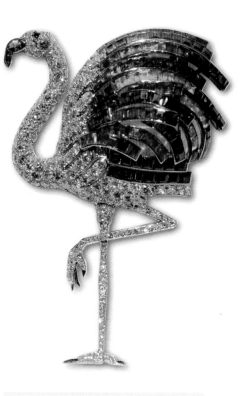

*Shop vintage for:* Good-quality paste diamanté and matching earring and necklace sets. It's worth visiting vintage fairs or hunting out jewellery experts who can show you Wallis jewellery replicas and you can also do your own research online. Hunt out good copies of Wallis's Cartier onyx and diamond Panther bracelet, which fetched a cool £4.5 million at auction in 2010, making it the most expensive bracelet ever sold at the time.

## Hats

Adrian of Hollywood designed two hats for Swedish icon Greta Garbo that were hugely influential during the 1930s: a floppy style that tipped down over one eye in 1930 and a pillbox shape in 1932. Women's headwear subsequently shrank in size and took on a rakish angle for the rest of the decade, often featuring netting over one eye – now known as a "fascinator". Solidly waved and lacquered hair was the perfect base upon which to anchor a beret or jaunty little hat that finished off the Mistress style.

# Beauty Guide

Wallis Simpson and Hollywood stars Joan Crawford and Bette Davis all wore their short hair meticulously waved and curled about their heads, then lacquered solidly for good measure. No escaping ringlets and tendrils for them – the look was super-neat. Wallis had naturally curly hair that she fought hard to control. Soft waves will do for a modern take on the Mistress. Brunette was the "in" colour and much easier to maintain than bleached blonde, and provided an antidote to the Jean Harlow look. Like many of the Hollywood greats of the time, Harlow never found a place at the Royal table. War put a stop to travel arrangements and by the time peace was declared, tastes had moved on.

OPPOSITE: The Duchess of Windsor's black silk ensemble by Christian Dior, circa 1949, has a lightly boned bodice with the tulle inner corset fastened to the front by hooks and eyes, a wide neckline, fold-over collar and three buttons. Severe but stylish, the piece is a perfect example of Wallis's Mistress look.

ABOVE LEFT: Wallis's twentieth wedding anniversary brooch in diamonds, rubies and emeralds was given to her by Edward in 1957.

ABOVE RIGHT: A flamingo brooch Edward gave Wallis for her birthday in 1940, and one of her favourite pieces, was made by Cartier, and is encrusted with diamonds, rubies, sapphires and emeralds.

### Beauty Tips

• Strong arched eyebrows accentuate the eyes and frame the face. Wallis emphasized hers to simultaneously balance out her large nose and draw attention away from a strong jaw.

• Black eyeliner along the lash line and mascara complete the eye make-up for this look and mirror the eyebrow shape.

• Full lips, coloured in red or coral shades, are essential for the sensuous Mistress.

• A touch of blusher softens the severe effect.

• Hair should be softer than Wallis Simpson's – keep it neat and sprayed, but off the face.

# The Mitford Sisters: English Aristo

Mention the name "Debo", Dowager Duchess of Devonshire, and one immediately imagines Deborah Mitford's family, the ubiquitous Mitford sisters and their enduring influence on the image of the smart English gel who is slightly quirky, self-sufficient and leads a semi-rural, impecunious life. Of course these women came from wealthy stock but the look they inspired depends on lots of charming, old-fashioned influences. In the film version of Dodie Smith's novel, *I Capture the Castle*, Rose makes the perfect English Aristo fashion heroine, as does the wonderful Linda in Nancy Mitford's own novel, *Love in a Cold Climate*. More recently, Jasmine Guinness and Alexa Chung have come to typify the modern version of this look, now known as "Granny Chic".

In the late 1930s the English aristocracy was enjoying its last days at the helm of society. Unbeknownst to the Tavistocks, Percys and Cavendishes, World War II would permanently destroy the class system of fealty that had endured for over a thousand years. The BBC television drama *Upstairs, Downstairs* remains a loosely accurate blueprint for the headcount in the average country house and in those heady days, young, aristocratic girls set the fashion tone in Britain. Enamoured of their American counterparts, English gels were both thrilled and saddened when William Cavendish, Marquess of Hartington and heir to the Duke of Devonshire, married Kathleen "Kick" Kennedy of the famous American clan in 1944. Within months of the young and beautiful couple's marriage, tragedy struck when William was killed in action during World War II and Kathleen surrendered her title to the wife of William's younger brother, Deborah Mitford.

After World War II, rising costs of labour, maintenance and materials meant money was scarce in the country and the "make do and mend" war ethic continued. Since then, an underlying, charming shabbiness has hung about the country houses and estates of Britain

> **English Aristo Lookalikes**
> Jasmine Guinness
> Stella Tenant
> Rosie Huntington-Whiteley
> Alexa Chung

OPPOSITE: A young Deborah Mitford goes for a brisk, chilly walk dressed in classic tweed jacket, wool skirt and walking shoes in 1940.

ABOVE: Stella Tenant, granddaughter of Deborah Mitford, models Dries van Noten tweeds and knits in 2004: very heritage style!

RIGHT: Fashion commentator Alexa Chung specializes in the "Granny Chic" look.

### Key Looks

- Long cardigan belted at the waist and worn over pencil skirts or jodhpurs
- Floral-print, 1940s-style summer dresses
- Shawls with everything
- Pussybow blouse
- Men's trousers and brown lace-up brogues
- Twin-sets and pearls
- Grandma's ballgowns
- Family jewels or fake tiaras for evening
- Tweed pencil skirts and floral-print blouses
- Victorian underwear and nightdresses worn as outerwear
- Hats, either small and pretty summery straws or fedoras and deerstalkers
- Silk scarves in Hermès prints, worn as headscarves à la Her Majesty Queen Elizabeth II
- Men's plain macs, belted at the waist
- An umbrella and a Labrador

but keep pieces small and groovy – a tweed or heavy wool kilt or straight skirt is perfect for the office. Muddy, heathery green or brown can be perked up with a shocking pink cashmere top or a yellow silk shirt. A flimsy, lacy top also looks good underneath a buttoned-up cardigan worn over tailored trousers. English eccentricity can work well if you keep these simple rules in mind.

Essentially, combine classic English pieces from men's and women's wardrobes: big sweaters with short tweed skirts, fitted hacking jackets over ball gowns … anything goes as long as it comes from the same stable of sensible, English stalwarts. Vivienne Westwood epitomizes the essence of this look with her bustle dresses, corsets, tweeds, knits and woollens fashioned into overtly feminine shapes that lend an exaggerated modernism. Other contemporary designers to stray into "Lady of the House" territory include Ally Capellino, Bella Freud and Nicole Farhi. Capellino's simple pinafores, ticking shirts and straw hats encapsulate life in the English countryside.

and to step into any of them is to inhale the familiar, slightly damp aroma that always hangs in the air. Hence the fact that handknitted sweaters, twin sets and big cardigans go with the look – it is impossible to thoroughly heat an English country house, so sweaters are essential!

But you don't have to go strolling through the countryside to make English Aristo your own: so long as you stick to form-fitting shapes, it can work equally well in town. As a rule of thumb, long and saggy, dramatic or voluminous clothes don't look good after a long trip on the bus or train. Commute in country lady chic,

# Style Guide

**The Palette:** The natural fabrics of this look dictate a soft, country mix of colours. Tweeds and woven wool tailoring in coppery browns and mossy greens form the backbone for this look, along with corduroy in mustardy yellow, bottle green or muddy brown and old-fashioned shades of lilac, violet and palest mauve, dusty pinks and flowery shades of scarlet. Argyle, tartan, herringbone and houndstooth provide pattern.

**Key Designers:** Liberty of London, Hermès, Victor Stiebel, Hardy Amies, Norman Hartnell, Harris Tweed, Jaeger, Pringle of Scotland, Dereta, Country Casuals; also Vivienne Westwood, Ally Capellino, Alexander McQueen, Ralph Lauren, Margaret Howell.

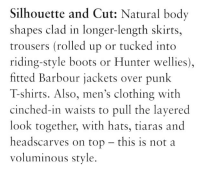

OPPOSITE: An American version of the English Aristo look by Claire McCardell, 1947.

BELOW: Argyle knits return perennially to the catwalk, here for Michael Kors in 2006. Mix patterns and shades of similar colours for an eclectic look.

**Silhouette and Cut:** Natural body shapes clad in longer-length skirts, trousers (rolled up or tucked into riding-style boots or Hunter wellies), fitted Barbour jackets over punk T-shirts. Also, men's clothing with cinched-in waists to pull the layered look together, with hats, tiaras and headscarves on top – this is not a voluminous style.

## Tweeds and Knits

Natural wools, tweeds, cottons and silks create this outdoorsy look, with absolutely no polyester, rayon or manmade fibres.

*Shop vintage for:* Quality goes hand in hand with English Aristo style, hence all the right labels including Pringle, Scottish Cashmere and Argyle knits. The look does not depend on perfection so splash out on a slightly bobbled or misshapen sweater if you love the colour, neckline or other detailing. As a general rule, the more quirky, the merrier. Shrunken lambswool can be quite fetching so long as you make the right decision on sleeves: long or pushed up above the wrists. Sleeves that are not quite long enough look more Orphan Annie

than country lady! Harris Tweed is the name to look for when it comes to hacking jackets, waistcoats, skirts or trousers. The latter might be slightly scratchy or even itchy, but can look great rolled up to ankle-length and worn over high-heeled, leather lace-up boots. Look for knitwear in pastel shades with pearly or gold buttons.

## Floral Prints

Prints feature heavily in this look, particularly old-fashioned rose- or peony-printed cottons or heavier curtain fabric cut down into clothing.

*Shop vintage for:* Small, sprig-like patterns in violets, yellows, grass greens, dusty pinks and washed-out primaries. Or look for large pink and red rose prints, which became popular in the 1950s but truly belong to this look. A full, rose-print 1950s skirt or pinafore dress in washed-out primary colours with a shrunken sweater would work perfectly.

## Eveningwear

Naturally, Vivienne Westwood designs have fallen into the collector's box for fans of English eccentricity. For eveningwear, the eccentrically English dresser goes all out: ballgowns, frills, feathers and all manner of furbelow are acceptable.

*Shop vintage for:* Great British designers of the early twentieth century include Reville & Rossiter (later merged with the House of Worth), Michael Sherard, Victor Stiebel for Jacqmar, and Norman Hartnell (the latter two designers both made clothes for Queen Elizabeth and Princess Margaret). It's still possible to uncover forgotten country-house gems by these under-appreciated genii at rural vintage sales or stores in out-of-way spots.

*Shop designer resale for:* Classic Westwood pieces, including bustles, corsets and bustiers. An original checked 1980s mini-crini is perfect for younger lovers of this look and offers endless possibilities. Long 1950s ballgowns in pastel satins and lace (pinks, powder blues, lemony yellows and mint green) fit well with the English Aristo.

## Accessories

No English lady is complete without a classic silk scarf. Work a floral, scenic or Liberty-print scarf as your key accessory by tying it loosely over the shoulders or knotting tightly at the neck. Wear with jodhpurs and a white shirt. Hosiery represents an important part of this look, which is after all more than a little bit "blue stocking". Wear knee-high or ankle socks over patterned tights, brightly coloured socks with flat brogues or woolly stockings in all shades for a quirky feel. Socks and heels can be a tricky look to pull off, but add an instant eccentric feel. Don't forget to pile on the estate jewels or good vintage costume-versions of pearls, cameo brooches, key chains and lockets.

*Shop vintage for:* Original Liberty print scarves, or any with a Harrods logo. Flat lace-up brogues and loafer-style shoes – tassles and buckles are acceptable, as are high-heeled lace-ups and two-tone spectator pumps, especially by British brands Russell & Bromley and Lilley & Skinner.

## Handbags

Good-quality, aged leather satchels, doctor's bags and Gladstones go well with this look, but any kind of old beaten-up leather bag works well. Be cautious when buying vintage designer bags, however. Even though the shop owner may well believe the bag to be genuine Louis Vuitton, it can be hard to tell unless the original packaging or at least the outer bag and authenticity

card are available. If you are not concerned about authenticity, there's no problem. Also, the prices of such items are sometimes only slightly less than if you bought them new. As a rule of thumb, study the detailing on a vintage designer bag. Look carefully inside for any seams that might be coming apart, a missing label, cheap-looking interior linings made of artificial silk or cotton instead of silk. Check zip fastenings and press studs for logos and solid workmanship. Check the designer's website for original features as a comparison or scroll through a site such as www.fashionphile.com, which specializes in only vintage bags.

*Shop vintage for:* Original H. Wald & Co silk bags for evening or leather military-style shoulder bags, messenger bags or cartridge and saddle bags for day. Also fabric-and-leather or canvas totes by Burberry or capacious carpetbags.

## Beauty Guide

English Aristo depends on a naturally beautiful complexion and a perfect bone structure. Creamy skin with a rosy glow is a must but you can cheat, of course. No need for a suntan with this look so instead, choose foundation in a creamy shade similar to your own skin. Choose a product with light-enhancing qualities and a cream blusher to rub on the apples of your cheeks. Avoid powder: it has a drying, ageing effect and no-one wants to look like a dowager duchess the day after a big night on the gin. A soft, gleaming complexion needs only a touch of mascara, preferably dark brown, and a dark, dusky rose-pink lip tint.

A chin-length bob works well with this look, even better if you have curly hair that can be chopped off and left to bounce around at shoulder height. Ideally, hair does not need to be overly "done" and blowdrys are definitely not needed. Neatness is abhorrent and eccentricity is fundamental to the English Aristo look. Consider Helena Bonham-Carter and Daphne Guinness, blue-bloods with a distinctly original approach to style. Both favour dramatic, Gothic elements. Bonham-Carter's bird's-nest coiffure is so quintessentially English that the actress frequently resembles characters from the 1960s St Trinian's films. Guinness, with her trademark white streak, traded her previously pretty but conventional blonde highlights for drama and presence. A messy up-do can update English Aristo chic, too. Wearing hair piled up on top of the head, secured with grips (bobby pins) but with tendrils falling down is flattering and modern.

Young English Aristos also favour a punked-up approach. If your style is more Geldof gal than Sophie Dahl, ripped-up tights and black eyeliner work very well with floral frocks, kilts and men's shirts worn as dresses. Don't forget Tilda Swinton's graceful, natural beauty, too. Her pale colouring and fine blonde hair suit the wistful mood of the Aristo look to perfection – the more natural your hair colour and skin tone are, the more this look will work on you.

### Style Tips

- Never wear black; instead choose natural colours to blend in with your country estate; for a modern twist, add a bright colour in a scarf or accessory.

- This is a covered-up look – no cleavage, no leg.

- Dresses should be below-knee, fitted and floral, worn with a skinny belt.

- Soft, squishy tapestry tote bags lend the requisite comfy look.

- Mix-and-match prints and textures in rusts, coppers, browns and bronze.

- Add lace detail – but ensure it's aged-looking and not bright white.

- Accessorize with cat-eye or round-rimmed glasses and a classic wristwatch.

FAR LEFT: Helena Bonham-Carter in her trademark Vivienne Westwood.

# Marilyn Monroe: Goddess

Marilyn Monroe may not have been a fashion icon in the conventional sense but Goddess style was an element of the look that made her an icon. As Hollywood sought to push the female form to ever more hourglass-shaped extremes, the "Blonde Bombshell" obliged with the most famous shape of them all. To get Monroe's curvaceous look, you don't need her body but you do need to understand how best to flatter your own assets. Finding underwear to enhance your curves is crucial before any shopping trips for this look. Monroe's figure became a blueprint for copycats that included Jayne Mansfield and Sophia Loren.

From the pink satin strapless and fishtail gown in the iconic "Diamonds Are a Girl's Best Friend" sequence from *Gentlemen Prefer Blondes* (1953) to running somewhat innocently along the beach in denim cut-offs and a chunky cardigan, Monroe was a natural Goddess. Moviegoers had no idea that beneath the sensuous aura, Norma Jean (her real name) struggled with her weight, lacked confidence and suffered all manner of personal demons.

To nail the Goddess look, it's essential to understand Marilyn's ultra-feminine style and graceful beauty. Underneath it all, she wasn't the out-and-out sex kitten so often portrayed. Her clothes might be form-fitting, her abundant cleavage frequently on display, but there was a truly angelic radiance about her, too. The Goddess look is not simply a question of pouring yourself into a tight dress and slapping on layers of scarlet lipstick: take time to find outfits that unleash your own ultra-sexy, inner Goddess.

Watch a few Marilyn movies to witness her full effect in action. Check out her plaid shirt and jeans in *Niagara*. For *Seven Year Itch*, Marilyn wore the famous white halterneck dress that blew up over her head as she stood on the subway vent. The dress

## Key Looks

- Halter-neck dress fitted to the waist with concertina pleats
- Black boat-neck dress with full net skirts
- Floor-length, fishtail dress, worn with elbow-length gloves
- Long-sleeve shirt with rolled-up sleeves and "boyfriend" jeans
- Defined and pointed breast shape
- "Po-boy" sweater and chunky, knitted cardigans
- Bucket-shaped handbag
- Clip-on earrings
- Cardigan knotted at the waist
- Ferragamo stiletto shoes

### Goddess Lookalikes
Jayne Mansfield
Diana Dors
Sophia Loren
Anna Nicole Smith
Scarlett Johansson
Eva Herzigova

FAR LEFT: Every Goddess needs to wear gold. Here is Marilyn in her most famous pose, wearing a hand-pleated lamé dress made by William Travilla for 1953's *Gentlemen Prefer Blondes*.

LEFT: A young Sophia Loren (left) and Scarlett Johansson (right) channelling their inner Goddesses.

> **"*I don't mind living in a man's world, as long as I can be a woman in it.*"**
>
> *Marilyn Monroe*

demonstrated that, contrary to popular folklore, the star did wear underwear! Her favourite dress was the shimmering sheath she wore for the final sequence of *Some Like It Hot*. From a squinting distance Monroe appeared to be naked but for a simple sheath of sparkles beginning on her breasts. Monroe loved her natural-looking shape in this dress and had a similar one made for her "Happy Birthday" song to President John F Kennedy at Madison Square Gardens in 1962.

Off-screen, Marilyn was photographed on the beach in a black-and-white patterned (and much-copied) cardigan. "Po-boy" sweaters (so called because the sleeves came up short midway between elbow and wrist) are typical of Marilyn's downtime look, as is a white mac, belted at the waist. Marilyn wore her clothes, not the other way round. Her clothes were worn to accentuate her glorious, full-on female body and this is the spirit of the Goddess look.

RIGHT: Marilyn Monroe takes time out from the set of *Niagara* in rolled-up jeans and cowboy boots.

OPPOSITE: An ivory silk jersey cocktail dress with asymmetrical drape, designed by Ceil Chapman for Marilyn Monroe, is made to cling to curves. Chapman designed her own line of cocktail dresses and gowns as well as costumes for film and television.

# Style Guide

**Palette:** Champagne and pastel colours with a hint of sparkle define the colour choices of the Goddess. Pastels look their best in strong, natural fabrics such as silk or Duchesse Satin. Good-quality finishing will ensure these shades look as classy, sexy and flattering as they ought to. "Ice cream" and pastel shades are notoriously "tacky"-looking in artificial fibres, such as polyester and rayon.

**Key Designers:** Orry-Kelly, Chanel, Levi's, Charles James, Ceil Chapman, Norman Norell.

**Silhouette and Cut:** Exaggerated hourglass with defined, pointed breast shape and rounded-out bottom, the curvier the better. Marilyn's weight yo-yo-ed but this did not matter because all her dresses were made to measure. Well-fitting clothes were part of the secret to her wonderful shape.

## Casual Separates

Goddesses can wear jeans, as demonstrated by Monroe, who chose styles that could be belted at the waist. Choose straight-legged styles with the legs slightly loose and belt at the waist. The trick with a successful girl-take on the Levi 501 is to buy them big and pull in with a belt. Seek out a soft, plaid shirt and wear knotted at the waist for an authentic, casual take on the Goddess look. Alternatively, sass up your jeans in a plain, white, men's T-shirt. Again, tuck in for a feminine shape and roll back the sleeves for a 1950s version.

*Shop vintage for:* The original "boyfriend" jean, the Levi 501. 501s enjoyed a popularity revival in the mid 1980s and purists still hunt them out now.

## Evening Gowns and Dresses

This is easy; choose from three key styles for Goddess chic: satin hourglass and floor-length, concertina-pleat halterneck and a shimmying sheath.

*Shop vintage for:* All of the above plus lucky finds from American eveningwear specialists including Ceil Chapman, Charles James and Norman Norell, or take a leaf out of Marilyn's book and have your dresses made. Goddess shape requires attention to your detail. Hunt out vintage stores that also carry fabrics, as many have tablecloths, curtains and home-furnishing materials from the 1950s (Jackie Kennedy's inaugural gown was made from heavy duchesse satin normally used for home furnishings to ensure it would keep its shape and hang perfectly).

Replicas of Marilyn's *Seven Year Itch* white, pleated dress are pretty easy to find but search for quality, too. Compromise on pleats if you can find a crisp cotton halterneck dress with a full skirt that does the job well. The trickiest look to find is sequin and mesh, sexy clinging dresses like those from *Some Like It Hot* or the one she wore for JFK's birthday celebration at Madison Square Garden. However, vintage stage and theatre costumiers may be a destination for clingy sequin numbers. The joy of vintage shopping can often be had searching out seemingly elusive garments. Specialist stores are the way to go.

## Shoes

It has been said that MM modified one shoe to give her that sexy hip-swaying walk, though this is unlikely considering the price and craftsmanship of her shoe choices. Famously quoted as saying "Give a girl the right shoes, and she can conquer the world," Monroe's choice of designer was Salvatore Ferragamo, the most famous being a pair of rhinesone-encrusted red shoes. One suede and crocodile shoe created for *Some Like it Hot* was designed in dozens of colours and materials for her.

*Shop vintage for:* Ferragamo stilettos from the 1950s are the ideal, but pricey, choice. Look for a heel height of 9 cm (3½ inches). Slingbacks and mules were also Marilyn's choices for eveningwear, so look for 1950s versions by Charles Jourdan or Frederick's of Hollywood.

## Accessories

The Goddess does not carry her own bag; her only accessory is a cigarette. This does not need to be lit; it can just be waved around. On-screen Marilyn was often adorned with jewellery but in real life she wore minimal accoutrements to feel and look as natural as possible.

TOP: Marilyn Monroe's iconic red Swarovski rhinestone shoes for *Gentlemen Prefer Blondes*, 1953, and a gold kidskin stiletto worn in *Bus Stop*, 1956. Both by Ferragamo.

ABOVE: Look for sparkling jewellery like this diamanté and gemstone bracelet to wear as a signature piece.

RIGHT: The pink satin dress by Travilla, worn by Marilyn in *Gentlemen Prefer Blondes*, has side slits and a big bow at the back.

OPPOSITE: Goddess beauty emphasizes lips, cheeks and eyes. Monroe's usual dark brown eyeliner, false lashes and beauty spot are all present in this publicity shot.

*Shop vintage for:* For jewellery, look for big, bold diamanté pieces, clip-on, non-dangling earrings or chandelier styles. Otherwise, try fun 1950s accessories, bucket-shaped bags, raffia half-basket, half-leather handbags and "tiki" Hawaiian print scarves. "Tiki" style was a fun theme born from movies set in Hawaii such as Elvis Presley's Blue Hawaii. The style included bamboo-covered home accessories, traditional Hawaiian flower strings and plastic flowers and fruit of all kinds, plus exotic, flower-print shirts for men and separates for women.

# Beauty Guide

Off-screen, Monroe was far more inclined to leave nature to itself and often went without make-up in private. When forced to face a crowd or paparazzi she would slick on a touch of coral lipstick and hide behind enormous shades, day or night, to prevent herself being pictured cosmetics-free. Monroe's natural beauty stood up well to the standard red lipstick and black eyeliner look of the time. A natural blonde who had faded to a reddish brown in adulthood, she had pale skin without the freckles often associated with such colouring. Monroe found it hard to tan and kept herself mainly covered from the sun, preferring a lighter complexion with creamy blusher accenting her apple cheeks. Monroe had the same make-up artist, Allan "Whiley" Snyder, all her life. This explains the consistency of her simple make-up look. She always wore brown shadow and dark eyeliner along her upper lid, with lashings of black mascara.

For Monroe, blonde hair was everything and she never returned to her natural shade after finally plunging for platinum in 1953, in time to film *Gentlemen Prefer Blondes*. For the last ten years of her life, Monroe wore her hair in the same simple bob. Gently layered around the ends so that it flicked up, she was not a fan of heavily rollered and lacquered styles. She was a sensuous woman and wanted touchable, sexy hair. Like Bardot, she favoured a slightly messed-up, informal look in private.

## Marilyn "Set" Hair

This style works best for jaw-to-shoulder length, layered lengths of hair and is a classic 1950s "roller set" look. It has been said that up to nine shades of blonde were tried on Marilyn before she settled on her platinum blonde. The hairstyle has been a look copied by Scarlett Johansson, Christina Aguilera and Katherine Heigl.

**You will need:**
Mousse
Setting lotion
Set of hot rollers
or a curling iron
Hair clips
Hairspray

1 After shampooing the hair, towel try gently, then apply gel mousse.
2 Create a deep side parting, section off and, using a round brush, blow-dry section by section to a smooth finish, curling under.
3 Then make a deep side part and section off into 2.5 cm (1 inch) sections. Spray each section with setting lotion.
4 Using a hot roller set, roll each section onto the roller. Wind sections around the face and at the forehead under toward the face, and wind those behind them backward toward the crown and nape of the neck.
    Alternatively, curl each section with a curling iron, following the same winding pattern, and secure each curl in place with grips (bobby pins) before moving on to the next section.
5 Leave until cool, then remove the rollers (or grips) and gently comb through each curl with a wide-tooth comb to soften. Mist with hairspray.

# Audrey Hepburn: Ingénue

Inspired by Audrey Hepburn, the Ingénue style features boxy shapes with feminine edges. A go-to evening style for any woman seeking an easy, chic fix, it also makes a great style for shoestring shoppers and students because 1950s and early 1960s garments still linger in shops, markets and online. Think Beatnik bars of the 1950s, smoky jazz clubs and gamine beauties with short, pixie haircuts or always-neat buns, ponytails and up-dos. The colour palette is based around black and the shapes flatter every feminine form.

Although there's no doubting Audrey Hepburn's natural grace and beauty, she owed much of her fashion choices to her costumier, Edith Head, who guided Hepburn toward the great designers Hubert de Givenchy and Cristóbal Balenciaga. They, in turn, created the shapes for which Hepburn's Ingénue style became famous and, if you adhere to their simple silhouettes, the look is easily and authentically achieved. Balenciaga's most famous design innovation was the "standout back". While the front of his gowns fitted perfectly, the back stood away from the body in a medieval princess way, giving the wearer a regal look and Hepburn wore this style in long and short versions. Givenchy created boxy designs for her, but they were never unfeminine.

Originally a ballet dancer, Audrey Hepburn was spotted by Collette, the Parisian boutique owner, on a railway station in France. Collette suggested the young girl should be in films and a star career was born. Hepburn epitomized the youthful spirit of 1950s style as the decade ended. When *Breakfast at Tiffany's* was released in America in 1959, it heralded a glimpse into the emancipated girl's future. The easy movement of the look reflects Holly Golightly's free spirit, even the impending freedom of women. Givenchy said at the time, "I've dreamt of a liberated woman who will no longer be swathed in fabric, armour-plated."

## Key Looks

- A fitted, not tight, structured silhouette
- Beatnik black turtlenecks and slimline slacks
- Princess-style, ballerina-length "New Look" dresses and pinafores
- Bateau ("Sabrina") necklines
- Shift dresses
- Pearls
- Court heels
- Elegant, simple eveningwear; column or A-line LBDs, worn with real jewellery
- A plain white shirt. These became a big trend in the 1950s after Audrey wore one in *Roman Holiday*. For the full-on Audrey look, tie it at the waist
- Flat pumps, which can be worn with anything from Capri pants to full 1950s-style skirts
- A long silk scarf in neutral colour so it can be worn with anything, and worn in every way possible
- Chic fitted suit

### Ingénue Lookalikes
Shirley MacLaine
Jean Seberg
Katie Holmes
Audrey Tautou
Natalie Portman

OPPOSITE: The elegant and poised Belgian-born British actress Audrey Hepburn poses in a film still from *Funny Face* (1957).

LEFT: Natalie Portman and Audrey Tautou imitate the Audrey Hepburn look naturally with their slight figures, luminous skin and gamine hairstyles.

His garments, he said, were light enough to "float on a body delivered from bondage." Although he was talking about corseted underwear, the metaphors now seem relevant to feminism – minis and bra-less liberation were just around the historical corner.

# Style Guide

**The Palette:** Black, red, bottle green, white, cream, the odd flash of yellow or orange. Audrey's favourite colour was said to have been pink, but she more often stuck to neutrals.

**Key Designers:** Hubert de Givenchy, Cristóbal Balenciaga, Christian Dior.

**Silhouette and Cut:** This is a petite look; a neat head, visible neck and boxy shape, revealing wrists and ankles, sum up the style. The waist is always present, clothes are never baggy and often skim the hips and stomach but a cinched-in waist is not as crucial to this look. The billowy shapes are flattered by being cut beautifully across the shoulders, around the arms and wrists, and stopping on or slightly above the knee. Boxy tops often give way to narrow pedal pushers stopping well above the ankle. Boat-necks, elbow-length sleeves and slightly shortened trousers always elongated and flattered Audrey Hepburn's tiny physique.

## Dresses and Eveningwear

The dress is a wardrobe staple for Ingénue style. Flirtatious but never too revealing, Hepburn's Givenchy shift dresses were often deeply cut around armholes, low at the back but never drew attention to cleavage. Breasts should be well supported for this look to create a curvaceously neat silhouette. Day dresses can be simple pinafores, as Hepburn's look in *Sabrina*, or smarter single-colour wool or jersey. Eveningwear is fantastic yet entirely controlled. Think black confection, lace and netting over pure black satin, bows, tight bodices, full skirts or simply cut, flattering cocktail dresses. The look is fitted, not skintight – Ingénues don't need to try too hard. Details such as the 1960s bow at the waist appeared on both day and evening dresses.

*Shop vintage for*: Designer originals by Givenchy, Balenciaga and Dior are now mainly consigned to the super-rich collector or museum costume collections. Gorgeous of-the-era copies are plentiful, though, and look for empire-line column dresses, long backless sheaths, or strapless gowns with very full ballerina-length dresses.

# Knits

Mohair, cashmere and bouclé knitted sweaters suit the Ingénue, ditto large roll collars, boat and slash necks and polo or "mock" polo necks (turtlenecks). Typical sleeve shapes are raglan, elbow-length or tightly fitted to the wrist, which add to the outline. Sweaters should be no longer than hip-skimming and will look tidy worn with above-ankle, narrow slacks or jeans. Ingénue style could incorporate a black beaded evening cardigan, possibly worn with the buttons at the back. Other 1950s detailing to look for includes Intarsia patterns. These are small motifs knitted in different coloured yarn within a sweater or cardigan, usually a flower, bow or butterfly shape.

*Shop vintage for*: Designer knitwear from the 1950s is the ultimate goal but sadly rarely available. However, many beaded evening styles can still be snapped up, presumably because they were always saved for best. Collectable and sometimes still available 1950s names include Grès, Nina Ricci, Balmain, Lanvin, Ballantyne (American designer Bonnie Cashin created a range for them in this decade) and Pringle of Scotland.

LEFT: An embroidered dress by her favoured couturier, Givenchy, in 1963 shows off her prim figure with its high Sabrina neckline and nipped-in waist.

RIGHT: Audrey Hepburn's Givenchy white point d'esprit ballgown from the 1956 film *Love in the Afternoon*.

## Style Tips

- Ignore trends. Stick with the classics and what suits you.

- Audrey's favourite casual style was a pair of skinny trousers, a polo neck and some flat shoes – all in black. She often wore this to and from the studios.

- Rarely in spangles or sequins, Audrey sometimes added a whimsical touch with a cute hat, scarf or some pretty bows.

- Givenchy's distinctive neckline "décolleté Sabrina" was created for Audrey – she favoured it to hide her collarbone and show off her shoulders.

## Trousers

The slimline black Capri was one of Audrey's core off-duty pieces, which helped create her neat, clean silhouette. In fact, a 2006 commercial for Gap used clips of her dancing from *Funny Face* with the tagline "It's Back – The Skinny Black Pant".

*Shop vintage for*: Black vintage Capris are likely to be faded but there should be plenty of brightly coloured versions available. Details include high waists, side zips, side slits at the hem and flat fronts. Look for cigarette pants too – these follow a similar narrow-fitting line but cover the ankle.

## Coats

This is a great winter style. Bright wool coats, fur collars and muffs and capes suit the silhouette well. Look for swing styles or boxy and billowy shapes but select knee-length, as any longer could look too huge and frumpy. Elbow-length or "bracelet" sleeves worn slightly above the wrist were styles of the time. Decoration to spot includes super-large buttons in the same colour as the coat; false, half-belts on the back; scarves attached with press-stud (snap) fastenings.

*Shop vintage for:* Many department stores sold well-made coats in these styles. Seek out US brands Neiman Marcus or Saks Fifth Avenue, Lord & Taylor (Tom Brigance designed for them in the 1950s) and UK brands Barkers, House of Fraser, Jaeger and Viyella.

## Shoes

No higher than 10 cm (4 inches) but not tiny kitten: that's the rule for Ingénue heels. Look for 1950s and 1960s evening styles in dyed satin or lace fabrics with stiletto heels, or flat pumps for casual day wear. When vintage shoe hunting take a tip from Hepburn herself, who always bought a half size larger than she needed to stop her toes and shoes bulging. Nothing looks worse than a bunion-shaped lump on a pointed-toe shoe.

*Shop vintage for:* A pair of original Roger Vivier shoes would be a true find. Vivier designed for Dior, first introducing the spindly stiletto to accompany Dior's New Look frocks in 1947. Ballet pumps, Audrey's favourite flats, were made for her in 1957 by Ferragamo but vintage Capezio will be more easily available. Other shoe names to spot-check include Mabel Julianelli, shoemaker to Sophia Loren, H&M Rayne, Rayne-Delman and Bally.

## Hats, Gloves and Scarves

While wide-brimmed and feathered hats are a little over the top, they may still work with a summer look. A hat also looks wonderful with a shift dress in the same colour. Scarves, sunglasses and gloves – both for day and elbow-length for evening – were very much part of Audrey's put-together look. The tortoiseshell sunglasses with green lenses worn by Holly Golightly were reissued by Oliver Goldsmith in 2011. A headscarf, knotted beneath the chin, was an Audrey favourite and lends a glamorous leading-lady touch when worn with sunglasses.

LEFT: Audrey's black "Beatnik" ensemble of sweater dress and tights, a variation on the black Capris and polo neck.

OPPOSITE: Audrey's much-copied formal look from *Breakfast at Tiffany's*: the tiara in her beehive and the pearl choker frame her face.

## Jewellery

Ingénue style is accentuated with a few dramatic accessories: huge pearls, big beads, a striking wrist cuff or set of bangles. Charm bracelets also add to the upmarket allure. For evenings, Ingénues can pile it all on, with matching earring and necklace sets.

*Shop vintage for*: Pearls and diamanté earrings in mint condition can be hard to find and pricey, but look for 1980s versions. Vintage tiaras to dress up your evening look are available from vintage boutiques and online dealers specializing in bridalwear.

# Beauty Guide

Audrey Hepburn's perfect bone structure presented movie make-up artists with the ultimate canvas for their work. Make-up supervisor Wally Westmore accentuated her eye make-up on *Breakfast at Tiffany's*, developing the screen look he first created for her in *Sabrina* (1954) and *Funny Face* (1957). Fans will know Hepburn's make-up was strong and exaggerated in the movie to emphasize Holly Golightly's character as a pretty but broken doll. Up close it is clear she was wearing a heavy foundation base to give a perfect china-doll complexion. This is a strong look that also, luckily, works beautifully on any face shape. Cheeks are rosy pink as were the lips, and eyebrows were well-groomed, pencilled and full.

Although the Ingénue look can be blonde, it really is a brunette or red-headed look. The whole point of Hepburn was that she was nothing like the other busty blonde stars of her day. She wore elaborate hairpieces or a simple ponytail, but the main key to her look was a wispy, short-ish fringe worn with height on the crown, created by a little backcombing beneath a top smooth layer. As a basic shape, everything else was secondary to this starting point. Hair accessories, including black velvet bows, clips and even a pinned-in blonde streak, adorned Holly Golightly's head, so give them a whirl, too, if you're copying her hairstyle.

**You will need:**
Tweezers
Brow powder shadow
and brush
Brow pencil
Brow wax (tinted or clear)

TIP: To avoid getting too much powder or wax on the brow, dab the colour onto the back of your hand first and swipe several times with the brush to load the brush with just enough colour.

## Groomed Brows

Audrey's brows were quite thick, flat and defined and extended well beyond the outer corner of the eye, which gave a dramatic accent to her face. Choose one shade darker than your natural brows to recreate this look.

1 To create the Audrey brow shape, the eyebrow should be slightly longer than the outer corner of the eye while the starting point should be aligned with the inner corner of your eye.
2 If your brows are thin or sparse, first define the shape by filling in with a brow pencil using short, wispy strokes. This will help you create the shape you want without it looking drawn on.
3 Using an angled brow brush and the powder, and starting from the centre of the brow where the colour is naturally deepest, brush in the direction of hair growth to fill in the entire brow and strengthen colour.
4 Now brush the wax on top to set the powder colour and tame any wayward hairs.
5 If you still have sparse areas or want a deeper colour, dip the same brush into the powder again and fill in the area.

### Beauty Tips

• Keep a clean foundation with little eyeshadow. The eyelid should be primed with preferably a pale grey or pinky-beige shade to enable eye-liner to "pop".

• Use a cream or fluid eyeliner to create a perfect elongated line along the upper lashes, which is then tapered upward and outward. It has the effect of a mini-face-lift, pulling the whole face upward, too.

• Pink cheeks and pale pink lips will help to emulate the fresh-faced Hepburn look.

• Keep the brow full and brushed. Pencil in any sparse areas to achieve the look.

• Avoid false lashes – Audrey's was a clean non-vampy look with lashes accented by mascara only.

• Audrey was the inspiration for Givenchy's L'Inderdit Perfume – spritz on to get a hint of Audrey!

LEFT: Hepburn on the set of *Sabrina* displays the talents of her make-up artist Wally Westmore – sharply angled brows, delicate eyeliner on the upper lashline only and coral lips accentuate her pretty pixie face.

# Grace Kelly: Ice Princess

Grace Kelly and Katharine Hepburn both starred as fictional heiress Tracy Samantha Lord in *The Philadelphia Story* and *High Society* respectively, albeit in different eras. Kelly went on to marry a real-life prince, Rainier III of Monaco, in 1956 and her cool, ice-blonde beauty was the perfect antidote to Hollywood's hot super-vamps. Her ladylike full-skirted dresses, sweeping down to mid-calf length, were reminiscent of Christian Dior's "New Look", sharply contrasting with Hollywood's skintight pencil-skirted silhouettes.

On and off-screen, Grace Kelly embodied a smart, upmarket brand of elegance that was to evolve as a blueprint for the buttoned-up, affluent American housewife of the 1950s. "Toney" is another word that sums it up perfectly. While there is no dictionary definition, it's safe to say that it describes the honed, toned features of America's self-made upper-classes. The look revolved around fitted dresses with matching jackets over the top, simple kidney-shaped hats plus pointed, stiletto-heel court shoes, mink stoles and satin gowns for evening. Conventional, smart and groomed, this look works well today for the office. Off-duty, Grace wore Capri pants with flat pumps or moccasins.

The crisp, simple silhouette of the Ice Princess look was enhanced by healthy-looking natural coloured or carefully dyed hair. A light tan or sprinkling of freckles demonstrated that even the most fashionably dressed American enjoyed the great outdoors. Horseriding and nautical or recreational sailing details crept into day clothes to emphasize a love of sporting pursuits. Princesses were definitely home birds, too, and an industry sprang up around lingerie and leisurewear. Negligées, peignoirs and matching nightgowns, Doris Day-style pyjamas, housecoats and lounging suits were all the terrain of American designer Sylvia Pedlar, who created silk and chiffon creations for the perfect princess in her boudoir. Gently-fitting nightgowns were worn with prettified nylon or chiffon negligées. Pedlar also designed some of the first lingerie ranges for Christian Dior and Hubert de Givenchy.

LEFT: Grace Kelly in a scene from *To Catch a Thief* in 1955 wears a cream chiffon gown with a "Grecian" style draped bodice.

RIGHT: January Jones, a.k.a. Betty Draper, the troubled but perfect-looking 1950s housewife on HBO's *Mad Men*.

FAR RIGHT: Gwyneth Paltrow stealing Ice Princess style at the 1999 Academy Awards.

***Ice Princess Lookalikes***
Babe Paley
Kim Novak
January Jones as Betty Draper
in *Mad Men*
Gwyneth Paltrow
Rosamund Pike

# Style Guide

**Palette:** Almost-white, pastel shades of mint, blue and pink, especially in satin or cotton sateen fabrics. Grace wore suits in creamy, beige woven wool and coats in bright red and green. Other colours include cream, camel and navy blue knitwear, the occasional flash of candy pink, banana yellow, or emerald green for eveningwear and special occasions.

**Key Designers:** Christian Dior, Jacques Fath, Charles James, Norman Norell, Sylvia Pedlar, Cristóbal Balenciaga, Hubert de Givenchy.

**Silhouette and Cut:** The New Look silhouette with an emphasis on full skirts and tiny cinched-in waists. Although many dresses were ballerina-length (falling to above the ankle), this was balanced by a more exposed décolletage – with off-shoulder, portrait and sweetheart necklines. With the return of the corset, tight-waisted bodices were kept in place, though with a more flexible nylon and elastic version – the girdle.

## Dresses

In contrast to the spare looks of the 1930s and '40s, Parisian designers such as Christian Dior, Jacques Fath, Balenciaga and Givenchy and their imitators, created classic Ice Princess styles. This was the era of the sexy and glamorous cocktail dress, when Betty Draper types dressed up for pre-dinner drinks with their husbands – Grace favoured chiffon and velvet versions.

*Shop vintage for:* Strapless is the only way to go for evening, plus full skirts stiffened with layers of net petticoats. Such dresses were not cheap, requiring yards of good-quality fabric. Day dresses were less full but still long and fairly flouncy; choose styles with turn-back cuffs, lapels and coat-like details. Choose summer dresses with square or sweetheart necklines and close-fitting short sleeves.

### Key Looks

- Full-skirted, longer dresses with masses of net petticoats
- Snug capes and shrug jackets
- Riding jacket, jodhpurs and riding boots
- Full "swagger" coats
- Coat dresses with button fronts worn with a handkerchief knotted at the neck
- White sunglasses with round lenses
- Headscarves worn over the head and knotted tightly at the nape of the neck
- Cashmere cardigans worn cape-like over the shoulders and buttoned at the collar
- Elbow- or bracelet-length sleeves
- Hermès Kelly bag or large square leather bags with metal snap clasps
- Lace-edged, full-length nightgowns with matching negligées
- Stockings and suspender belts

RIGHT: Grace Kelly's dresses from the "Grace Kelly: Style Icon" exhibition at the Victoria & Albert Museum, London, in 2010. The floral cocktail gown is for evening while the button-through is a classic 1950s day dress.

OPPOSITE TOP: Pearls and white gloves make the perfect Ice Princess accessories to this New Look pink lace and net dress from 1952.

## Separates and Knits

Givenchy created the Bettina blouse in the mid 1950s, which became a favourite for Grace Kelly and Audrey Hepburn. A simple, fitted shirt with huge bell-shaped sleeves, it looks good worn with snugly fitting Capri pants, a pencil skirt or full, gathered waist skirt. A word on pencil skirts: Ice Princesses choose gracefully touching-where-they-fit-only, straight skirts with small back kick pleats to allow for movement. The fine-knit cashmere twinset, originally a brilliant idea by Coco Chanel for chilly spring days, was reborn in the 1950s – Grace Kelly wore her cardigan as a cape, top button fastened at the neck.

*Shop vintage for*: Cashmere twinsets and snug round-neck sweaters from Pringle, Ballantyne, Dalton, Hadley and Bonnie Cashin, as well as beaded and embroidered cardigans from Helen Bond Carruthers. Many copies of the Bettina were made, so hunt out this flattering, elegant sleeve-shape.

## Outerwear

The "topper" is the key Princess shape – a shorter, hip- or three-quarter length version of the "swagger" coat. Both styles fitted neatly across the shoulders but then dramatically flared out. For evening, full satin coats with enormous collars that stood away from the shoulders were worn.

*Shop vintage for:* Fitted and flared button-up coats to wear over day dresses – look for brightly coloured versions in red or blue. Details on swagger coats and toppers might include a half-belt at the back, a double-breasted front with no collar and two oversize buttons. Proportions are important for authenticity, so it's worth hunting down longer-length 1950s garments.

## Casual Clothes

Off-screen Grace Kelly relaxed in preppy classics including "Chino" style trousers, Capri pants and crisp, white shirts accessorized with a leather belt and neckscarf. Kelly also wore men's-style shorts with a shirt knotted at the waist.

*Shop vintage for:* Men's oversize V-neck sweaters and good-quality, well-fitting men's Chino trousers, Capri pants, ladies' gingham-print shirts plus short, swingy cardigans.

RIGHT: Capri pants and sleeveless polo neck make a cool, casual summer ensemble.

## Shoes

This was the age of the satin, pointed-toe dance slipper, dyed to match a frock, and gold or silver stiletto evening sandals. American designer Mabel Julianelli was famous for her "barely there" shoes – stiletto heels with simple, very thin straps on top – the forerunners to modern evening sandals. Toe-thong straps and Japanese-style "flip-flops" were popular. Grace Kelly wore a flat leather version for relaxing in Monaco after her wedding.

*Shop vintage for:* Pointy stiletto pumps and slingbacks from Rayne, Mabel Julianelli, Charles Jourdan and Bally. Sparkles and glitter look best with confectionary-style dresses, so seek out anything strappy on top with a slim heel. The Ice Princess look requires a ladylike foot – no platforms or clunky shoes!

## Handbags

Women began to carry around more paraphernalia in the 1950s and lipsticks and eye make-up came in small, durable palettes that could be stored alongside powder compacts in neat make-up bags. Ladies who lunched kept pocket date diaries and address books. More women drove cars and carried their own keys, so the need for bigger bags grew. Chunky, boxy shapes made from Lucite, a pearlized form of Bakelite, were fashionable alongside bags made from woven raffia, bamboo and natural materials. Quality leather goods became highly covetable, too. Émile-Maurice Hermès made handbags from saddle leather at his eponymously named family business. In the 1930s he created a large flat bag for his wife Julie, perfectly sized for fitting into a car door pocket but expandable. Grace Kelly was photographed with one of these bags in 1956, which prompted the company to name the bag after her. She

OPPOSITE: Multicoloured shoes reflect the 1950s trend for a colour-matched look. Fruit-inspired shades – peach, apricot and lemon – were considered fresh and new. These late 1950s designs are by Charles Jourdan, Rayne, Bally, Dolcis, Lilley and Skinner and Dior.

LEFT: Each Hermès Kelly bag is handmade from start to finish by just one person.

**Style Tips**

• With a strapless evening gown, wear a coat pushed back behind the shoulders like a shawl or wrap.

• Wear a simple string of pearls like a choker – ask a jeweller to shorten for you.

• Strapless dresses should be cut straight across or only slightly curved above the cleavage.

• Wear a snug cardigan, buttoned up and tucked into Capri pants or a twinset paired with smart pressed slacks or full skirts.

• Practice the rules of etiquette. An Ice Princess will always know which fork to use! Read Emily Post's *Etiquette* or Amy Vanderbilt's *Complete Book of Etiquette: A Guide to Gracious Living* (first published in 1952).

famously hid her first pregnancy behind her Kelly bag for months before announcing it to the press. Grace had coloured, canvas and leather as well as the original tan, saddle-hide version. The boxy, briefcase-type bag is synonymous with Kelly chic, as is a black valise-style bag by American manufacturer Mark Cross, which she used in the film *Rear Window*.

*Shop vintage for:* Choose 1950s handbags fashioned from woven raffia for summer or square-shaped snap-shut versions with a neat, gilt clasp in calf, crocodile or snakeskin, in structured, frame-box styles. Although vintage original Hermès Kelly bags are expensive, look for that same shape from other designers such as Mark Cross, Koret, Jane Shilton, H Wald, Caron of Texas and store brands. Beautiful but pricey, the best Lucite handbags are by Wilardy, Llewellyn, Gilli Originals and Patricia of Miami.

## Accessories

Headscarves were key accoutrements to 1950s ladies. Necessary for holding elaborate, lacquered hairstyles in place, colourful silks were popular. Hermès and Liberty of London produced the most famous prints although there were many copies. Grace Kelly liked to knot her scarf beneath her chin or tied round the neck, perfect for keeping her hair in place on Riviera outings. Just before they married, Rainier ignited another fashion trend when he bought Grace a matching necklace and bracelet set from Van Cleef & Arpels in New York, consisting of three-tiered pearls with diamond clasps. Accessory-wise, the Grace Kelly look embraces the 1950s fashion for elbow-length sleeves, charm bracelets and ladies' wristwatches.

*Shop vintage for:* Oversize gold-coloured costume jewellery with enamelling or coloured stones, oversize pearls, big-link chains and gold bangles. Also, look for a small plain gold ladies' watch with a brown leather strap for day and dainty, diamanté-encrusted versions as evening. Hunt out original 1950s costume jewellery by brands Ciro, Monet and Adrien Mann. Henkel and Grosse were the German designers of Dior costume jewellery from 1955 and any H&V items from that era are collectable now. There are several good dealers who specialize in vintage Hermès scarves, though the price is high; for an appropriate alternative version, seek out 1950s silk scarves with countrified equestrian prints, mimicking the Hermès horse-saddle imagery.

# Beauty Guide

Grace Kelly's look was that of the quintessential ice blonde. However, her almost bare-faced beauty can be achieved on any colouring, as the key is grooming. Americans are expert at the art of looking immaculate and this should be the foundation for a Princess look. That means having every beauty box ticked, from perfectly plucked eyebrows to a smooth complexion, pearly white teeth, neat nails and not a hair out of place. Try a French or America-style manicure to mimic Grace Kelly's fresh look; the American style has creamy, instead of brilliant white nail tips, and a beige rather than pink base. Having a professional manicure is an easy way to feel instantly groomed.

Grace Kelly's 1950s waved hair was always glossy and perfectly sprayed into place. While it was pretty, the same look might seem dated now. Try a slightly longer version with looser waves for a more modern take but keep the glow by finishing with a high-shine styling product. An easy option would be a Betty Draper bob, slightly layered to flick up at the ends, just long enough to be pulled back into a short, neat ponytail. If your hair is long, try a neat chignon at the back of your neck for a clean outline.

Most importantly, this look is a healthy one so make sparkling eyes and rosy cheeks a focal point of the Ice Princess face. Close inspection of Princess Grace photos reveal she wore plenty of make-up but the overall effect was ultra-clean and fresh. Eye drops will add sparkle while natural brown or grey shadow colours are best for eye definition. Try dark brown mascara instead of black and define cheekbones with a pinkish-tinged blusher, preferably a cream to allow for a soft sheen rather than a powdered effect. The Grace Kelly face may sport a light tan but as a rule it's shaded from sunworshipping evidence and prettily rosy. Lips are rosy red but chaste-looking.

ABOVE: Clean, immaculate and groomed applied to both clothes and beauty in the Ice Princess look. Not only do the coat, suit and hat match, but so does the lipstick. The swagger coat – a Kelly favourite – and suit are by Jean Patou, 1954.

OPPOSITE: The fresh-faced American girl in the mid 1950s. Grace Kelly appeared in ads for Max Factor and topped America's Best Dressed List in 1956.

**Beauty Tips**

• Choose natural, barely
  perceptible make-up, but
  with full-coverage foundation
  and a coral blush.

• Choose pinks or corals for lips.

• Carefully define eyes with
  natural taupe, brown eyeliner
  and dark brown mascara –
  black can be too heavy.

• Push a flipped-back bob
  behind your ears and secure
  with sparkly hairgrips.

## The Sleek Bob

Grace's glossy golden blonde hair was cut in a chin-length blunt bob. Hers
was a chic, "done" look, though gently curled or flipped at the ends. It
has a lot of volume on the top but is sleeker at the sides and with the curls
at the bottom and to the back. The hair sweeps away from the hair line
toward the back of the head and shows off the ears and earrings. You really
do need hot rollers for this look and a to-the-shoulder or above hair length.
For a true retro experience, roll damp hair in sponge rollers and leave
overnight rather than using hot rollers.

**You will need**
Rat-tail comb
Paddle brush
Hot Rollers
Hair grips (bobby pins)
Hairspray or high-shine
finishing spray

1 Working on at least day-old hair, create a side parting (Grace's was on
  her left), and section your hair with the comb.
2 Wind each section in the hot rollers, winding away from the face. The
  very bottom back pieces should wind under, but the remaining sections
  should all be wound away from the front hair line.
3 Leave in for at least 25 minutes, depending on how easily your hair
  curls, then remove from the rollers.
4 Spray with hairspray and gently brush out with a paddle brush.
5 Now brush the hair back away from the face to create smooth height
  at the top. Spray for hold and shine.
6 Secure the hair behind one or both ears with grips (bobby pins) or
  decorative clip to expose the ear.
7 If your hair is too long, make the curls at the bottom tighter using
  curling tongs or lightly backcomb to shorten.

# Elizabeth Taylor: Hollywood Glamour

Gorgeous glamour epitomizes the style of Elizabeth Taylor. Expensive, elegant and forever feminine, it was her insistence on the finest finishing touches that separated Taylor from the mass of 1960s Hollywood stars. "Face, breasts, waist" was her mantra and she dressed to accentuate her three top assets. The double-Oscar-winning actress performed on and off screen with dazzling brilliance, a complicated character mix of brains, beauty and caprice.

From an early age, Taylor was destined for stardom. Her carefully put-together look originated from a love of costume and the leading role. Never seen in public unless fully dressed and accessorized, Taylor always made an entrance with perfect hair and make-up, adorned by the most splendid jewellery. One of the world's most beautiful women, she was not a devotee of any one designer, preferring to choose her wardrobe according to fashion and, in true movie-star style, have clothes tailor-made.

The young Taylor was creating fashion waves on-screen from her earliest starring roles. A white, strapless evening dress of silk petal-sprinkled tulle worn in *A Place in the Sun* (1951) was one of the most copied gowns of its time. Thanks to the ingenious costumier Edith Head, Taylor secured her own special place in the fashion sun from the moment the movie launched. Later she was dressed in simple yet striking 1950s cuts, with a tiny waist and expansive cleavage, by top costumier Helen Rose to star opposite Paul Newman in *Cat on a Hot Tin Roof* (1958). Givenchy supplied the Taylor wardrobe for Terence Rattigan's *The V.I.P.s* (1963); however, it was as the young Egyptian queen in *Cleopatra* (1963) that Taylor would really shine. The most expensive movie of all time was shot in Rome and was to transform her into one of the world's finest actresses; it also sparked one of Hollywood's greatest romances between Taylor and her leading man, Richard

## Key Looks

- Wide-cut V-neck dresses
- Kaftans and turbans in vivid prints, especially Pucci
- Bejewelled empire-line evening gowns
- Plunging necklines
- Draped, hourglass gowns
- Extravagant head-to-toe matching ensembles, including hats made of the same fabric as dresses
- 1970s prints in bright colours
- Elbow-length gloves
- Jewellery sets of matching earrings, necklace and bracelet, such as the 1957 ruby and diamond set by Cartier, a gift from husband Mike Todd
- Large, sparkly chandelier earrings
- Extravagant headpieces.

## Hollywood Glamour Lookalikes
Joan Collins
Catherine Zeta-Jones
Kate Beckinsale
Kim Kardashian

OPPOSITE: A film still of Taylor from *Last Time I Saw Paris*, 1955. "Face, breasts, waist" was Elizabeth Taylor's beauty mantra, all shown off to perfection here. She loved jewel colours including the emerald green she is wearing in this shot.

FAR LEFT: Actress Catherine Zeta-Jones' dark beauty and classic, film-star dress sense make her a natural style successor to Elizabeth Taylor.

LEFT: Kim Kardashian, a radiant brunette, has a Taylor-style, hourglass look that makes her millions. High-fashion status eludes her but she has tons of glamour.

ABOVE: Silk palazzo beach pajamas from Pucci, late 1960s. To steal Taylor's style, accessorize with jewelled sandals and a turban. There were plenty of Pucci imitators at the time so search for secondhand knock-offs.

Burton. Costumes were not only splendid but also reflected early 1960s high fashion. Draped silk dresses accentuating curves were the central building blocks of the *Cleopatra* wardrobe, with bejewelled collars, strapless, cutout and V-shaped necklines, plus armlets adding detail. Twentieth Century Fox's costume designer "Renie" (real name Irene Brouillet) won an Oscar for her sumptuous efforts. Throughout filming, Taylor's weight yo-yoed, causing her ensembles to be repeatedly altered to fit. What remained constant, however, was her tiny waist, drawn in every day of the production by a dresser brought in specifically for the task. Even now, *Cleopatra* is an extraordinary spectacle and a must-see for movie fans and fashionistas alike.

Elizabeth's voluptuous figure added to her allure; her skin had a smooth, healthy look, and her fame coincided with a beneath-the-surface revolution in lingerie. Thanks to Dior's "New Look" of 1947, which required a small waist to offset a full skirt, the corset made a return, albeit in a softer version. Composed of stretchy elastic fabric known as Lastex, with easily fastened, concealed buttons, the corset or panty-girdle (as it was often built onto a pair of knickers) assisted in the return of the hourglass figure. New Yorker Frederick Mellinger's famous store, Frederick's of Hollywood, was known for lingerie in sensuous, colourful constructions that flattered the figures of strumpets and starlets including stripper Betty Page. Among the first to introduce underwiring and padding to brassieres, Mellinger also produced a line of less-appealing buttock pads that also sold well. Designed to add curves to skinny bottoms, it's unlikely Liz had need of such help. To get her look some suffering is necessary: you simply must have a waist!

Off-camera, Taylor led a colourful life as an international jetsetter. The underlying tension in *The V.I.P.s* reflected the real-life emotion between the beautiful actress and her lover, Richard Burton. Elizabeth's need for passion, love and drama was always reflected in her clothes. A trip to the Italian Riviera would warrant an entire beach wardrobe from Pucci, complete with matching turbans and towels. Her pear-shaped 69.42-carat diamond, a gift from Burton and now known as the Taylor–Burton Diamond, is one of the largest in the world. Stylistically, Taylor did nothing by halves. She adored Balmain and Halston, particularly Balmain's exotic take on the hippie look during the late 1960s. Instead of cheesecloth and cottons, Balmain fashioned his kaftans, trouser suits and shift dresses from gold- and silver-embroidered brocade or vividly coloured silk damask. A love of excess sometimes took the star to clothing extremes: white, daisy cut-out hot pants complete with matching boots were the sort of all-matching garb that only Elizabeth could get away with in 1971, ditto her Pierre Cardin headdress of white icicle-inspired crystals, flowers and spikes from 1967.

Showbiz was Elizabeth Taylor's world and she dressed, loved and lived as she pleased. Throughout her life the extremes of the star circuit passed for "normal" and she formed enduring friendships with some of its most notorious characters, including Michael Jackson, Rock Hudson and Liza Minnelli. Part of Taylor's allure was her aura of tragedy. Widowed in 1958 following her third marriage to Hollywood producer Mike Todd, she went on to suffer a series of debilitating illnesses yet always appeared looking immaculate, if sometimes frail. After illness and age finally claimed her fabulous figure, Taylor maintained her exceptional beauty and glamour right up until her death in March 2011 when the screen legend made her final entrance, having left specific instructions to be 15 minutes late for her own funeral.

BELOW: Many fans believe Taylor looked her most radiant in *Suddenly Last Summer* (1959), showing that she could be a barefoot, natural beauty with wild hair, red lipstick and a perfectly fitting swimsuit.

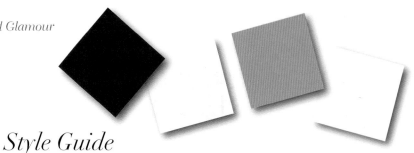

*ABOVE:* Elizabeth Taylor in New York, 1976: the opulent kaftan-style dress could be Balmain or possibly handmade for the star. Here she takes a hippie look and transforms it into something ultra-luxe.

## Style Guide

**The Palette:** Opulence, splendour and patterns dominate, alongside Taylor's trademark poppy red. Look for bright white jersey in long or draped, Grecian shapes and ice blue, a colour Taylor loved wearing to enhance her violet-blue eyes.

**Key Designers:** Emilio Pucci, Hubert de Givenchy, Pierre Balmain, Roy Halston.

**Silhouette and Cut:** The hourglass silhouette. Designed to always enhance and accentuate Elizabeth's fabulous face, breasts and tiny waist, her line usually involved an extremely cinched-in waist, plunging neckline and knee-length or full-length skirt.

## Dresses

With true glamour, Elizabeth Taylor brought the 1960s evening dress to life. A pale blue satin gown she wore to the Academy Awards, 1970, featured everything that was wonderful about her style. The simple design was essentially a vest-shaped top, albeit cut into a wide, deep "V" with the straps thinning on the shoulders. A tightly fitting bodice leading to a full skirt completed the ensemble, accentuated by the 69.42-carat Taylor Burton diamond, mounted into a necklace by Cartier after Taylor declared the diamond too big for a ring.

*Shop vintage for:* Eveningwear from the 1960s to really cut a sophisticated dash. Look for perfect-condition silks in mint green, pink, cream or ice-blue; also seek out white lacy or crochet styles to wear casually; very "Summer Liz", they reflect her love of exotic places and sunshine. You might even find the odd, 1960s bridal gown to make an ideal "Late-Night Liz" party outfit.

## Kaftans

Another unforgettable Taylor fashion moment includes a pink kaftan and matching turban. Look for late 1960s, early 1970s pieces inspired by the ethnic elements creeping into high fashion by designers such as Yves Saint Laurent and Ted Lapidus as well as the more traditional fashion houses of Lanvin and Dior.

*Shop vintage for:* Asian-inspired kaftans in rich reds, purples and silvery blues with golden-threaded embroidery or printed patterns. Also look for scarves and wraps in similar fabrics.

> TIP: Avoid LBDs. Taylor shone in colour and almost never wore black until much later in life. She was not a fan of the easy or simple route to dressing and would have balked at the thought of an unobtrusive black dress.

## Accessories

Taylor relied on upmarket accessories including Chanel bags and sunglasses, elegant gloves, huge jewels and her trademark elaborate headdresses, including a white feather and Bulgari emerald concoction from 1962, the waist-length, flower-bedecked ponytail she wore for her first wedding to Richard Burton and the white crystal and diamond crown borrowed from the set of *Boom* in 1968.

*Shop vintage for:* Matching shoes and bags by leatherwear designers Hermès and Gucci plus designer versions from Chanel, Ted Lapidus and Dior. Taylor always preferred a boxy, structured bag which she liked to match with boots and shoes. Look for chiffon headscarves in plain, light colours to wear as a hair band or turban or hunt out a matching hat and dress set. Clever traders will archive such items together for resale so you might strike lucky at higher-end vintage stores.

## Jewellery

*My Love Affair with Jewelry* was Elizabeth Taylor's book published in 2003 about her lifetime obsession with jewellery. In particular, Taylor's husbands Mike Todd and Richard Burton loved to buy her precious adornments. Her favourite pieces included the Taylor–Burton diamond and "La Peregina", a huge drop-shaped pearl that once belonged to Anne Boleyn. Taylor loved big, colourful pieces such as her "Lamartine" bracelet by Van Cleef & Arpels, featuring yellow gold, platinum, diamond, coral and amethyst.

*Shop vintage for:* 1950s or 1980s pieces in chunky yellow gold with coloured stones or good-quality fake diamonds. Costume jewellers Adrien Mann in the UK and Kenneth Jay Lane in the US made splendid versions. Look for brooches to pin provocatively near a plunging neckline and long chandelier earrings to draw attention to the neck.

### Style Tips

- If you are lucky enough to own any precious jewels, pile them on!

- Maintain a tan but make it fake.

- Throw a coat over your shoulders, cape-style.

- Smoulder in silken lingerie, like Maggie in *Cat on a Hot Tin Roof*.

- Dress in colour: Liz eschewed white for a canary-yellow gown to marry Richard Burton the first time and was rarely seen in black.

- Wear your jewels with everything, even casual jeans, or (as Liz has said) with fur, perfume and nothing else.

- Emphasize the bust – wear padded bras and body-shaping underwear to achieve the hourglass silhouette.

- Always dress to be seen – Elizabeth always worked high-octane glamour; casual was not her style.

ABOVE: After gaining a penchant for glamorous headgear in *Cleopatra* (1963), this 1969 shot shows a typical Taylor turban-style hat. Note also the brooch enhancing her coat, possibly her Bulgari emerald, a gift from Richard Burton.

LEFT: Look for matching costume sets (called "parures") to accessorize a formal dress. This set features red rhinestones and tiger's-eye cabochons and is the highly collectable Juliana jewellery, by William DeLizza and Harold Elster of New York.

## *Beauty Guide*

From the moment Taylor first appeared in front of the cameras, she was a natural star. Her perfect heart-shaped face and sparkling violet eyes framed by a born-lucky double layer of eyelashes instantly made her one of the big screen's most sought-after faces. Although the actress's star was on the ascent in the 1950s, Taylor's beauty was largely indistinguishable from her peers and the Hollywood uniform of short, curled hair and red lips did not enhance her features to their best, individual effect.

The revolutionary spirit of the 1960s freed Elizabeth's look from Old Hollywood to New. She grew her naturally curly hair and

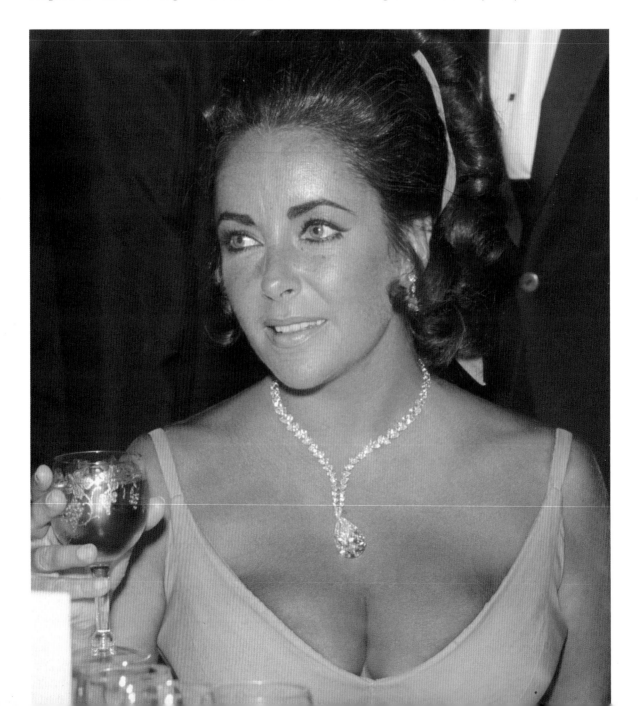

had it straightened, then flicked up the ends to meet the new decade. Taylor's hair could be coarse but this made it perfect for backcombing and the bouffants so popular at the time. Elizabeth accessorized her longer hair with a scarf worn as a hairband and a side-swept fringe. For evening she wore elaborate hairpieces, tiaras and even the occasional wig. Another change in decade saw her eschew her trademark deep red lips in favour of pale pink gloss, relying on Hollywood make-up-artist tips to bring out her best features. For example, her jawline was soft and sometimes even a little podgy but she compensated for this by balancing out her face with immaculate eyebrows (canny beauty tricksters know that strong brows are the framework for the face and draw the attention upward). Taylor always wore her brows enhanced and immaculately groomed. After *Cleopatra*, her eye make-up remained heavy and dramatic for public events throughout her life, yet she never looked brash.

OPPOSITE: Elizabeth Taylor at the 42nd Annual Academy Awards in 1970 wearing the Taylor–Burton diamond. Cartier created the diamond necklace and mount for the rock because it was too big for a ring, "even for me" said Taylor.

> **"Enough is never enough."**
>
> *Liz Taylor*

## Winged Eyes

Liz Taylor's *Cleopatra* in 1963 set the standard for a decade of mega-wattage eye make-up. The winged eyeliner and blue eyeshadow became her trademark look on screen and off. Her make-up was old-school Hollywood – panstick was used as a base – so choose a very matt foundation if you want to recreate the look. Full, dark brows were balanced by peachy cheeks and lips.

1 Apply a pale cream or taupe shadow from the lashline to the brow. If desired, follow by a violet shadow on the lid and into the crease.
2 Starting at the inside corner of the eye and using a very fine-tipped, black liquid liner, draw from the inner corner outward across the top lashline, stopping short of the outer edge.
3 To achieve the Cleopatra "wing" at the outer corner, use a black gel liner and brush. Draw the angle in first, then build up the thickness of the line, extending it toward the brow.
4 Line the lower lashes with the gel liner and brush, as close to the root of the lashes as possible. Join to the top eyeliner at the inner and outer corners.
5 Line the inner waterline of the lower lashes with a white liner to brighten the eyes.
6 To soften the look, gently blend a powder shadow over the eyeliner using a liner brush.
7 Finish with several coats of black mascara or apply false lashes to imitate Liz's thick lashline.

**You will need:**
Cream and violet powder eyeshadow
Black liquid and gel eyeliners
White eyeliner
Black mascara

# Jackie O: American Classic

When Jackie Kennedy arrived at the White House in 1961, her reputation as America's "First Lady of Style" was already established. It might be surprising to know that she fought hard to shake off this clotheshorse image, preferring to be respected for being a great public servant. Somehow she never quite succeeded and her understated elegance, grace and style shaped fashion.

In keeping with the family heritage, Jacqueline Lee Bouvier loved all things French and spent a year of her college education studying in Paris. After her marriage to John F Kennedy on 12 September 1953 in Newport, Rhode Island, she favoured top Paris fashion houses for her wardrobe, including Chanel, Balenciaga, Dior and Givenchy. However, there was a glitch during Kennedy's presidential campaign when a bill sent to Joe Kennedy for his wife's and daughter-in-law's couture was accidentally made public. Pat Nixon, wife of rival Republican Richard, issued a statement in which she declared simple American clothes were good enough for her, alerting Jackie to a possible backlash. Following this, Jackie turned to Diana Vreeland from *Harper's Bazaar* for advice: "I like terribly simple, covered-up clothes," she told her. "I must start to buy American clothes and have it known where I buy them." Vreeland directed the future First Lady to the fashion experts at New York store Bergdorf Goodman (and incidentally where the young Roy Halston was millinery designer). Halston went on to create several of Jackie's early pillbox numbers.

However, Jackie could not settle on any one designer and experimented with many, including Mainbocher designs. "I just look like a sad mouse," she concluded of herself in the Duchess of Windsor's austere look. Jackie was eventually introduced to Oleg Cassini, a family friend of the Kennedys. He sketched out designs

### American Classic Lookalikes
Michelle Obama
Nancy Shevell
Carla Bruni
Kristin Davis as Charlotte in
*Sex and the City*

OPPOSITE: Here Mrs John F. Kennedy is shown boarding a commercial aeroplane for a flight to Palm Beach, Florida in 1961. Jackie looks immaculate in this Oleg Cassini coat suit with her trademark Halston-designed hat, pearls and white gloves. Note the folder and business-like bag with jewelled handles, the perfect combination of busy but glam working mother.

ABOVE: Carla Bruni-Sarkozy, arriving for the G-20 Pittsburgh Summit in September 2009, clearly studies Jackie's First Lady style and makes it work using modern French designers including Chanel, Christian Dior and Yves Saint Laurent. Bruni softens Jackie's severe lines with lighter fabrics.

LEFT: No other First Lady since Jackie has made such a fashion statement in the White House. Mrs Obama sticks to Jackie's favourite knee length for skirts and dresses and often steals her cue and wears white to important occasions. She also encourages and supports fledgling American designers and high-street brands alongside modern greats.

## Key Looks for 1960s

- Sleeveless, fitted shift dresses with matching coats
- Coordinating pillbox hat, shoes and bag
- Simple designs, nothing too decorative
- Belt in the same fabric as the dress
- Pearls and stud earrings by Van Cleef & Arpels
- White shoes and matching bags for summer
- Big button details on coats and jackets
- Form-fitting evening dresses with a touch of frothy chiffon, beading or overlaid lace and a long, plain satin skirt, preferably by Valentino
- Matching capelet (cape) or tippet (stole)

## Key Looks for 1970s

- One-shouldered evening dresses by Halston
- Double-breasted black leather trench coat
- Black polo-neck sweater, particularly worn with white jeans
- Chanel A-line skirt suits with gilt buttons and nautically striped edging
- Hermès headscarf tied Queen Elizabeth II style to keep her hair in place
- Oversized "O"-shaped sunglasses by Nina Ricci
- Rectangular bags with chain handles by Chanel and Gucci
- Twin sets
- Flared trousers
- Loafer-style shoes with small heels by Ferragamo

loosely based on the work of her favourite French designers and understood the aesthetic for a simple "always covered-up" style. Although the garments evolved into a classic look, today their styling seems dated and somewhat formal. Jackie demanded heavy fabrics that would not crease or ride up during formal occasions. Some might even describe the snugly fitting waists, armholes and lengths she preferred as unforgiving. However, a Jackie-style dress and matching coat suit still makes for perfect wedding-guest chic.

On 20 October 1968 Jackie married the wealthy Greek shipping magnate Aristotle Onassis, almost five years after the assassination of her beloved husband and four months after the assassination of her brother-in-law, Bobby Kennedy. She chose a Valentino dress from the famous 1968 "White" collection as her wedding gown.

Throughout the 1970s Jackie wore Chanel suits, polo or turtleneck sweaters, easy items from a classic wardrobe consisting of black shirts, white jeans, double-breasted coats in camel or black leather, and the odd funky or splendid evening dress. Despite her slim physique, she never lost her love for "covered-up" clothing but occasionally indulged in the 1970s fashion for one-shouldered evening dresses. She never sought to reveal too much leg or cleavage, though. Memorable outfits include the printed Pucci empire-line mini-dress that she chose to wear for her fortieth birthday and the black leather trench coat in which she was photographed as she held stepdaughter Christina Onassis's arm after the death of the child's father.

In 1976, Jackie returned to New York, where she took up a role as a book editor at Random House. Again, her wardrobe was a mix of pared-down classics, items she never deviated from. Fashions came and went, but Jackie remained permanently in style.

RIGHT: A sketch of a coat designed by Oleg Cassini, Jackie's personal designer during the presidential years, for her inauguration wardrobe. A soft-finish wool in fawn colour with a removable collar of Russian sable, the semi-fitted shape has a restrained flared hemline. An appliquéd band follows a fluid shape from neck to hem.

# Style Guide

**Palette:** From pretty pastels to ultra-sophisticated neutrals, depending on your favourite Jackie era. Early 1960s styles included pastel pink, peachy coral and navy blue, but for her later "Onassis" style, look for classic neutrals of white, taupe, camel and navy.

**Key Designers:** Roy Halston, Oleg Cassini, Emilio Pucci, Valentino, Chanel, Hubert de Givenchy, Cristóbal Balenciaga, Christian Dior.

**Silhouette and Cut:** The Jackie silhouette is small and lightly fitted, no matter what your size. Garments should be pared down to the minimum amount of fabric needed for movement. This is a "covered-up" look and never sexy or revealing – no visible cleavage or leg allowed!

## Shift Dresses

The cornerstone of Jackie's wardrobe during the 1960s, the shift dress gave way to separates in the 1970s. Whether a Diane von Fürstenberg wrap-dress, Pucci print dress or formal gown, they all shared the same perfectly fitted form.

*Shop vintage for:* Original 1960s shifts. More boxy than later versions, these were often made from heavyweight fabrics, which retained their shape even with movement. Hunt out fabric first and style second as you may find a dress or coat that could be altered to fit. A good tailor widens the scope of your treasure or consider dressmaking classes.

BELOW: This 1962 photograph shows how high-street fashion companies re-created Jackie's look using everyday fabrics and slightly less structured tailoring to suit the lives of ordinary women. The looks are still sexy and chic as befits the *Mad Men* era. One model wears a grey-and-white checked suit with matching hat, purse and pumps, another a blue woollen suit by Junior Sophisticates with bright navy lizard shoes, and a third in a red-trimmed blue suit by Townley with red lizard walking shoes by Millerkins.

## Summer Prints

In the 1970s Jackie favoured American designers, among them Lilly Pulitzer, a New Yorker who re-located to Florida. Inspired by the colours of Palm Beach, Pulitzer opened a store selling bright quirky prints that appealed to the cream of American society, and became known as the "Queen of Prep". Former First Lady Jackie O was very impressed with Pulitzer's upmarket resort prints and society connections and quickly added them to her own wardrobe, along with similar prints by Pucci and Valentino.

*Shop vintage for:* Vintage Pulitzer dresses, Pucci resort styles and Herbert Sondheim sundresses. Pulitzer still sells many original designs, so look for their label on colourful, heavy cotton or jersey summer clothing.

## Eveningwear

After moving to Europe in 1968, Jackie lightened up her evening style. She married in Valentino's famous "White" collection and carried this lightweight mood, sticking with the designer for many evening outfits of elaborate embroidered or lace-worked fabrics cut in simple ankle-length or mini sleeveless dresses. During the 1970s she gravitated toward American designers, most notably Halston.

*Shop vintage for:* Dresses in heavy fabrics such as brocade or heavy white cotton crochet or lace styles layered over silk or cut into formal but simple shapes. Also 1970s Grecian-style, long and draped jersey dresses in silky sheens. Look up pictures of original Halston designs and hunt out copies in vintage stores. Jackie O wore these styles with simple gold cuffs and strappy gold sandals.

TIP: There is an extremely lucrative market for vintage, pre-1997 Chanel costume jewellery, when Chanel made costume jewellery at their factory in France. After 1997, manufacture transferred to Italy, where the process became industrialized and materials changed. Of course the quality is just as good, but purists prefer the old-fashioned, hard-as-nails Chanel glass pearls and glossy yellow gold-gilt, pre-1997.

ABOVE LEFT: First Lady Jackie Kennedy standing on the grounds of the Taj Mahal during a visit to India in 1962. The printed dress was a rare departure for Jackie during her early years, as she normally preferred the simple ease of dressing in plain-coloured fabrics. Cassini made her several versions of this dress in different colours and fabrics for her India trip.

ABOVE RIGHT: Standing at the bottom of a swimming pool, a young woman models a Lilly Pulitzer shift in Palm Beach, 1964. A favourite designer of Jackie's, Pulitzer continues to dress Manhattan's elite off-duty ladies today. Choose one of her shifts, kaftan tops or cocktail dresses for instant East Coast style.

## Coats and Outerwear

A coat or wrap, almost always in fabric to match the dress, is classic Jackie O style. From her greige-coloured inauguration outfit in stiff, but warm knitted twill lined with sable to a pink, heavy lace brocade evening gown and matching wrap, the look is quintessentially Jackie.

*Shop vintage for:* Suits of matching coats and dresses in good-quality fabrics. Look for bracelet-length sleeves and oversized covered buttons. Double-breasted 1970s designer coats also reflect this classic choice (well-fitting men's coats from the same era might fit the bill, too). Source garments by other successful designers of the time such as Ted Lapidus, Guy Laroche and Bill Blass.

## Shoes and Bags

Jackie followed the 1960s trend for matching shoes and bags in the White House and up until she left the US. Often seen with document cases or notebooks, Jackie also opted for her own version of her friend Grace's Kelly bag, in shades of cream, white, red and black. In the 1970s she chose Louis Vuitton , Gucci and Chanel shoulder bags. She liked comfortable shoes but always wore a slight heel to compensate for her diminutive height.

*Shop vintage for:* Classic, low court shoes or a flat sandal, such as Jack Rogers' Navajo style. For winter, buy loafers with heels in patent leather or dainty versions of the golf shoe complete with tassels and heels instead of toe-caps. Other top-quality 1970s shoe designers to look for include Charles Jourdan, Maud Frizon, Gucci, Dior and Pierre Cardin. Choose saddlebag shoulder bags with long straps and logo buckles by Hermès and Gucci, large, square handbags with snap clasps and Kelly-style bags; there were many copies of all of these. Also hunt out 1970s Chanel bags – this was the decade when styles became roomier and had chain straps.

## Jewellery and Sunglasses

*Women's Wear Daily* kicked up a storm when Jackie swapped her classic, three-row string of pearls for long Chanel beads, and her pearls are a look that is stolen time and time again. Jackie loved simple jewels by designer Jean Schlumberger, who designed for Tiffany's and made pieces for Gloria Guinness and the Duchess of Windsor. Jackie's favourites were her yellow gold and white enamel bracelets and a strawberry brooch, featuring exquisite rubies, given to her by JFK on their first Christmas in the White House. Jackie always wore the same large, rounded sunglasses by a series of different designers, the most famous being the Nina Ricci 3203.

*Shop vintage for:* Classic items with a twist. Simple rows of pearls can be ageing, so opt for lots of long, slim lengths. Find huge brooches to adorn dresses and coats. For sunglasses, look for round frames from Foster Grant, François Pinton and Nina Ricci.

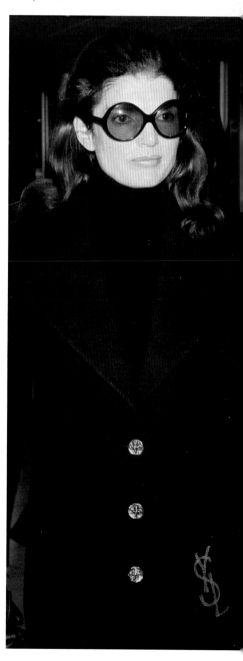

BELOW: Jackie Onassis at Heathrow Airport, London, 1970, wearing her trademark Nina Ricci sunglasses. Note the YSL logo on her navy blue coat and the effortless chic of a black polo neck.

# Beauty Guide

Beauty-wise, Jackie always subscribed to the same simple rules. She sported a slight tan all her life without ever looking too bronzed. After forcing her naturally curly hair into a short cut for years, she succumbed to hairdresser Kenneth's suggestion that she grow it out into a more manageable bob when she arrived at the White House. This could be set on the giant rollers Kenneth created for her and more easily controlled via the extremely fashionable "Italian look". This slightly bouffant bob, raised at the crown and curled at the ends, was to become Jackie's favoured style. She grew it slightly longer in the 1970s but the essential shape remained.

Jackie always looked fresh-faced and natural thanks to her perfect cheekbones. Jackie's eyes were wide-set, so she ensured her eyebrows were pencilled in across the natural corners of her eyes to bring them closer together. Overall, she preferred the classic, balanced look of a plain eye and coloured lipstick. Favourite hues were red for White House functions and 1960s shades of peachy coral for daytime. This became her palette for the rest of her life, varied only by the shade of her skin.

## Beauty Tips

- Backcomb your hair and anchor a sparkling brooch at the crown for evening.

- Tanned skin gives a permanent, healthy jetset look, so choose a tinted moisturizer or bronzer.

- Soften sharp, square bone structure with a touch of blush to outline the apples of the cheeks.

- Black eyeliner, a touch of sparkling grey at the corners of the eyes plus pink or neutral lips complete the pared-down signature look.

- A flipped-up bob keeps short hair youthful and swingy.

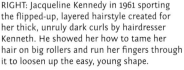

RIGHT: Jacqueline Kennedy in 1961 sporting the flipped-up, layered hairstyle created for her thick, unruly dark curls by hairdresser Kenneth. He showed her how to tame her hair on big rollers and run her fingers through it to loosen up the easy, young shape.

LEFT: Jackie O's natural features – a strong, square bone structure and very wide-set eyes, required only a touch of enhancement from make-up. Coral lipstick, creamy blusher and simply shaded-in eyebrows created a youthful, preppy look that Jackie stuck to throughout her life.

**You will need:**
Fine-tooth comb
Light-hold volumizer
Wide-barrelled curling tongs
Hairspray

## The Flip

Jackie's bouffant flip – a teased style with a lot of volume on top, extending to the jawline in a big upward-curled flip – was a popular look in 1960s America, also sported by Mary Tyler Moore and, more recently, Condoleezza Rice. If a flip is done on hair that is too long, however, it will tend to droop, so the style is best achieved on chin-length bobs, either with a fringe (bangs) or without. The 1960s Flip can be worn secured off the face with a hairband or scarf.

1 Section the hair and apply a volumizer spritz to the roots. To achieve lightness and volume, ensure you have not used too much product in your hair, which will weigh it down.
2 Working in sections using curling tongs, wind each section upward to create a flip curl. Apply hairspray before going on to the next section.
3 Backcomb ("tease") the hair at the top, smoothing it in a barrel shape over the crown and slicking it down into a smooth flip. Spray in place.

# Brigitte Bardot: The Bombshell

Brigitte Bardot was the original Bombshell; her attitude and looks created a special chemistry that ignited the fuse of modern glamour. Hot on the heels of the gussied-up 1950s, Bardot pulled the rug out from beneath the feet of the red-lipsticked, heavily styled stars of the time, such as Liz Taylor, Ava Gardner and Sophia Loren, who were sporting short, tightly permed hairstyles, strong make-up and über-corseted figures. Europe's sexily "undone" antidote to Hollywood vamp-glam, Bardot made her 1953 on-screen debut in *Bikini Girl*, a Hollywood B movie, but it was producer Roger Vadim who truly put her into orbit in 1957 with *And God Created Woman*.

In *Babydoll*, a 1956 film sold on the child-woman stereotype, she was young and naïve yet radiating sensuality – this also happened to be Bardot's natural look, which was enhanced during her early career with pretty 1950s dresses cinched tightly in around her tiny waist and cut very low in the front, often with a teasing glimpse of provocative lace or underwear. Bardot was naturally slender and full-breasted, which she accentuated with stretchy, fine-knit sweaters, V-necks, plunging necklines and a tiny waist.

The Bombshell is not a designer look; instead it revolves around the overall effect of gorgeousness from the girl in question. Girls like this don't need precious enhancements and wealthy accoutrements. This look should always be thrown together, with only one accessory, and for Bardot this was often a knotted scarf around her neck or a straw hat. Bardot lost out to Catherine Deneuve as a fashion muse to Yves Saint Laurent, even though she wore his designs, including YSL trenches and trouser suits. Bardot also lost a husband to Deneuve, but that's another story. Never a total fashionista, Bardot's cool style was all her own, not the product of image-makers.

OPPOSITE: An early shot of Brigitte Bardot, showing her natural, light brownish-red hair colour and thick waves. Note her Repetto pumps, simple pencil Capri pants and black polo neck with jaunty neckerchief.

FAR RIGHT, TOP: Claudia Schiffer, looking radiant and proving the longevity of Bombshell style. Here, simple black mesh and Bardot hair need no other embellishment.

FAR RIGHT, BOTTOM: Nancy Sinatra, around 1967. The original go-go girl, Sinatra took Bardot's looks and rocked them on the pop music scene with her video for "These Boots Are Made for Walkin'". An American Bardot with a belting voice, Nancy shunned the hippie-dippy vibes of the West Coast, took off for Vegas and redefined American glamour.

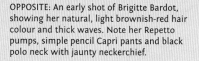

ABOVE: Duffy, the Welsh singing sensation and fledgling Bardot-style Bombshell. Her youthful, relaxed take on the Bardot look originates from a love of retro style and music rather than an urge to be perceived as a sex-bomb.

***Bombshell Lookalikes***
Goldie Hawn
Nancy Sinatra
Claudia Schiffer
Sienna Miller
Duffy

# Style Guide

**Palette:** Black, white, beige, cream, navy-and-white matelot stripes.

**Key Designers:** Dorothée Bis, Christian Dior, Jacques Esterel.

**Silhouette and Cut:** The silhouette is an exaggerated hourglass. Clothes are secondary to the overall effect of dazzling, youthful gorgeousness. Accentuated in every item of clothing, the body is everything to the Bombshell. Yet the curves are sexily outlined, rather than va-va-voom.

## Skirts

The waist is crucial for the Bombshell look. It doesn't need to be tiny, but it does need to be pulled in and accentuated with a leather belt. Loop one through a full skirt for a classic look that's also current. Tight knee-length pencil skirts or simple, denim A-lines are also very Bardot.

### Key Looks

- Black tights worn only with an oversized black mohair sweater
- Gingham-checked sundresses with full skirts
- Clingy sweaters worn with Capri trousers
- Belts to emphasize the waist
- Flat shoes or barefoot
- Midriff-revealing hip-slung trousers or jeans
- Unbuttoned frilled blouses
- Breton nautical tops paired with skinny jeans or very short shorts
- 1970s-style waist-cinched khaki trench coats

**❝***Every age can be enchanting, provided you live within it.***❞**
*Brigitte Bardot*

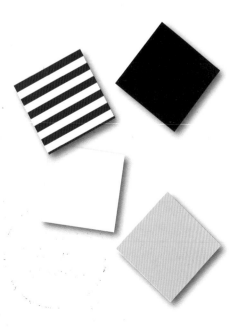

*Shop vintage for:* Pencil skirts (no longer than the knee), full "gypsy" skirts from ethnic sellers, denim A-line styles by jeans-makers including Brutus, Falmer and Lee Cooper.

## Dresses

Bardot made pink gingham famous when she got married for the second time, wearing a dress fashioned from the simple fabric. Early in her career she wore 1950s-styled, flouncy dresses in blue gingham check or light cotton, often revealing a glimpse of lingerie or white broderie anglaise petticoats.

*Shop vintage for:* Prom dresses from the 1950s with sweetheart necklines, full skirts and petticoats, as well as full dresses in cotton poplin and blue chambray fabrics. Hunt out summery styles rather than eveningwear. For evenings, Bardot loved a black feather or a white fur wrap, casually thrown over bare shoulders.

## Lingerie

While American underwear at the time was functional and effective, manufactured from Latex and all the latest stretchy fabrics, French lingerie was considered to be far more feminine and sexy. French lace-edged camisoles, mini-slips, suspenders, French knickers (tap pants) and softly structured satin brassieres offered a sensual alternative to tight corsetry. Bardot's natural shape meant she needed little help in retaining her curves and instead wore lightly underwired bras and lingerie purely for prettiness's sake.

*Shop vintage for:* Lacy lingerie and broderie anglaise petticoats to hang below full skirts and peep from necklines. Look for Frederick's of Hollywood or Maidenform labels on chiffon babydoll nighties or peignoirs. Victorian lace nightgowns, petticoats and camisoles can all be incorporated into this look.

## Trousers

Hip-slung to reveal the midriff and short enough to show an ankle, the navel was integral to Bardot's look and, whenever possible, the young Bardot revealed this highly sensual body part. In the late 1960s and early '70s she chose longer flares but they always started below her navel, low on the hips. Bombshells might well wear worn trousers with an open frilly shirt and gold sandals. The cut is strictly body-skimming, but you don't have to be super skinny; this shape actually suits a curvaceous figure.

*Shop vintage for:* Slimline trouser suits with fitted jackets from André Courrèges, Pierre Cardin and Paco Rabanne. Boys jeans and trousers from Lee or Levi's and late 1970s Capris from Thierry Mugler, Christian Dior or Geoffrey Beene. Ensure trousers are fitted and finish on the hips; no pegging or baggy shapes.

OPPOSITE: Bardot wears a full gingham skirt with petticoats on display in *Come Dance With Me,* 1959.

BELOW: God certainly created this woman. Bardot with her newly blonde locks in a typical come-hither pose.

BELOW: Bardot poses with a male model on a French beach, circa 1964, at the height of her fame. Here she relies on her favourite fall-back outfit of stretchy sweater and cords with a man's belt cinching in the waist, a knockout casual look.

OPPOSITE: A floppy hat was a trademark Bardot accessory for bad-hair or hot days. She owned black, white and chocolate brown felt and woven raffia versions and steered the "hippie hat" into mainstream fashion.

## Knitwear

Bardot rocked a sweater like no one else. She loved a simple deep V-neck or slashed boat neck. A snug little cardigan worn over a silhouette-enhancing T-shirt in navy and white stripes was also key to the look. She was once photographed in a snug-fitting cream Aran sweater, accessorized with a yellow daisy in her hair.

*Shop vintage for:* Fine knits, cashmere sweaters and cardigans with small buttons. Choose V-necks or crewnecks. Try Sonia Rykiel, Dorothée Bis and Chloé for French – often fine-knit and fitted – detailing. Look for original Aran or Scottish wool cable knits in creams and taupes, too.

## The Mackintosh

This features in so many cute vintage looks. A white Mac worn over a black sweater is about as easy a classic, casual look as you can find. Bardot wore it sexily, coat pulled in tightly at the waist, over bare legs and knee-length leather boots. She also wore tan, cream and beige leather versions. Yves Saint Laurent's safari style was hot toward the end of Bardot's film career and she often chose jackets with patch pockets and belts in that style.

*Shop vintage for:* Short, fitted 1970s trenches. For authentic period coats, look for labels Burberry or Aquascutum and menswear labels including Lord John and Burton.

## Shoes

Bardot begged Parisian ballet pump manufacturer Rose Repetto to make her a flat pump as comfortable as a dance shoe for everyday wear. A pump was created that helped Brigitte feel the earth beneath her feet; she wore shoes as little as possible – going barefoot was a quintessential part of her bohemian, sex kitten attitude, although she occasionally favoured a kitten heel. Flat pumps look good with a touch of ankle showing, crucial to the look.

*Shop vintage for:* Repetto, Russell & Bromley, or Anello & Davide ballet shoes. Kitten-heeled pointy-toe courts and black kitten heel boots from the 1980s, sold by Shelley's in the UK, as well as 1960s originals by Jaeger and Dolcis.

## Accessories

Bardot rarely wore jewellery, opting to keep her sensational shape the focus of her look with simple, figure-hugging clothing; a stretchy hairband or simple knotted scarf added a girlish accent. She sported the Riviera look of big floppy hats or cheeky caps, and sunglasses with white or black plastic frames in rounded, huge shapes.

*Shop vintage for:* 1960s and '70s collectables including Biba floppy-brimmed hats, Ted Lapidus sunglasses, Pucci printed silk scarves, Pierre Cardin and Gucci leather belts (men's are better for this look), and gold hoop or gypsy-style dangling earrings.

## Beauty Guide

Bardot's beauty appeared to be simple, tousled and sexy but behind the scenes, the Bombshell look required considerable maintenance to work. Cheating is positively encouraged. No natural blonde, Bardot's natural hair colour was reddish brown and she had tawny eyes and brows. When she finally went all the way blonde around 1960, the impact was super-powerful. Full and pouty lips, a perfect nose and huge, slightly squinty eyes stood out against fair hair, giving her an almost too-beautiful-to-be-true look. In her most iconic shots, Bardot shows off the ultimate Bombshell combination: long blonde hair and smoky eyes. However, unlike Audrey Hepburn's Ingénue or Liz Taylor's Hollywood Glamour, the essence of the make-up is "undone". Bardot's messy beehive looked artless but was perfectly shaped and coiffed, with long tousled lengths falling down her back and short tendrils across her forehead, flattering her face from every angle. The look requires lots of backcombing ("teasing") on the crown before hair is pulled back and secured over the top. Bardot often wore a thick black hairband, a look that works much better on already-backcombed hair.

Bombshell beauty focuses on the eyes – huge, deep and sexy. Eyeliner is black and smudged over with a deep grey or metallic eyeshadow to soften the shape. Hagop Arakelion, the make-up artist on …*And God Created Woman*, was responsible for Bardot's trademark look. He knew that the face should be flawless in order to carry off heavily eyelined eyes, otherwise the look could be trashy. The dark kohl-lined eyes, balanced with an innocent pale lip created a look to go back to time and time again. Try as they may, even Kate Moss and Sienna Miller can't live up to the sex kitten that is Brigitte.

TIP: For a sexy Gallic look tie a silk scarf at the side of the neck using a square knot and wear with a boat-neck or V-neck sweater. Keep the scarf small; a large man's handkerchief will do the trick.

## The "Cat Eye"

1 Bardot didn't have super-arched eyebrows, but they were tidy and appropriately fit her face shape. Make sure to tweeze any strays in order to start with a neat eye palette.

2 Fill in the brows with a brow shadow and brush or pencil.

3 Apply a neutral taupe eyeshadow on your lids. You may want to put a lighter colour or highlighter on the browbone under the arch.

4 Draw the "cat's eye" – the most essential part of Bardot's beauty regimen. Apply a thin line of black liquid liner beginning from the inside of your eye all along your upper lash line. Keep as close to the lash line as possible. When you reach the outer corner of your eye, flick the brush upward as you extend past the edge of the eye. Be sure to taper the line at the end, thinning it out to a point as it reaches its end point. It's better to start with a thin line and repeat until you reach the preferred thickness. Bardot used quite a thick line.

5 Use a pencil eyeliner to line the lower lids, drawing the liner from the inside to the outer edge.

6 Glue on false lashes, either as a strip or individual lashes. When applying strip eyelashes, trim the edges if necessary to fit your own unique eye shape and make sure the outer lashes are longer to further emphasize the "cat eye".

7 Apply mascara over the false lashes. This will help blend the false lashes with your real ones. Only apply mascara on the upper lashline.

## Pouty Lips

1 Line the lips with a nude or nude-apricot lip liner close to the outside edge of the lips to create a fuller appearance.

2 Apply matte lipstick with a brush. Use a nude or nude-apricot matte lipstick that matches the colour of your lip liner. Bardot was often photographed in apricot-coloured matte lipstick.

3 Lip gloss is optional. In her movies, Bardot had the natural shine from seductively licking her lips, which were naturally plump. To achieve a pouty look, apply a clear lip gloss in the centre of the bottom lip only.

RIGHT: The Bardot Face. A wide black hairband completes this most iconic of make-up looks. Keep this next to your make-up mirror if you are a fan and get to work. See our guide for copying the Bombshell cat's eyes and luscious, natural lips to perfection.

**You will need:**
Tweezers
Brow shadow or brow pencil
Taupe or other neutral powder eyeshadow
Highlighter
Black liquid liner
Black pencil liner
False lashes
Lash glue

TIP: Use a wet cotton swab if your liquid liner appears too harsh at the edges or to thin the line into a more tapered shape.

**You will need:**
Lip liner in nude or peach
Matte lipstick in nude or peach
Clear lip gloss

# Twiggy: Ultra Mod

Less is more when it comes to styling this 1960s look. Miniskirts are in almost everyone's wardrobe but it's what goes above and below that makes shopping fun for the vintage fan. The Ultra Mod look depends on a solid A-line shape: long legs, low heels and short or neatly shaped hair.

The first model to break out of the traditional, ladylike breed of fashion clotheshorse, Lesley Hornby's cool came directly from the streets of London. The great models of the 1950s may have originated from humble beginnings but almost all managed to snaffle a marchioness at the very least. "Twiggy", as Lesley was called, was part of the new, younger classless generation. She had the requisite regional accent: Cockney. At a shoot for the *Daily Express* in 1966, London hairdresser Leonard chopped off Twiggy's then long, Jean Shrimpton-ish locks. The subsequent photo's were so new and modern-looking that Deirdre McSharry, fashion editor of the *Express* at the time named Twiggy the "Face of 1966". Twiggy's mesmerizing face, characterized by deep blue eyes and a cupid's bow lip that curled up toward her nose in a pixie-ish way, made her a modelling enigma until the 1970s, when she appeared with David Bowie on the cover of his album *Pin Ups*. Showbiz beckoned and Twiggy made records and starred in films, most notably *The Boyfriend*.

Designer names to seek out from this exciting era are led by Mary Quant. Reading the beat of the street, Quant was already well established by 1966. A few years earlier, she had set up Bazaar boutique in the then slightly shabby backwater of London's Chelsea. It was the beginning of the boutique shopping concept and she began selling her own designs alongside those of other designers to a young and groovy clientele. Quant's approach was modern and practical: she just made the clothes and then sold them in Bazaar instead of roping her wagon to the fashion train

*Ultra-Mod Lookalikes*
Edie Sedgwick
Peggy Moffat
Agyness Deyn
Emma Watson

OPPOSITE: Twiggy knocked rivals including Suzy Parker and Jean Shrimpton off the covers of most British magazines during 1966–68.

ABOVE: Vidal Sassoon's famous five-point-cut, seen here on Peggy Moffat, defined the 1960s. Mary Quant also had the cut although Twiggy's was a softer, more 1920s boy-crop.

FAR LEFT: Emma Watson's Twiggy-style chop of her long, Hermione Granger-locks catapulted her into the fashion firmament.

LEFT: For a while Agyness was hailed as the new Twiggy as she captured the youthful spirit of the times.

*Key Looks*

- Straight or A-line dresses in fabrics that hold their shape, such as Crimplene
- Op Art colours: black, white and primaries
- Mid-calf boots with pointed toes and flat heels
- Plastic-belted trench coat
- Knitted jersey mini-dresses with matching tights
- "Wet look" PVC coats
- Skinny-rib knitted sweaters, especially in stripes or solid bright block colours
- Patent-leather square-toed shoes and "Pilgrim" shoes with buckles
- Suede or leather minicoats
- Sheepskin coats
- Dresses with low-slung, wide loops to hold a hipster belt
- Plain or button-up A-line miniskirts
- Tunic dresses worn over polo-neck sweaters

RIGHT: Models for veteran French designer Yves Saint Laurent present his Mondrian dress at his retrospective haute-couture show at the Pompidou Centre in Paris, January 2002. At the age of 65, legendary French designer Saint Laurent bids adieu to fashion with a presentation of more than 300 outfits from a career spanning 40 years.

OPPOSITE: Twiggy poses in a "crossover" evening dress with Mod styling, circa 1967, fashioned from silky fabric rather than the decade's classic jersey. The dress features Fortuny-style pleats and a pretty tie neck. Exposed shoulders peeking from a cutaway, high neck were a late 1960s key look. Low-heeled, shiny gold shoes and lightly backcombed hair complete the glamorous evening look.

of "showing" twice a year and designing collections months in advance. A key face on the London scene, she also created a cosmetic range with the distinctive daisy logo.

Another key proponent of the Ultra Mod look was Cilla Black, a Liverpudlian friend of the Beatles who worked the cloakroom of the Cavern Club to help support her dream of becoming a singer. Similarly to Twiggy, Cilla shunned the beehive and had her trademark thick red hair cropped into a boyish short "back and sides". Her long, lean frame attracted the attention of designer Caroline Charles, who had been an assistant to Mary Quant and who had a flair for transforming a fun trend such as crochet (popular at the time) into high fashion. Taking a lace bedspread from her mother's house, Caroline turned it into a fitted ankle-length dress for Cilla. Now a permanent exhibit at London's Victoria & Albert Museum, the dress encouraged a whole industry of copies in its day. Today, few models have the lasting impact of Twiggy but in recent years Kate Moss, Agyness Deyn and Rosie Huntington-Whiteley have all epitomized modern British beauty.

## Style Guide

**The Palette:** Primary and monochrome colours – the art movements of Pop and Op Art – were to become synonymous with this period; for example, Yves Saint Laurent's Mondrian print dress in red, blue and yellow squares outlined in black on white. Also strong shades of mustard yellow, turquoise, royal blue, pink and orange.

**Key Designers:** Mary Quant, Caroline Charles, Marion Foale and Sally Tuffin, Paco Rabanne, André Courrèges, Rudi Gernreich, Yves Saint Laurent, Pierre Cardin.

**Silhouette and Cut:** Boyish and gamine. Short A-line dresses or coats with neat hair and long legs on view. An alternate silhouette is a skinny-rib, stretchy dress worn over same-colour tights, or the double "A" – a short, flared-out coat and bell-bottom trousers.

## Artificial Fabrics

The 1960s saw an artificial fibre revolution, alongside experimentation in non-traditional fabrics including PVC, glass, paper and metal. Pop-Art-inspired circles and squares found their way into clothing design. Square-shaped miniskirts and sleeveless tops held their shape when fashioned from metal or chainmail by such French designers as Paco Rabanne, Pierre Cardin and André Courrèges. Closer to home, artificial fabrics with roots in oil chemical compounds, including Crimplene and other heavy, textured nylons, held their shape well and were durable and easy to produce.

*Shop vintage for:* Man-made, acrylic skinny-rib knits, knitted short-sleeved tops and rollover polo necks (turtlenecks). Also, knitted artificial jersey-like fabrics and polyester; trousers made of Crimplene and poly-cotton shirts and blouses.

## Dresses

Short dresses followed the miniskirt and Twiggy was the face of Mod fashion. A-line shapes were most popular, followed by straight shapes with a band of contrasting-coloured fabric across the midriff or straight up the front panel. More extreme versions were made from see-through plastic with nylon coloured edging. Stiff fabrics including very heavy jersey dresses came with graphic cut-outs or appliquéd-on flower or Op Art shapes. Necklines styles included a slightly raised band (the "mock" polo) or round-shaped and slashed boat-neck styles. Armholes were very deep and shoulders were narrow. As the '60s progressed, more traditional fabrics came into use for the new styles. Silks, velvets and cottons helped Mod fashion's transition into mainstream style.

*Shop vintage for:* Quirky designs with see-through cut-outs in the style of Rudi Gernreich. Original Gernreich might be hard to find, but fun replicas may be quarried from vintage fairs. Scout out designs with patch pockets in contrasting colours or featuring edging in patent leather or PVC. Short pinafore dresses to wear over polo necks and tights make cute finds, too.

## Separates

Jackets, bell-bottom trousers, miniskirts and waistcoats made up the Mod look. Bell-bottoms were ankle-length, so keep ankles exposed for an authentic Mod feel. Tweed and heavyweight miniskirts are period styles, as are primary-coloured A-line minis.

*Shop vintage for:* Look for robust miniskirts and flared jeans or the collectable slimline Sta-Prest trousers. Also find funnel-neck jackets, short, straight bomber styles and three-quarter-length PVC or patent leather macs. High-street brands in 1960s Britain included C&A, which made fun, high-quality versions of fashionable looks. American department stores including Macy's, Sears and Marshall Field's all carried their own, good-quality versions of the Mod look.

## Shoes

Low kitten heels and flats were the order of the day. Vintage 1960s shoes can be hard to source because supplies have already been plundered by collectors through the years, so scavenge in out-of-the-way stores and vintage fairs.

*Shop vintage for:* Square-toe shapes with large buckles, low-fronted lace-ups, patent kitten heels, mid-calf zip-up boots, slingbacks and block heels from Russell & Bromley, Roland Cartier or boutique brands Young Jaeger and Way In at Harrods in the UK, or Marshall Field's in the US.

"*People always think of me as the Sixties'
Girl, but I never think of myself that way...
I've always felt that some part of me came
from the Twenties and Thirties, the eras I
feel most comfortable with.*"

Twiggy (Lesley Hornby)

### Style Tips

• Pick coloured miniskirts and
mini-dresses, especially decorated
with bows, ribbons, buttons,
patch pockets and zips.

• Accessorize with a square
or rectangular-shaped framed
handbag or go "Space Age" with
a clear plastic version.

• Choose strong graphic geometric
patterns and shapes in your
clothing – circles, squares,
rectangles and stripes, bull's-eyes
and polka dots.

• Wear dangling earrings
constructed of silver balls or
primary-coloured acrylic in big
circle or rectangular shapes.

OPPOSITE: Models in 1967 demonstrate an
easy, stylish but everyday version of Twiggy's
look: on the left a yellow-striped choirboy
smock and on the right a smock dress of red
with a yellow flower print, both by Michele
Rosier for Pierre d'Alby. Matching tights and
Mary Jane shoes make a fashion statement –
the colour-blocking technique started here!

LEFT: Twiggy, mid 1960s, in a typical, fun pose.
Bright yellow top, big hoop earrings and knee
socks: a school uniform phenomenon is born.
The 1960s were a time for change, and even
traditional items, like the tennis shoes Twiggy
is wearing, came in bright or acid colours.

## *Beauty Guide*

Twiggy's short, boyish crop was "the" hairstyle of the 1960s. Although long, full hair stayed in style for a few more years, modern women lopped off their locks in droves. It is worth noting that this slightly longer-on-top-crop is easy to maintain and a very simple way of looking young and chic. It's also a style that looks good on most face shapes; if you always wear your longer hair pulled back in a ponytail, the crop might suit you, as the effect is similar.

Although her hair was cut by legendary London hairstylist Leonard, Twiggy did her own make-up and would have used high-street products from Max Factor and Rimmel to create her legendary look. If you decide to create the dramatic 1960s make-up, simple hair is a must. Twiggy's eyes were made up with a double layer of eyeliner encircling light blue shadow, with long false lashes for extra drama. It was an effect that was quickly bastardized into a rather messy street look that hung around until the fresh-faced 1980s. Twiggy was also famously down-to-earth and friendly and had a youthful energy. It's a happy-go-lucky, easy, fresh beauty that requires minimal foundation and even the odd freckle.

LEFT: A close up of Twiggy's ultra-modern make-up in 1965 reveals it took some work to apply but that all the lines add up to her trademark "O"-shaped features. Despite her skinny physique and heart-shaped face, she hid her angles with cleverly drawn-in lines.

## Monochromatic Mod Eyes

The eye look for this time is pale with strong liner and heavy false lashes, sometimes worn two at a time on both top and bottom lashes. Lips were minimal, in soft colours or frosted shades. Warhol-style metallic silver and monochrome lend a Pop Art quality. The lower lash line is always exaggerated, but remember this is Twiggy, not Dusty Springfield!

1 Colour the entire eyelid with white eyeshadow, up to the browbone.
2 Apply silver to the centre of the eyelid.
3 Blend black eyeshadow into the crease of the eyelid to create a graphic line. Extend the black under the eye as well.
4 Using black gel eyeliner, line the upper lashline from the inner corner to the outside and under the lower lashline.
5 Trace over the powder crease with the gel eyeliner in short strokes and sweep around until the edges meet. Build up black colour in the outer corner.
6 Concentrate the mascara on the centre of the upper and lower lashes to make the eye open out and look more circular than "cat eye".

**You will need:**
White, silver and black powder eyeshadow
Black gel eyeliner
Black mascara

TIP: Trim the lashes to fit the length you need, or glue on individual lashes to build up density exactly where you want it.

## False Lashes

This is best done on lashes that have been coated with a layer of mascara as it helps the false lashes stick. For that really eye-opening 1960s look, choose lashes that have heavy fringing to the centre of the eye, rather than too much at the outer corner. This results in more of a round-eye look.

**You will need:**
Set of top and bottom lashes
Eyelash glue, such as Duo adhesive
Tweezers

TIP: Use the end of a make-up brush to press false lashes securely in place – this avoids getting glue on your fingers.

1 Remove the top false lashes from the packaging and bend slightly to shape.
2 Evenly apply a thin line of glue along the base of the false lashes. Once the glue is slightly dried and tacky, you are ready to apply.
3 Holding the lashes with the tweezers align the lashes to the top edge of your natural lashline, pressing firmly into the corners. If using your fingertips, hold the lashes at either end and press into the inner and outer corners.
4 For the bottom lashes, apply in the same way on top of your lashes, as close to the base as possible.
5 Finish with several coats of black mascara, then curl the lashes.

# Jean Shrimpton: British Classic

Jean Shrimpton represented the high end of British style in the 1960s. Smart and glamorous without any Hollywood pizzazz, her English prettiness radiated worldwide. With naturally coloured mid-brown shoulder-length hair and a pale, English complexion, on paper she sounded ordinary. In the flesh Shrimpton was everything but average. Her naturally full hair was effortlessly fashionable, ditto her slimline silhouette. She favoured simple styles, uncluttered by the baubles and brights of Pop fashion. Known as "The Shrimp", she was the upmarket version of Twiggy and crossed boundaries where the youngster from South London did not. Her look and that of her fellow modelling superstars including Sarah Stuart (who later married the Aga Kahn) and Patti Boyd was less Mod and more classic than the fashiony faces of Twiggy and Penelope Tree.

Jean Shrimpton was born in High Wycombe, Buckinghamshire, England, and spoke the Queen's English without any kind of regional accent. She was the photographer David Bailey's muse and wife, and together they created some of the most stunning shots of the 1960s. "Twiggy was a product," Bailey told one interviewer, "but Jean was the real thing". Shrimpton famously wowed Australians with her appearance at the Melbourne World Cup in 1965, wearing a dress that stopped 10 cm (4 inches) above the knee. She was lucky enough to be able to cross over between the highly fashionable, young world of her then boyfriends David Bailey and Terence Stamp into sophisticated fashion circles. In 1968 she modelled in an advertisement wearing a beige, Chantilly lace dress by the American designer Bill Blass, which prompted a run on stores carrying the dress and thousands of copies being produced.

An enduring image of Jean features the model sitting on the floor, legs splayed out like a young deer, wearing a suit with

### Key Looks

- A short shift dress with pumps and a small handbag
- Dresses with a matching jacket over the top
- Duffel coat
- Mac, headscarf and sunglasses
- Mini-striped tube dress
- Nude-coloured lace mini-dress
- Lightweight blouses and dresses with narrow bodies and full, voluminous sleeves
- Ankle-length "hobble skirt" evening gown
- Slightly flared, ankle-length jeans
- Oversized accessories
- Large, face-framing hats in winter

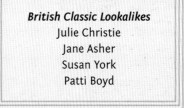

### British Classic Lookalikes
Julie Christie
Jane Asher
Susan York
Patti Boyd

OPPOSITE: Jean Shrimpton in relaxed pose circa 1965. A pretty button-through dress with plain tights and Mary Jane shoes shows an easy anytime outfit for fans of "The Shrimp".

FAR LEFT: Model Patti Boyd married Beatle George Harrison but left him for Eric Clapton who famously wrote his song "Wonderful Tonight" for her. She was a classic 1960s beauty in the style of Jean Shrimpton, favouring pretty hair and make-up without the harsh lines of the trendy Mod look.

LEFT: Julie Christie on the set of the 1966 film *Fahrenheit 451*, wearing a Pop Art-inspired dress and typical 1960s earrings. Christie was Britain's Bardot though her sensible English attitude and chic, classic looks prevented her from taking on the Bombshell head-to-head.

hat and handbag. It is the kind of outfit the Queen Mother might have worn, albeit a shorter version, but it indicates the aristocratic backbone running through British fashion in the 1960s. This classic element is now internationally synonymous with understated, expensive dressing, usually referred to as the "ladylike" look. Super-smart, yet traditional British brands such as Jaeger (where Jean Muir started her career), Viyella and Marks & Spencer catered toward the market for this look. These companies manufactured endurable wardrobe staples for those who had to conform to society's rules a little more than the anti-establishment generation. It simply was not possible for everyone to be a rebel in the 1960s and Shrimpton embodied a subtle, English sexiness that eventually found it's way on to the big screen, particularly in Bond film characters – from Miss Moneypenny's librarian chic to Pussy Galore's blonde bouffant and black suede boots.

Thanks to Shrimpton's global popularity alongside the success of the Beatles, Mary Quant and all things Mod, British fashion gained recognition on the world stage for the very first time. Street style cemented interest from foreign press and buyers and the positive vibes rippled out to boost the business. John Bates was the British Yves Saint Laurent, designing some of the shortest and earliest mini-dresses, string-vest dresses and catsuits. He pushed new boundaries in British design, featuring cut-outs, mesh panels, clear PVC details and metallic leathers in his work. In 1964 the Northumberland native started his company Jean Varon, creating famous looks for Jean Shrimpton that included empire-line evening dresses with elaborately decorated tops and slim-fitting skirts. Alongside Jean Varon, other British design labels were gathering force. Belville Sassoon, an amalgamation between two young designers, Belinda Belville and David Sassoon, created a range of elegant, colourful womenswear, focusing on the formal end of the market. Their matching coat and dress ensembles, bridal gowns and evening dresses were worn by society women.

## Style Tips

- Choose one large accessory as a focal point, such as a large, cross-shaped pendant, a huge brooch of semiprecious rocks or a man's wristwatch.

- Carry a small, handle-top handbag and match your gloves to your hat.

- Simple shift dresses keep the look crisp, neat and ladylike. They work best with bare legs and slingback shoes.

- Pair elbow-length gloves with a simple, slightly hobble-skirted evening gown by British designers John Cavanagh or John Bates.

- For an informal look, sling a wide belt around your hips over a sloppy sweater.

- Go barefoot to summer garden parties.

OPPOSITE TOP: Twiggy in a 1969 pose wearing a Foale & Tuffin dress. Marion Foale and Sally Tuffin were English designers who created Swinging London's most wearable looks from their Carnaby Street boutique. This dress evokes the spirit of the 1930s with wide frilled sleeves and a wrapover style.

OPPOSITE FAR RIGHT: A mini-dress by Pierre Cardin in turquoise crepe, circa 1967–68, demonstrates the simple A-line shape that dominated fashion at the time.

OPPOSITE: A mini-dress and cape by Pierre Cardin in organdy, circa 1960. Capes were essential items of 1960s outerwear. Despite the designer's love for the cape, it has never quite cemented itself as a practical fashion garment – perfect for a night out or a totally retro look, though.

# The Style Guide

**Palette:** This is more classic than other 1960s looks, so choose neutral creams, beige, black and white for daywear and pink, coral, mauve or creamy custard yellow for the evening.

**Key Designers:** Mary Quant, John Bates, Bill Blass, Belville Sassoon, Caroline Charles, Jean Muir, Burberry.

**Silhouette and Cut:** Natural contours, fitted clothing; a coltish style – all long arms and legs, with no lumps and bumps.

## Day Dresses

Classic 1960s A-line shifts make this look work. As do shirt-waisted, YSL-style button-up dresses. The pinafore came out of the kitchen and into high style, worn over a white chiffon blouse or a black polo neck for drama, and in Prince of Wales check or wool tweed at Jaeger. Mod versions carried front zips with large hoop pulls in contrasting colours such as orange, chocolate and cream jersey.

*Shop vintage for:* Suits featuring lightweight dresses with matching coats for a classic, formal English look. Shift dresses from the 1960s will be less structured than their 1950s counterparts and should fall on or just above the knee.

## Evening Dresses

Look for pretty early 1960s evening gowns with long, straight skirts, a split in the back and a flattering slash or straight neckline. For inspiration, look at Cecil Beaton's creations for Audrey Hepburn in *My Fair Lady*; many of the dresses in the movie feature this return to the "hobble" – an ankle-length, narrow skirt first made popular by Paul Poiret in 1920s. Choose those made in more than one fabric such as silk and velvet or satin with a richly embroidered but same-coloured upper bodice.

*Shop vintage for:* Look for 1960s originals by Jaeger, Belville Sassoon and Debenhams. Designers Mollie Parnis, Norman Norell and Vera Maxwell created similar looks for the American market.

### Coats and Outerwear

The 1960s saw the emergence of fabulous, enduring British brands in solid shapes, such as the duffle, Mackintosh and cape.

*Shop vintage for:* Duffel coats by Gloverall, originally made for the navy but popularized by the Beat Generation as warm, comfy cover-ups, in heavy wool with wooden toggles. Also look for Mackintosh raincoats by Burberry, Lord John and Hepworths.

### Shoes and Bags

Low heels were popular, such as square-toed, slip-on pumps with block heels or kitten-heeled slingbacks in cream or white for summer and black or chocolate brown for winter. Long, flat leather or suede boots with kitten heels were worn over the knee. Reptile skin accessories look good with the classic look but there were some great fakes available at the time, too.

*Shop vintage for:* Classics from Rayne, Russell & Bromley, Charles Jourdan and Roland Cartier. Don't forget the lace-up suede desert boots worn by Shrimpton and lots of arty types in the 1960s; those by Hush Puppies and Clarks were the best-known brands. Look for "ladylike" small, boxy-shaped handbags in black patent or highly polished chocolate brown.

## *Beauty Guide*

Jean Shrimpton's 1960s look called for a lighter style of make-up than the popular 1950s pan-stick face. A natural complexion with big, expressive eyes was key. Jean Shrimpton's only beauty bug was the dark circles beneath her eyes, which were evident in later model shots. Instead of heavy black, painted-on eyeliner, lighter, prettier looks came into style for daywear thanks to "The Shrimp". Cosmetic companies began manufacturing easier-to-use products for girls on the go, including eyeliner pencils, mascara in a tube and sticks of concealer. This made a difference to the look, allowing for greater precision and more choice. Soft, brown eyeliner was Shrimpton's style, along with naturally arched eyebrows instead of the painted-on peaks of the past. Her naturally pouty lips were left largely untouched by anything other than a light, pastel pink shade to accentuate the fullness.

With the demise of the tight perms of the 1950s, full, natural hair was in style for the first time in history, and Shrimpton's naturally thick hair made it easy to create signature looks including her bouffant crown and flicked-up ends. Less structured and set than the Jackie Kennedy Onassis "flip", Shrimpton's version was longer, more modern and paired with a girlish fringe. Her natural mid-brown colour was easy for hairdressers to match and she often wore hairpieces for parties, shoots and special occasions to add length, height and fullness; pretty soon, hairpieces became available in Woolworths and other high-street stores.

OPPOSITE: Low, block heels were the new and comfortable replacement for the old-fashioned stiletto, which had completely gone out of fashion by the mid 1960s. Here are vintage models from Pierre Cardin, 1969; Gina, 1960s; Charles Jourdan, 1966 and 1970; and Gina, 1960s.

LEFT: Jean Shrimpton with her huge doe eyes, flip hairstyle and fringe, wearing the "tam-o-shanter", a favourite fashion shape for hats in the 1960s.

### Beauty Tips

- A brunette version of the classic English Rose, Shrimpton was the original face for Yardley cosmetics – study the original advertisements for make-up and hair looks to copy.

- A made-up version of natural beauty (the precursor of the "no make-up make-up" look) with added emphasis on the eyes.

- Dramatically arched brows keep the eyes the focus of the face.

**You will need:**
Hair serum
Medium-size paddle brush
Blowdryer

## The Fringe

Jean Shrimpton's fringe (bangs) was blunt-cut and arched at the edges, but not too heavy. Although she usually wore it straight down on the forehead, there are many other pictures of her with a longer grown-out sideswept fringe and backcombed crown. If the fringe has a really soft edge, you can sweep it to the side as it grows out and it will sit naturally flat, tucked behind an ear.

1 If your hair is wavy, add a tiny drop of serum to the fringe before you begin. Always blowdry a blunt fringe before the rest of your hair.
2 Using a paddle brush, dry the fringe using a side-to-side sweeping motion. Do not wrap the hair around the brush. You want the fringe to sit flat on the forehead, and not achieve a big bouffant fringe.
3 Finish drying the rest of your hair as normal.

# Marianne Faithfull: Rock 'n' Roll Girlfriend

One of the most enduring 1960s British rock-chick images is the young Marianne Faithfull, clad in a frilled shirt, high-collared, double-breasted peacoat and huge, square-shaped sunglasses. Faithfull turned the tables on the ordinary girl's moment in the sun, in the late 1960s. Cilla, Twiggy and Sandie Shaw were all enjoying a fruitful reign until the Rolling Stones' girlfriends began stealing their headlines. Clad in velvet frock coats, floppy hats and floor-length frills, Marianne Faithfull and model Anita Pallenberg, the exotic girlfriends of Mick Jagger and Keith Richards, created one of fashion's most enduring looks. In fact it was a raggle-taggle collection of clothing from vintage stores and London's cool boutiques including Granny Takes a Trip and Hung On You that helped foster the image.

The Stones' girlfriends were not dressed by the couture names of the 1960s. Theirs was a much more eclectic style, both of living and dressing. At a time when the Stones were being busted for, among other sins, peeing on the grass verge at a motorway service station and smoking cannabis, few designers would have wanted to align with them. A very different set of circumstances governed fashion in the 1960s, and although it was cool to be outrageous and flamboyant, taking rebellion into illegality scared off some members of the fashion establishment.

Faithfull has been a muse and inspiration to countless designers and models since her arrival on the rock scene in the 1960s. At times, Kate Moss, Sienna Miller and film stars including Sarah Jessica Parker have all been spotted in versions of her 1960s look. A talented singer, Mick Jagger wrote "As Tears Go By" for her and theirs was a musical as well as a loving liaison. Faithfull's

***Rock 'n' Roll Girlfriend Lookalikes***
Anita Pallenberg
Mary-Kate and Ashley Olsen
Kate Moss
Daisy Lowe

OPPOSITE: Marianne Faithfull and her son in 1969; Faithfull is clad in true Rock 'n' Roll Girlfriend ensemble of floppy hat, fur coat, flared jeans, snakeskin boots and tapestry bag.

ABOVE: Anita Pallenberg, a woman with the coolest credentials ever. Former girlfriend of Brian Jones and Keith Richards, Pallenberg was a fashion force in her own right.

FAR LEFT: Single-handedly responsible for every major London look of the last 15 years, Kate Moss remains an edgy, rock-star's princess despite her married status.

LEFT: Showbiz twins Mary-Kate and Ashley Olsen may be peddling one of fashion's most expensive labels with The Row but their love of vintage with a rock 'n' roll edge makes them strong contenders in this lookbook.

look evolved during her period with the Stones and pretty soon paparazzi were chasing Jagger's pretty girlfriend to see what she would be wearing next.

At the time, designers with an ear to the street loved the looks worn by Faithfull and her friends. Hard to put together for ordinary fans and young women on 1960s budgets, Barbara Hulanicki spotted a gap in the market for a mass-produced version of the vintage-inspired looks so popular among the rock 'n' roll crowd and set about creating an entire store based on the concept. Thus was born the London store, Biba.

Hulanicki's surreal images of girls with halos of curls, darkly made-up, doe eyes and 1920s style cupid's bow lips gave the Biba look a unique eccentricity that still resonates. The company took the retro elements of Marianne Faithfull's looks and paired them with even more romantic imagery from further back in time. Casting back to the age of Art Nouveau and Art Deco, Hulanicki captured a spirit born of the twentieth century. A touch of darkness combined with the careless, live-for-the-moment magic of the flapper girls embodied the spirit of Biba. Strictly for women, although male rock stars including the late, great Marc Bolan were fans, too, key pieces included fitted velvet jackets, tightly wound scarves or velvet chokers, black satin frilled shirts and skinny bell-bottoms. A large, cloche-crowned hat, folded back and pinned, completed the look.

ABOVE: This late 1960s dress in Art Deco print rayon is from Biba, the vintage designer of choice for the Marianne Faithfull look. It has a pussybow neckline and puffed sleeves.

RIGHT: Models wearing Biba fashions, complete with folded-back brimmed hats, circa 1970, in a fashion shoot for the *Daily Telegraph*.

### Key Looks

- Fin de Siècle-style high necklines with frilly detailing
- Beaded cuffs, wrist to elbow
- 1920s flapper-style adornments, such as long strands of pearls
- High, beaded collars
- Buttons extending down the front of long dresses
- Ostrich feather boas
- Shaggy astrakhan fur jackets
- Velvet headbands with flowers attached
- Wide-brimmed floppy hats with the front pinned back
- Cloche hats
- Moon and stars motifs

BELOW: A late 1960s Ossie Clark silk top with a blue-and-red Celia Birtwell print on a cream field. Clark's floaty creations were a hot favourite of London's rock-star royalty in the late 1960s and early 1970s.

# Style Guide

**The Palette:** Black, chocolate, navy blue, beetle-bluey greens, rust-brown, fuchsia pink, various hues of purple, yellow, orange, mustard, bottle green.

**Key Designers:** Ossie Clark and Celia Birtwell, Biba, Granny Takes a Trip, Mr Freedom, Annacat (called "the Biba of Brompton Road"), Hung On You.

**Silhouette and Cut:** Closely fitted body-skimming torsos with billowing legs and arms or tightly fitting sleeves with big, feather-trimmed cuffs. The blazer over long bell-bottoms in close-fitting cuts was a shape shared by boys and girls.

## Dresses

The "Romantic Bohemian" look evolved in the late 1960s and by the early '70s designers including Balmain, Valentino, YSL, Gina Fratini and Dior were all creating versions of the look. With partner Celia Birtwell, Ossie Clark showed designs at evening fashion shows where groovy young Londoners fought for seats to see models including the transsexual Amanda Lear. Clark's bias-cut dresses featured '40s-style shoulder pads, puffed sleeves, flat fronts, deeply cut V-necks and tiny buttons designed to be left undone.

*Shop vintage for:* Renaissance-style maxi-dresses by Ossie Clark, Biba and Annacat; chiffon dresses and velvet pinafores by Gina Fratini.

## Separates

While Barbara Hulanicki designed beautiful dresses, she also revolutionized the market for separates by making it possible for those earning meagre wages to afford a little Biba style, even if they couldn't buy a top-to-toe look. Mixed prints and textures, such as corduroy, satin, brushed denim and dark-coloured floral cotton prints in the same piece of clothing were often seen.

*Shop vintage for:* 1930s cream Belgian lace and silk camisoles and slips, delicate chiffon and silk blouses. Bell-sleeve blouses with deep cuffs and high collars in Biba shades of purple, moss and ink.

### Style Tips

- Combine Biba "auntie" colours of mulberry, ink, rust and plum.

- Fuse your eras: take inspiration from Victoriana, Art Nouveau, Art Deco and the Golden Age of Hollywood.

- Wear a hat – a 1920s cloche, 1960s floppy brim hat or velvet fedora.

- Wear dresses and skirts either extremely short or super long.

- Add a low-slung wide leather belt to jeans, shorts or dresses.

- Rock a pair of vintage lizard-skin boots.

LEFT: Turquoise silk blouse from British boutique, Granny Takes a Trip, 1967-8. This King's Road boutique, with half a Cadillac sticking out of the wall inside, mixed art and fashion to become London's hippest clothiers.

> *"Rebellion is the only thing that keeps you alive."*
> *Marianne Faithfull*

## Jackets and Coats

Dandy fashion evolved from young, broke artistic types raiding secondhand shops and making their finds look stylish. The covers of the Rolling Stones albums *Their Satanic Majesties Request* and *Beggars Banquet* sum up the look to perfection. Military style peacoats and Victorian gentlemen's frock coats were worn by both sexes. Accessorize with the all-important frilly cuffs and high ruffled necks.

*Shop vintage for:* High fashion designers including clever YSL picked up on the trend as did British high-street brands including Bus Stop and Chelsea Girl.

RIGHT: A young boutique worker in true Faithfull style, London 1972. She wears a velvet coat, blouse with the prerequisite frilly tie-neck and cuffs and platform-heeled clogs with striped socks.

## Stockings and Shoes

Stockings and tights in black, purple or bottle colours and a pair of lace-up, granny boots add to the authenticity of a Biba-esque look, as do black fishnets or holey-patterned hosiery. To avoid resembling Nancy from *Oliver Twist*, ensure the look is worn with a low belted waist or a shift-straight tunic top and the length is short. A sexy expanse of thigh clad in funky hose is a crucial element of the Biba look. By contrast, you can go long but ensure it's super-long, trailing over your platforms.

*Shop vintage for:* 1940s-style platforms by Biba or Terry de Havilland and knee-high, lace-up granny boots, especially in two-tone colours.

## Jewellery and Accessories

Victorian semiprecious, carved jet jewellery makes the perfect addition to the Biba-esque wardrobe and is highly collectable, too, as it is increasing in value. Originating mainly from the Whitby area of northern England, jet was a great favourite among Victorian ladies who embraced all things black after the fashion of Queen Victoria, who wore carved jet brooches and beads following the death of her husband, Prince Alfred. Other accessories include velvet chokers with pearls, bows or fake jewels sewn at the centre and brooches and earrings featuring ostrich feathers. Wear an ostrich boa or wrap a long silky scarf several times around the neck.

*Shop vintage for:* Long strands of pearls or beads, Victorian jet beads and brooches, velvet chokers, long silk scarves, square-frame sunglasses by Polaroid, Ray Ban or cheaper chainstore brands, and ostrich-feather fans, earrings and boas.

# Beauty Guide

Marianne Faithfull's beauty look relied on a heavy fringe with the rest of the hair long and straight. Unlike other 1960s babes she wore it down and loose without backcombing or adding hairpieces. Later on, she sported the pageboy – keeping the same heavy fringe but in a long bob style.

Slightly Bardot-esque but more edgy, smudgy make-up replaced clean, feline lines and long, natural lashes worked instead of false versions. Pale lipstick and a few freckles completed her look. Pale and interesting is key to this look: eyes and lips should stand out against a delicate canvas. Use purple, pink and red hues for eyeshadow and add black kohl, pink blush and natural lips.

LEFT: Marianne Faithfull, circa 1973, wearing an Ossie Clark dress and sporting a "pageboy" bob, an easy way to add retro cool.

### Beauty Tips

- Faithfull's heavy fringe has made a comeback in recent years – make sure the length just covers the eyebrows.

- For a subverted take on the English Rose, keep the face pale with coral lips but amp up the look with dark, moody eyes.

- A smudged smoky eye gives the "just rolled out of bed" look – try Biba colours of blackish purple, sapphire or mulberry.

OPPOSITE: Marianne Faithfull and Anita Pallenberg, the world's coolest women demonstrate the full Rock 'n' Roll Girlfriend wardrobe: wide leather belt, mini-dress, black leather boots on Anita and hat, velvet wrap and ankle-length flares on Marianne – and, of course, feather boas for both.

RIGHT: Marianne in the film *La Motorcyclette* by Jack Cardiff, 1967, perhaps the most iconic and most-copied photo of Faithfull ever taken. The film is packed with ideas for any groovy girl's leather-influenced wardrobe.

# Talitha Getty: Boho Contessa

Pick up any upmarket fashion magazine from the 1970s and you will spot this glamorous take on the hippie look. Boho Contessa evolved from the ethnic fashion movement of the late 1960s and early '70s and in recent years has enjoyed a rebirth. Celebrities Nicole Richie and Cameron Diaz are Californian girls who occasionally rock Boho Contessa back to her roots.

Such eccentric styling originally required the insouciance of the über-rich to carry it off. Although the hippie look had reached the provinces, the extravagant ethnic fabrics and discarded wardrobes of wealthy ancestors formed the basis of the Boho Contessa's wardrobe and were decidedly different to a cheesecloth kaftan from a high-street shop. During the 1960s, young heiresses frequented palaces in Morocco and mixed local market finds with their inherited splendour.

The step-granddaughter of the Bohemian artist Augustus John, Talitha Pol became one of London's most celebrated beauties of the 1960s. Though courted by ballet superstar Rudolf Nureyev, she met oil heir and philanthropist John Paul Getty Jr (whose father was reputedly one of the richest men in the world) at a dinner party after Nureyev failed to accompany her. They were married soon afterward in Rome in 1966.

Sometime muse to Yves Saint Laurent, Talitha Pol was the original rich hippie who befriended numerous fashion names including Diane von Fürstenberg (whose granddaughter is named after her) and was renowned for her eclectic style. She followed the hippie trail to Marrakech in 1969 and was famously photographed by Patrick Lord Lichfield wearing a splendid, multicoloured embroidered coat over white pantaloons and boots, with her husband wearing traditional Moroccan dress in the background.

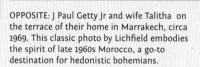

### Boho Contessa Lookalikes
Nicole Richie
Donyale Luna
Simone d'Aillencourt
Marisa Berenson
Veruschka

OPPOSITE: J Paul Getty Jr and wife Talitha on the terrace of their home in Marrakech, circa 1969. This classic photo by Lichfield embodies the spirit of late 1960s Morocco, a go-to destination for hedonistic bohemians.

TOP: The German-born Veruschka von Lehndorff's unconventional beauty made her the perfect Contessa Boho pin-up.

FAR LEFT: Nicole Richie, along with LA cohort stylist Rachel Zoe, revamped the West Coast Boho look, bringing the kaftan back into fashion. Shawls, gold jewellery and sparkly sandals comprised the Richie "rich" look.

LEFT: Rolling Stone Brian Jones and American model Donyale Luna in 1968: *Time* magazine declared 1966 "The Year of Luna" in the US while Twiggy dominated in the UK.

Throughout the 1960s and 1970s, exotic models such as Veruschka (the German supermodel) and Marisa Berenson (the "Queen of the Scene") were pictured with their long hair flowing over tanned, naked (or nearly naked) bodies in fashion journals. Born Vera von Lehndorff, Veruschka arrived in London in the early 1960s, looking to escape a somewhat traumatic childhood in Nazi Germany, and was eventually photographed by Richard Avedon, Francesco Scavullo and Franco Rubartelli. She was also famous enough to play herself in Michelangelo Antonioni's legendary movie *Blow-Up*, uttering the immortal phrase, "Here I am". Stunning Simone d'Aillencourt travelled to India in the late 1960s, where she posed for Henry Clarke with her ankles and wrists tethered by exotic chain jewellery, her hair styled in an enormous beehive and covered in rich beading. Six-foot tall Donyale Luna was a mix of French, Irish, African and Mexican ancestry, who eventually left modelling to concentrate on movies and appeared as sorceress Enotea in Federico Fellini's 1969 classic *Satyricon*. For decades the movie has been the source of inspiration for numerous high-end fashion designers so fans of this vintage style should take note.

Designers soon picked up on the trend for dressing boho beauties. Ossie Clark and Celia Birtwell shared a flat with Jimi Hendrix for a time and dressed the bohemians in richly coloured, body-hugging styles. White crochet, purchased dirt cheap from craftswomen plying their wares beside the Venice canals or on the beaches of Greece or Ibiza, was a favourite for beachwear. Boho ensembles included a large poncho over a bikini, always worn with a wide-brim, hippie hat. British designer Caroline Charles created equally beautiful versions of the rich hippie look for an upmarket clientele, including actress Elizabeth Taylor. Internationally, the house of Pucci became the Boho Contessa's label of choice, although Bill Blass, Pierre Balmain and Yves Saint Laurent all produced appropriately opulent lines.

### Key Looks

- Long, lean silhouette
- Ultra-long maxi-skirts or flares draped over high, wooden clog-style shoes
- Flared ankle-skimming jeans over jewelled flat sandals in summer
- Slimline kaftans with beaded embroidery around keyhole necklines
- Large, semiprecious stone rings
- Tibetan and Indian silver jewellery
- Chiffon gypsy-style dresses worn off the shoulder with long, tiered skirts; also crochet dresses
- Lace-up leather waistcoats
- Shaggy fur-trimmed coats
- Wide brim hats in summer and Cossack styles for winter
- Headscarves in exotic colours, turban-wrapped
- Loosely crocheted poncho worn over a bikini
- Tight, knee-length calfskin boots
- Ethnic scarves and Spanish silk gypsy shawls with copious fringing and tassels
- Middle Eastern textiles

RIGHT: An Yves Saint Laurent gypsy-style outfit, 1969. Patchwork, quilting and strong colours were key components of the Boho Contessa look, a flash of satin or ribbon adding that ultra-luxe edge.

# Style Guide

**The Palette:** Rich and splendid midnight blues, purples and gold and black offset by tan or gold embossed leather, white leather or chocolate brown patents. Missoni's multicoloured knits from the 1970s, with browns, creams and oranges being the distinctive cues, add the finishing touch.

**Key Designers:** Ossie Clark and Celia Birtwell, Yves Saint Laurent, Thea Porter, Diane von Fürstenberg, Balmain, Missoni, Pucci.

**Silhouette and Cut:** Always super-long and lean, flaring out at the ankle and designed to emphasize the body shape. Necklines are low-cut, though the cleavage looks natural and "free" rather than full. Long sleeves, voluminous and gathered at the wrists or tight and trailing down over the hands, play a key part in the outline.

## Dresses

Luxury is vital for the Boho Contessa – absolutely no polyester, cheap cotton, heavy jersey or Crimplene. The floor-length dress is a staple piece, especially worn with a fur wrap for evenings or a close-fitting denim shirt during the day.

*Shop vintage for:* Look for long, figure-hugging Missoni-style knitted dresses or floaty multicoloured chiffon gowns you can belt at the waist with a wide gold or bronze leather corset belt. Don't forget the essential kaftan, but keep it long and body-skimming or sensuously thigh-length with bejewelled edging and a plunging V or keyhole necklines. Search for the exotic designs of Italian couturiers including Emilio Pucci, Emanuel Ungaro, Maria Antonelli, Giorgio Fabiani and Tiani (a young Karl Lagerfeld was their designer) – they created splendid kaftan costumes for Elizabeth Taylor in *Boom*, 1968.

## Outerwear

Ethnic looks reigned, such as heavily embroidered coats from Peru, Afghanistan or India, as well as tunics, tabards, cloaks, capes and ponchos. All were high-end, beautifully decorated or original pieces, never high street. Long leather and suede coats are also part of this look.

*Shop vintage for:* Hunt out fitted suede jackets in purple, bottle green or chocolate brown. Look for narrow lapels, blazer-style, from British high-street labels, such as Chelsea Girl and Miss Selfridge, as well as Ossie Clark and Foale & Tuffin. Don't forget capes and ponchos (blanket or loose-knit styles) too, especially those by Bill Gibb.

## Separates

Contessas chose a mish-mash of 1960s jeans in ankle-length cuts, Pucci-esque Capris, leather waistcoats, fur gilets, long cardigans by Missoni or Sonia Rykiel, huge Afghan coats and their grandmothers' fur coats and wraps.

*Shop vintage for:* Heavy damask and curtain-style fabrics, often made up into trouser suits in the 1960s, would be a great find as would fine lawn cotton blouses or Pucci beach trousers.

### Style Tips

- Look for fringing, tassels and mirrored sequins on bags, scarves and hems.

- Keep the look ethnic at all times – sourcing original items from holiday locations such as Morocco, Goa or the Middle East adds an authentic touch.

- Wear stacks of bangles up your arm, or an upper-arm bangle.

- Layer and mix colours, prints and materials while keeping an overall balance in mind.

- Keep the look long by wearing ankle-length dresses and skirts or tunics over skinny jeans for a modern style. No minis!

- For a less full-on look, stick to one focal piece – such as an amazing cape or dress – and go easy on the rest of the pieces. It's not difficult to overdo this look with excessive styling.

OPPOSITE: An Indian silk, empire-line Thea Porter dress with crimson sleeves trimmed in black velvet, late 1960s. Thea Porter's Soho boutique was the centre of Boho style in the late 1960s and her designs incorporated luxury Eastern fabrics including printed velvets, woven silks and chiffons.

LEFT: A model wearing an Afghanistan goat-skin jacket from Mallory & Church, 1968. Boho style could not be mass-produced so small boutiques flourished. Anyone who could get their hands on exotic Asian or North African garb could get rich, until the high street on both sides of the Atlantic caught up. Soon Macy's and C&A were producing their own cheaper versions.

OPPOSITE: Essential accessories for the Boho Contessa look: gold bejewelled sandals and a woven gold scarf.

BELOW: Verushka sitting on a inlaid Moroccan platter, wearing a bikini made from gold chains, with gold chains veiled over her body, 1968. Styled by Giorgio di Sant' Angelo, her whole body is covered in gold Bio-Miracle foundation, her eyes are made up in gold eyeshadow and her hair is coiled into gold dreadlocks.

## Jewellery and Accessories

Pile it on is the rule of the Boho Contessa: less is simply less. Boho Contessas favoured body jewels and Indian-inspired tummy, toe and ankle chains over conventional earrings, necklace and bracelet sets. Multiple bangles worn Grecian style above the elbows and golden, glittery headdresses or broken but precious tiaras also featured. Silk scarves in ethnic prints or bright colours were wound around the head, turban-style, or worn long and loose. Espadrilles, leather sandals, beaded flats and embroidered Turkish shoes also suit the look.

*Shop vintage for:* Splendid estate jewellery would be wonderful if you already have some in your possession, otherwise source costume copies with the right sprinkling of ethnic splendour. Seek out bone bangles, brass or silver rings with semiprecious stones and enormous chandelier-style earrings. Tibetan pieces with bells attached or bangles, necklaces and collars in solid silver lend the appropriate ethnic feel. Look for huge semiprecious stones set into chunky silver rings or chokers, Navaho silver and turquoise pieces and stacks of African wooden bangles. For footwear, shop market stalls for modern-day espadrilles, leather thong sandals and traditional Turkish shoes or Indian juttis and kolhapuris.

TIP: Scarves are a key look for the Boho Contessa. Choose Pucci-style versions and warp them around your head turban-style, or tie your hair in a low ponytail and wrap a folded triangle of the scarf around crown, knotting at the nape of the neck.

Alternatively, wear a scarf as a sari. Wrap an oversized long scarf around your waist, cross it over in front of you, twist, then tie at the back of the neck. Secure it at the waist with a tan or gold macramé leather belt.

## Beauty Guide

This is a luxurious look: hair needs to be clean and glossy, skin tanned and make-up carefully applied for a natural glow. Boho Contessa's large, extravagant jewellery calls for minimal make-up (avoid red lips and overdone black eyeliner) and simple hairstyling, although you can embrace backcombing, too. During the late 1960s many Contessas wore their hair in enormous "Marie Antoinette" bouffants, with long locks trailing down their backs. Such updos required hair pieces and serious amounts of cash and attention, but you can do a simple version if you naturally have long hair by backcombing the front section of hair, securing it at the crown, and allowing the rest of the hair to fall down the back.

RIGHT: This James Galanos 1965 evening gown displays a classic Boho pattern – a Harlequin, printed silk of blue, red, white and pink with matching over-sheath. Note the classic boho princess-style bouffant in this shot, coupled with classic chandelier earrings: a perfect evening or special event combination.

# Françoise Hardy: Euro Chic

The simple style of 1960s Parisian street culture makes this a perfect relaxed weekend look. Throw on straight white jeans, a black polo neck, add a slick of eyeliner and voilà! It's ideal for heading down to Rome on the back of a scooter. For inspiration look no further than French chanteuse Françoise Hardy. Impossibly pretty Hardy recorded her own compositions of romantic torch songs and easy-listening classics, beginning in 1963. Her sound sums up that other romantic, rebellious moment in French history, the late 1960s, when Parisian students took to the streets in protest at their government's supposedly right-wing, authoritarian bias. The lovely Hardy was courted by every major rock star of the day, from Mick Jagger to Bob Dylan, who travelled to Paris in search of the singer and even wrote a poem about her. Eventually, she married a Frenchman, the singer and actor Jacques Dutronc.

Hardy couldn't have dressed in a more simple or understated style for the 1960s and 1970s, yet she remains an archetype upon which a whole look is based, albeit one less obvious than Brigitte Bardot's Bombshell look. She chose masculine shapes, including a full leather biker's ensemble for one memorable photo shoot, and a black tuxedo with a bootlace tie for an evening out. A typical Hardy look is a pair of ankle-length, slightly flared jeans over Cuban-heeled boots with a fitted black T-shirt – understated sexiness. Plain necklines and an amazing bone structure eradicated the need for further decoration: she was ultra-cool and delivered her music standing or sitting stock still by the microphone. Hardy left

## Euro Chic Lookalikes
Jane Birkin
Patti Smith
Charlotte Gainsbourg
Jean Seberg
Carla Bruni
Lou Doillon

OPPOSITE: François Hardy in Paris around 1969. Wearing Chanel pearls with a T-shirt and jeans – an ultra chic, casual combination that works beautifully today.

ABOVE: France's First Lady Carla Bruni-Sarkozy's guitar gently weeps as she rocks her own upscale version of Hardy chic.

FAR LEFT: A confirmed Francophile, Patti Smith's naturally cool androgynous look has spawned thousands of imitators.

LEFT: Lou Doillon, daughter of Jane Birkin and sister to Charlotte Gainsbourg, represents the modern image of Euro-cool with an eclectic fashion style based on vintage finds and designer originals.

## Key Looks

- Flares with white pumps
- Mohair roll-neck sweater
- Black polo neck worn beneath a brown suede jacket
- Shaped white T-shirt with almost-elbow-length sleeves
- Fitted black shirt with black frills
- High or round necklines
- Monochrome patterned skirt
- Lightweight black leather biker jacket and matching leather jeans
- Cuban-heeled boots
- White skinny-rib sweater, white jeans plus white ankle boots with a low heel
- Oversize, plastic-framed sunglasses
- Long white, fitted crochet dress
- Short cotton shift dress
- Belted trench coat

the bopping around to other singers and eschewed the go-go-girl culture by avoiding all things Mod, gimmicky and glitzy. She remains as much a poet as a musician and epitomizes the classic Euro Chic mix of brains plus beauty. For a while, her favourite outfit to perform in was a simple, above-the-knee, A-line skirt with a fitted black sweater and low-heeled T-bar pumps.

While Hardy remains our Euro Chic cover girl, others have adopted and adapted her style through the years. Jean Seberg cropped her hair to star as Joan of Arc in 1957's *Saint Joan*, and although born in Iowa, USA, she remains another archetype of Euro Chic. A typical Seberg look might be a stripy, sloppy sweater worn over cropped jeans or a lightweight cardigan thrown casually over a simple, square-necked 1950s-style summer cotton dress. Seberg was frequently photographed in roll-neck or cowl-neck sweaters, which are especially flattering to shorter hair, adding length and interest to the neck. Another favourite was a cosy, heavy-knit cardigan such as an Aran style with a turned-up collar and big wooden buttons, worn fastened. At a time when almost every other movie star sported big, bigger or the biggest possible hair, Seberg went against the grain and hung onto her charming Jeanne d'Arc boy-crop.

Seberg and Hardy share the Euro-themed spotlight with the Gainsbourg gals. British-born actress Jane Birkin met French singer-songwriter Serge Gainsbourg on a film set shortly after her divorce from composer John Barry. Her intense, sexually charged relationship with Gainsbourg was played out in public and Birkin represented the sexed-up side of Euro Chic. Although she sported many cool looks, most involved at least a modicum of nudity – fine for St Tropez but perhaps harder to pull off elsewhere. Euro Chic is usually a covered-up look. Bare legs work, but cleavage does not. Birkin's daughters, actress and singer-songwriter Charlotte Gainsbourg and model and actress Lou Doillon, are the modern exponents of the look. Francophile Patti Smith travelled to Paris with just her raincoat and a few bits of men's clothing in 1969. Although she took her look back to New York, the idea of men's trousers and shirt with a raincoat over the top has cemented itself as a classic. Paris was, and remains, at the centre of European style – a homing point for poets and a magical place that encapsulated the free spirit of the 1960s.

LEFT: Françoise Hardy stood still in front of her microphone and allowed her simple songs to tell the story. The dress could be an early Missoni. A vivid pattern like this looks amazing when everything else – hair, shoes, make-up and accessories – are played down.

OPPOSITE: 1969: Another girl on a motorbike. Hardy takes a fashion-forward approach to biker classics, swapping stud-free patent leather, loose flares and sleek boots for heavy metal and leather.

# Style Guide

**The Palette:** Neutral. Black and white for shirts, polo-neck sweaters and T-shirts; beige for Macs and coats, creams for knits.

**Key Designers:** Agnès B, Joseph, Chloé, Chanel, Missoni.

**Silhouette and Cut:** This is a feminine, school-girlish shape with narrow, fitted clothing. Nothing frilly, billowy or full – pared-down, sexy chic.

## Separates

Choose dresses and skirts in simple cotton lawn or seersucker in A-line shapes. Despite the onslaught of the miniskirt, Hardy favoured a longer, just-above-the-knee length for skirts and dresses. Hers was an acutely simple style. Pure silk and natural knits including lambs' wool and mohair are also core to the Euro Chic look. Pair narrow white jeans with close-fitting, long-sleeved T-shirts or skinny-rib sweaters.

*Shop vintage for:* White jeans by Levi's – source original, straight-legged 501s or men's straight white jeans for an easy take on this look. Late 1950s or early 1960s summer dresses in lightweight cotton – the simpler and smaller the print, the better.

## Outerwear:

Men's leather jackets are great with this look, especially original, slim-fitting blazers or even a narrow trench. A boxy, brown, brushed leather men's casual jacket will work, too. Michael Caine's "Harry Palmer" style of coat suits this look perfectly. Outerwear fabrics are heavy but soft, with blanket-style wools, brown cowhide for jackets and black leather for the odd trench coat or cap.

*Shop vintage for:* A black wool duffel coat with toggles, a men's knee-length, off-white 1960s trench coat, a short leather or sheepskin jacket or a fitted black wool coat.

### Style Tips

- For Seberg chic, turn up the collars on coats and shirts.

- Keep the silhouette long and lean.

- Wind a scarf around your head as a headband.

- If you have the figure, wear black footless tights as trousers with a simple boxy top.

- Try a snug-fitting, narrow-legged men's suit in a dark colour.

- Wear brogues or boys' Cuban-heel ankle boots.

- Carry your worldly goods in a brown leather schoolgirl-style satchel.

- The ankle is emphasized, so show off footwear.

- Wear leather driving gloves on cold winter days.

RIGHT: French actress Françoise Hardy at Brands Hatch to film John Frankenheimer's racing drama *Grand Prix*.

BELOW RIGHT: Slightly beaten-up, brown leather accessories from the late '60s and early '70s will add instant, arty-looking kudos to any outfit. Take a chic-leaf from ultra-cool former French *Vogue* editor Carine Roitfeld and ditch high-fashion, exorbitantly priced designer bags from your wardrobe altogether. Vintage is far more Euro Chic.

BELOW: Hardy sports a YSL safari jacket and matching skirt, teamed with groovy cropped white ankle boots, a white polo neck and a squishy shoulder bag. The perfect outfit for posing moodily, 1960s-chanteuse style, on a pavement near you!

## Accessories

Hats form a key link in the Euro Chic chain – perfect for those "just got out of bed with an unnamed rock star" days. Wear hair long and messy underneath.

*Shop vintage for:* The ubiquitous beret aside, also look for peaked leather caps with brims or wider brimmed Homburgs and straw trilbies. For shoes, look for original 1960s T-bars, "Pilgrim" pumps (with buckles) and slingbacks – all with low stack or kitten heels – and for boots, search for period Cuban-heeled or Chelsea boots. For handbags, choose satchel or saddle-style bags with long shoulder straps and hunt out slouchy "hobo" styles in good-quality brown or tan leather.

# Beauty Guide

No beating about the bush here, this is a brunette look. Shoulder-length hair, bluntly cut to sweep over the shoulders, is given a choppy fringe (bangs). For extra texture, feel free to have the occasional home-chop with a pair of sharp scissors but never, ever brush or comb Euro Chic hair. Nor do you need hair accessories other than the occasional same-colour hair elastic for days when only a rough ponytail can save you from a shampoo.

Like most sexy, tousled styles leaning heavily on natural beauty, the Euro Chic look relies on cosmetic enhancement. Lips and eyes are the emphasis, with a heavy eyelid providing the hinge-factor for the face. Dark brown, black or graphite grey eyeliner covers the lid, ending in a sharp flick at the far corners of each eye. Lashings of mascara plus the odd falsie dotted along the outer upper lashline complete this sexy look. Euro chicks perfected the art of the Meaningful Stare, which necessitates that the eyes are made up just enough to emphasize shape and colour but not to look overdone. Lips are nude, matte and pouting – in fact, lipstick is almost dry, so leave the gloss at home and adopt a naturally pale, full look.

ABOVE: Françoise Hardy, circa 1970, with heavily outlined eyelids and pale pink lips. Despite the amount of make-up, she manages to look fresh and natural – which could be due to the innocent pie-crust collar and the absolute precision of her make-up. No smudgy lines or messy streaks, the look is crisply chic. A choppy fringe and long, straight locks enhance Hardy's gorgeous face.

# Bianca Jagger: Studio 54

While punk took hold of pop music, something far more sophisticated was happening on the dance floors in the 1970s: jetsetters from around the world flocked to groovy Studio 54 and the queues to get into the converted dancehall on Manhattan's West 54th Street became legendary. Most jetsetting of all was Nicaraguan-born wife of Mick Jagger, Bianca, who was central to the New York social scene. While the city streets deteriorated into an urban war zone complete with warring drug barons, gangsters and muggers, disco drove everyone to party hard. Like the fall of Rome, dancers grooved while, at times, the city literally burned.

Bianca Pérez-Mora-Macias met Mick Jagger at a party after a Rolling Stones concert in France in 1970 and in 1971 the couple were married in St Tropez with Bianca wearing a white skirt suit by Yves Saint Laurent with nothing under the jacket. Along with Liza Minnelli, Elizabeth Taylor and other doyennes of the New York social scene, Bianca loved Roy Halston Frowick's ("Halston") sensuous, ultra-simple designs. Originally a milliner for Bergdorf Goodman before branching out into garment design, Roy Halston eventually established his own label and created slinky gowns for the Studio 54 set. His signature was draped, languid dresses and separates fashioned out of luxurious fabrics including silk crepe de Chine, knitted silk jersey, satin-finished polyesters and ultrasuede. Halston broke high fashion's mould by frequently working with artificial fibres. Despite a dalliance

> ### Studio 54 Lookalikes
> Margaret Trudeau
> Jerry Hall
> Donna Summer
> Sister Sledge
> A Taste of Honey
> Alison Goldfrapp

OPPOSITE: Nicaraguan actress, model and human rights activist Bianca Jagger sports an asymmetric gypsy-style top of frilled white linen lace in this photograph by Norman Parkinson from the 1970s. Bianca brings high style to this lingerie-inspired look.

BELOW LEFT: Jerry Hall performs on stage with Bryan Ferry, London, 1977: her leggy, sleek style was the blueprint for the disco era. Though Hall looked fabulous as Bryan Ferry's favourite accessory, she left him at the end of 1977 for his arch rival, Mick Jagger.

ABOVE: Alison Goldfrapp performing on the Pyramid Stage at the Glastonbury Festival in 2008. Goldfrapp revamped disco musically and stylewise for a new generation. Her glitter-based make-up, 1970s retro outfits and sweet singing style have made her a thoroughly modern muse.

LEFT: Donna Summer's sultry, x-rated sounds revolutionized dance music with their sexually explicit noises! Donna Summer's splendid look of gleaming skin, huge hair and lips and a body to die for made her a disco diva for a generation, here shown in 1979.

courtesy of André Courrèges, Paco Rabanne and Pierre Cardin in the 1960s, artificial fibres remained a strictly downmarket phenomenon until Halston changed everyone's view: he loved to use fabrics that stretched and bounced with wear while snapping back into place. Halston's styles are referenced in fashion collections from every major designer of our times, and form the basis for the best slinky night-out look.

As well as eveningwear, his ultrasuede "shirtwaist" dress was among the most popular, sharing the spotlight with Diane von Fürstenberg and her iconic wrap-dress. Halston loved dressing women of all sizes and adored many of his female customers. "You have to have something for the woman who is overweight," he told the *New York Times* in 1978, "a loose tunic and pants is good because it elongates the body. You have to have something for the woman with hips – the princess line works for her."

Disco divas began to fill the pop charts: Sister Sledge, Donna Summer, Thelma Houston, Gloria Gaynor and A Taste of Honey all emerged from the scene with extravagant wardrobes. Harem pants, Lurex capes worn with feathers or giant flowers in the hair, the Studio 54 look was wholly theatrical and purely for fun. Halston's gowns were mixed up with ghetto accessories including gold jewellery, snakeskin shoes and belts, plus lots of fur. Disco style spread across the Atlantic and by the late 1970s, Christian Dior, Yves Saint Laurent and Thierry Mugler were producing their own versions. Silk jersey fabrics plus jewel-coloured straight jackets with narrow lapels, slash-neck vests and tailored trousers with tie-around waists formed the core of the look. Ever more vibrant colours followed, including pink, purple, jade green and turquoise. British-based designer Antony Price took everything a stage further by adding tailoring and menswear to the nightclub phenomenon. Although just as important to the British eveningwear fashion scene as Halston had been in the US, many British retailers lacked the necessary flair and vision to really push Price's designs, with the result that he remained an exclusive, upmarket clothier.

As the sumptuous Studio 54 look filtered down to the street, more accessories were piled on. Halston's original designs required no more adornment than a tan and high heels but soon all sorts of accoutrements flooded onto the scene: long strings of beads worn across the body, narrow belts doubled up and wound twice around the waist, Lurex hosiery or scrunched-down socks with satin trousers, pillbox hats and floral hair slides. Every girl looks gorgeous in the Studio 54 style: the colours, sheens and sparkles of the fabrics, combined with matching make-up and body-elongating high heels, mean this look will always be a winner.

### Key Looks

- Tie-wasted tapered trousers in silky fabrics
- Silver and gold metallic mesh vests and T-shirts
- One-shouldered dresses with long skirts, with an asymmetric, same-fabric frill
- White fur wraps
- Lurex or sparkly fishnet tights
- Silver or gold strappy sandals
- Simple strapless dresses with elasticated waists in slinky jersey
- Harem pants tied at the ankles
- Sequins and Lurex vests beneath silk shirts or worn with tight spandex jeans or leggings
- Draped, Grecian-style, crepe de Chine dresses
- All-in-one jumpsuits with elasticated waists, preferably hooded
- Oversize T-shirt knotted on the hips over footless tights and legwarmers – a glitzy version of dance-school chic

OPPOSITE: Beverly Johnson modelling a Halston dress, circa 1978, made of pastel vertical pieces of flowing material, probably chiffon, with a neckline plunging into a V-shaped waist. Halston remains the name most synonymous with disco-era fashion.

# Style Guide

**The Palette:** Studio 54 colours are jewel-bright fuchsia, teal, jade green, electric blue, emerald green and black. Two-tone silks, sequins and glitter-shot Lurex or shiny silver spandex add to the mix.

**Key Designers:** Roy Halston, Bill Blass, Geoffrey Beene, Giorgio di Sant'Angelo, Perry Ellis, Christian Dior, Thierry Mugler, Antony Price.

**Silhouette and Cut:** A long, fluid, feminine silhouette with blurred outlines caused by reflective fabrics in the disco lights.

## Dresses

Shimmering or gleaming fabrics are key to the Studio 54 look– don't be afraid of polyester and other artificial fibres. This is a night look relying on texture, allure and durability; simple silk may not withstand the rigours of the dance; you need stretch! Look for lightweight fabrics, even lingerie slips in shiny silk that you can cinch at the waist with a thin metallic belt. Length also works if the slits are high enough, so don't be afraid to rummage for finds among full-on eveningwear. Think Stephanie, played by Karen Lynn Gorney, in *Saturday Night Fever*, twirling about in her one-shouldered, knee-length frock, an asymmetric frill and flower corsage pinned to the waist.

*Shop vintage for:* Vintage Halston gets snapped up quickly, though you may find some pieces from the diffusion line he sold through JC Penney's in the 1980s, or from countless imitators. Founded by Sarah Jessica Parker, Halston Heritage is the new line based on the original, and sells many beautiful copies.

RIGHT: This Christian Dior red slit-thigh dress with blouson bodice in silk jersey is from the mid 1970s. Designed to reveal tantalizing glimpses of the disco diva's form as she danced, Marc Bohan for Dior created upmarket European versions of Halston's winning dance-floor looks.

LEFT: French designer Yves Saint Laurent shows his 1979 spring-summer women's haute couture collection in Paris. The model is wearing a cream version of his "Le Smoking" dinner suit.

## Trousers

Formal, flared trousers with high waists were worn with skinny, barely there sequin boob tubes, Lurex or satin vest tops and the occasional tuxedo jacket. If you have the figure for skintight spandex leggings or jeans, try them with an oversize silk shirt and a thin metallic belt around the hips. The jodhpur style, with bow-tied ankles and a high waist, was also a key look.

*Shop vintage for:* Designer trousers by Marc Bohan for Christian Dior, Ungaro, Geoffrey Beene and Thierry Mugler – they require a waspy waist to prevent the wearer from looking clownish. Keep your eyes peeled for barely-worn satin jumpsuits with zippy details to wear unzipped over shimmering lingerie.

## Tops

Slinky ruched tops with long sleeves, leotards, draped silk sleeveless tops and bandeau tops to be worn beneath lightweight satin jackets were all popular choices. Wear a satin tuxedo jacket with nothing underneath, like Bianca on her wedding day.

*Shop vintage for:* Versions of these styles from the 1980s and 1990s can work with the Studio 54 look, as well as original 1970s pieces. Also look for asymmetric vests, loose chiffon tops with shoulder-tie straps and lingerie-style silk camisoles.

### Style Tips

- Scrape hair to one side, balanced out with just one long gold earring.

- Keep glitter in your bag ready to dab on or throw!

- Wear beads diagonally across your body.

- Try glittery ankle socks worn with stilettos.

- Make a simple turban from sparkling net fabric.

- Dust highlighter over arms, shoulders and cleavage for a glowing look.

- Mirrored sunglasses are a fabulous nightclubbing look.

- Carry an ornate, Oriental fan.

- V-shaped dresses cut to the navel reveal expanses of tanned skin and piles of necklaces but this is a look for flat-chested girls only – absolutely no cleavage.

- Customize any garment with a wide, good-quality belt in bronze metallic leather.

- Finish off with a feather boa.

## Shoes

By the late 1970s towering spindle heels overtook the platform – Bianca wore gold metallic Manolo Blahniks for her famous birthday celebration in 1977 at Studio 54. For the dance vibe, don't forget dance-school chic: add footless tights beneath a lightweight skirt or pull legwarmers on over your ankles to wear with stilettos.

> *Shop vintage for:* Strappy stilettos in gold or silver by Terry de Havilland, Charles Jourdan or Manolo Blahnik.

## Accessories

Peacock feather hair accessories or earrings, metallic mesh-style earrings and extra-long chain earrings can still be found at specialist vintage jewellery stores. Flowers and feathers were big news, and inexpensive. Pin your hair back with a flower corsage or clip one to a belt. For jewellery, wear long feather earrings, long strands of beads or jewelled collars, or choose big gold hoops, thin gold chains and fine bangles. There's only one rule: make your bag a clutch style – and keep it small and shiny, too!

> *Shop vintage for:* Diamanté returned to the fashion spotlight at the end of the 1970s, so hunt out big shapes with small stones. Clutch bags by Judith Leiber, Manolo Blahnik and Chanel are high-end choices, but look for styles with sequins, beads and gemstones or in bright shiny colours or metallics.

# Beauty Guide

Apart from the odd sprinkling of glitter and shine, this is a more natural look than you might expect. Tanned skin was crucial for the gleam, cheeks shone with glimmering coral and pink tones, while highlighter became a key component in every make-up kit. Frosted or shiny white highlighter was the cosmetic world's big invention and women blended it on brows or cheekbones for added luminosity under the lights. Lips were coral, pink or *au naturel* and super glossy. The disco era saw the advent of lip-gloss and roller-ball-topped bottles of sticky, cherry-flavoured shine. Eye make-up was electric: vivid blues, greens or pinks with blue mascara and lots of sparkle and glitter dust sprinkled across lids and cheeks. Lashings of black, blue or purple mascara were worn to match the eyeshadow.

Hair is left wild and free, regardless of colour, style or shape. Hairstyles didn't last long under the lights, anyway! A chin-length wavy bob, slightly 1930s-style, was favoured by Bianca Jagger and allowed natural curl and movement. Long-haired women plaited their tresses into tiny plaits (braids), then wound them around their heads or else scraped their hair up into a high ballerina bun or into a side ponytail. Long hair was rolled at the front to softly mimic the classic 1940s look.

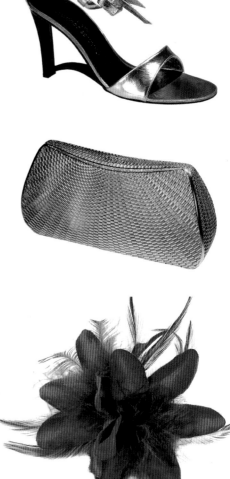

TOP: Gold leather Charles Jourdan sandal with a tied ankle strap, from 1979. Jourdan's designs were fashion-forward but available at concessions in department stores.

CENTRE: Evening clutch bag from 1975 in silver and gold metalwork. Clutches came out of retirement and returned to fashion via the disco era. All a girl needed was keys, lipstick and enough cash to get home, as true disco divas got free entrance to clubs and drinks bought for them.

BOTTOM: Orchids and other exotic flowers made perfect disco accessories, tucked behind one ear.

TIP: Use your highlighter to create an all-over body shimmer by applying it on the bony areas of the body – along the collarbones, the tops of shoulders, and down the arms and the shins to create an illusion of length.

LEFT: Bianca Jagger mixed romantic elements of fashion with masculine tailoring, as was perfectly executed in her wedding outfit of white tuxedo jacket and long white skirt. Her 27th birthday party, when she rode a horse into Studio 54 became the club's most legendary night, ever. She divorced Jagger after he left her for Jerry Hall in 1978 but quipped, "My marriage ended on my wedding day".

## Strobe-Light Make-up

Highlighters are available as creams, oils or powders and under various names such as "illuminators" and "shimmers", but they all perform the same function – to catch the light and define the face. For extra impact, start with a layer of cream highlighter and then dab powder highlighter on top to intensify the effect.

**You will need:**
Tinted moisturizer
Shimmery bronzing powder
Highlighter

1 Using a tinted moisturizer that matches your skin tone (rather than a full-coverage foundation), apply from the centre of the face blending outward in long strokes. Apply quickly and lightly to achieve an even coverage.
2 Apply the bronzer under the cheekbones, taking the colour up onto the temples and blending into the hairlines.
3 Dab on cream highlighter where light will naturally hit the face (see illustration right) – the centre of the forehead, under the arch of the brow, on top of the cheekbones, in a thin line down the length of the nose and on the chin.

# Grace Slick: Combat Chic

Ever since 1960s revolutionary babes Grace Slick of the rock band Jefferson Airplane and Oscar-winning actress Jane Fonda were photographed in US Army surplus clothing, combat gear has enjoyed an in-and-out style history. The two young women, dressed in vest tops, dogtag necklaces and combat trousers painted a tough, sexy picture of a look that works as well for a fashionista's day off as denim. Having morphed into the fashion label "Utility", the look is here to stay.

As lead singer with the band, Grace Slick was one of the first female rock singers of the modern era. She started out as a model but, after discovering her own voice, decided to start a band with her husband Jerry Slick and his brother Darby. Her haunting, strong voice was so powerful on tracks such as "White Rabbit" and "Wheels On Fire" that it was amazing she did not become a bigger star overseas. Multiple line-up changes obscured the success of the Jefferson conglomerate which changed it's name numerous times, ending up as just Starship. Grace, meanwhile, carried on wearing her fashion-free wardrobe.

To tour with a rock band in the 1960s, especially during the 1967 "Summer of Love" was to "rough it" in the original sense of the term. Sleeping on buses, in cheap motels or under the stars, the scene was no place for a designer wardrobe. Grace Slick wore clothes she picked up in California street markets and borrowed from the boys. Thanks to the Vietnam War, America was doing big business in used military clothing and it was possible to pick up cheap army surplus in most towns. On the tall, gorgeous Grace, with her tangled black curls, deep tan and blue eyes, it was a fashion statement.

**Combat Chick Lookalikes**
Jane Fonda
Loretta Swit as Houlihan
in *M.A.S.H*
Fergie from the Black
Eyed Peas
Rihanna

OPPOSITE: American rock singer Grace Slick, the lead vocalist of the band Jefferson Airplane, wears combat green, but here in the uniform of the Girl Scouts rather than the US Army. She was also famously pictured wearing a military jacket with a hand grenade attached, after appearing on *The Tonight Show* in May 1968.

ABOVE: Stacy "Fergie' Ferguson, the Black Eyed Peas singer, frequently rocks a combat-inspired look onstage, glamming it up with lots of blinging jewellery, full hair and stunning make-up.

LEFT: American actress Jane Fonda photographed during a performance of the anti-war road show *F.T.A.* (Free the Army) in New York, 1971. The title of the show, which also featured actor Donald Sutherland, is a play on the expression "Fuck the Army". Fonda's combat fatigues spawned a generation of copycats on college campuses around the US.

### Key Looks

- Man-size parka with fur hood over skinny trousers or a short dress
- Flak-style jacket
- Snug-fitting, combat-style khaki trousers
- Converse trainers or lace-up trench boots for casual
- Spiky or wedge heels for a glammed-up look
- Loose combats with a bare midriff or tight top
- Naval jacket or peacoat with brass buttons
- Shiny gold or silver accessories with combat green
- Long military-style coat, fitted to the waist
- Shorts with bare legs and military boots
- Khaki shirt worn over a white vest as a jacket
- Parachute silk shirts with heavy cotton trousers
- Layered, fine knits or string vests in sludgy creams, greens or white
- Neon vests, leggings or lingerie peeping through combat green
- All-in-one flying suit with elasticated waist and zips at ankles

Different versions of combat style emerged with changing times. In the UK in the 1970s, high fashion sent glam-rocking Bryan Ferry fans hunting for military shirts, pencil skirts and high heels so they too could dress 1940s style like Roxy Music backing singers. Later on, punk queen Jordan (Pamela Rooke, who worked in Malcolm McLaren and Vivienne Westwood's legendary Sex shop on Chelsea's King's Road) was photographed in ripped flying suits. Combat clothes were cheap, easily sourced and aggressive-looking – a perfect match for the gritty sounds of punk. Old Royal Air Force flying suits were unzipped to the waist or held together with the ubiquitous safety pins of the era.

High-fashion designers jumped into the army surplus pool with gusto on the back of New Wave music. Elements of formal military dress were snatched by New Romantic rockers and worn with eye make-up (the boys) and Dr Marten boots (the girls) for an irreverent take on dress costume. Designer Katharine Hamnett's parachute silk shirts of the early 1980s featured army-style detailing; they also came in heavy cotton drill.

Today, most designer houses, such as Louis Vuitton, Jean Paul Gaultier, Michael Kors and Chloé, have displayed elements of the look in recent seasons and that's not to mention the "Houlihan" cargo jeans and "Earhart" trousers by luxury denim-maker J Brand. By keeping an eye on the latest designer trends, it's easy to recreate Combat Chic for a fraction of the high-style prices.

RIGHT: Tommy Hilfiger's styling, here on the catwalk in 2002, shows how to feminize the combat look with a crisp white tank in a silky fabric and a low-slung belt.

OPPOSITE: Form-fitting army fatigues make a glamorous alternative to a T-shirt and baggy trousers. Team with long tousled hair and lots of eye make-up to feminize the look.

# Style Guide

**The Palette:** Camouflage colours – hunter green, olive, sand, beige, brown, khaki – with a dash of neon or orange.

**Key Designers:** Katharine Hamnett, Vivienne Westwood, Michiko Koshino, Jean Paul Gaultier.

**Silhouette and Cut:** Traditionally this cut is slim and fitted, '70s style, or else tiny on top balanced by baggy trousers. Too much khaki, however, and you resemble an extra from Ridley Scott's *Black Hawk Down*! The trick is to tailor current fashions with your own individual style to ensure you always look up to date in this gear. For example, although girl group the All Saints always appeared cool in 1990s combats and Timberland boots, today the same ensemble seems dated.

## Trousers

Key to the combat look, trousers can be easily obtained from vintage military outlets but it's good to have a style idea prior to shopping. Looking for something snug and fitted to wear with flats, or a loose style to belt at the waist and team with heels for a night out. Take along the belt you plan to wear or even the shoes to check out your look before you buy.

*Shop vintage for:* Look for stylish combat styles from the 1980s and 1990s by designers such as Jean Paul Gaultier, Michiko Koshino and Kenzo for Chloé. Hunt for white or cotton drill naval trousers, too – these manly shapes look cool with Converse sneakers or Keds and a simple blazer for a downbeat spring look.

## Shirts

Military shirts play a huge and versatile part in the Combat Chic look. Patch pockets or epaulettes are essential details to look for, as are loose shapes and sleeves that can be rolled up. Wear a large heavyweight version as a jacket, loosely belted over a white vest with long white flares for a contemporary look. Alternatively, copy Grace Slick's idea and wear a vintage Girl Scout top as a jacket – or go the whole way and wear the Girl Scout dress – sexily unbuttoned at the front. Big military shirts look perennially cool tucked into a black pencil skirt, Lauren Bacall-style, or worn loose over short shorts and belted at the hips.

*Shop vintage for:* Army surplus and Girl Scout shirts from the 1970s, or any designer "Utility" range from recent years.

## Outerwear

*Gossip Girl* socialites wear fur-trimmed parkas over their evening gowns to keep out the NYC cold, so why not try a men's parka over a sparkly mini-dress the next time you hit town? High-street stores often carry patch-pocketed, waisted, heavy cotton "Platoon" jackets in army green. Don't buy them! Instead, visit vintage fairs or online stores for authentic versions.

*Shop vintage for:* Parkas with fur trim, long fitted military coats in navy or green with belts and double fronts, army or airmen jackets in leather or sheepskin. Arctic, Desert and Mountain Force clothing in whites, greys and patterns as well as standard shades of green from vintage military-wear specialists. Track down Marc Jacobs' versions of Platoon jackets from his fall 2010 collection in "nearly new" stores. Scan men's military sections for small-sized naval peacoats and blazers.

RIGHT: Punk rock singer and poet Patti Smith wears an ammunition belt and military decorations over a white T-shirt in true "rock revolutionary" style.

## Accessories

Beware of overdoing it. You may have liked the movie *Private Benjamin* but seriously, let's not steal Goldie Hawn's look – mix up your military! For example, team a Platoon jacket with a sleek black leather bag to look more urban sophisticate and less *G.I. Jane*. Another good 1970s look that goes well with military influences is tooled brown leather, so hunt out 1970s belts and bags with this embellishment. Canvas messenger bags with leather edging from Mulberry or Gucci are also great with this look.

*Shop vintage for:* Source brown leather belts, canvas belts, worker boots, across-the-body messenger bags, RAF silk scarves, Arctic soldier "trapper" hats, green army caps, vintage Ray-Ban Aviators and dogtags.

BELOW LEFT: Military dogtags or simple chains and medallions that mimic their style make perfect accessories for the Utility or Combat Chic look.

BELOW RIGHT: Tooled handbag designed by John Bates in collaboration with leatherwork artisan John Williams, from early 1970s. Tooled leather has a chunky, retro vibe which adds fashion kudos to any combat-coloured look. Hunt out satchels or shoulder flap bags in this traditional style.

# *Beauty Guide*

Grace Slick's strong features needed nothing more than a smudge of black eyeliner to rock them up a touch. A California dweller, she had a permanent tan and always looked healthy despite her hard-living lifestyle. A fake tan looks wonderful with the Combat Chic look, but try and choose shades closest to your own skin to avoid looking porn-star bronzed. Bright orange or coral lip shades look cool, as does a thick line of vibrant green or blue eyeliner underneath lashes. Pale princesses also shine with red, 1940s-style lips and scraped-back hair.

You can afford to glam up a bit. Take inspiration from former French *Vogue* editor Carine Roitfeld and rock a messy, natural hair with heavy black eyeliner for a pure sexy-cool look. A short crop hairstyle or scraped-back hair looks fabulous with a tight, crewneck T-shirt and combat-style shorts. Grace's thick, wavy hair was long at the start of her pop career and she wore it loose down her back with a heavy fringe (bangs). As the 1960s progressed and she became more involved with anti-war protesters, she cut her hair into a layered, shaggy style – more edgy and less girly.

---

### *Beauty Tips*

- Grace Slick's bright blue eyes were the feature of her face, and she always wore eyeshadow and liner. To make blue eyes "pop", choose colours in golds, coppers, violets and blues.

- Dark blue liner and mascara also enhance blue eyes, but black adds drama too.

- Grace wore her fringe (bangs) very thick and long over the eyes or gently sideswept.

# Joan Jett: Rock Chick

Rock Chick is a fun, fancy dress idea for some people but for others it's a way of life. Wherever you fall on the spectrum, this is a hard-edged look and one of the most enjoyable images to put together on the vintage circuit: you can stay trad with Joan Jett's "borrowed-from-the-boys'" basics or punk it all up, Sex Pistols' style.

Rock guitarist Joan Jett moved to Los Angeles with her parents in the early 1970s and quickly became obsessed with Brit-based glam rocker Suzi Quatro. Suzi wore leather biker gear and black leather all-in-one jumpsuits to perform while her burly, all-male backing band rocked along sulkily behind her. Her songs "Devil Gate Drive" and "48 Crash" were a world away from the music produced by other female artists at the time. Up until then, rocking girls stuck to the hippie looks favoured by Janis Joplin and the Mamas & the Papas. Despite more female singers and musicians than ever before, women still didn't play in rock bands in the hard-rocking sense. Most of the women in rock were solo artists who strummed a guitar while standing by a mike, Joni Mitchell style. Otherwise, they did a lot of bopping around as backing singers, adding pretty harmonies. Joan Jett, like Suzi Quatro, was neither pretty-pretty nor a dancer.

After learning the guitar in high school, Joan got herself a black leather motorcycle jacket and started hanging around LA's music clubs. Inspired by the music of Quatro and British band the Sweet, she cut her hair into her trademark "short-on-top" mullet and auditioned for various bands. Jett was eventually put together with Cherie Currie, Lita Ford, Jackie Fox and Sandy West to form The Runaways. Their success, or lack of it, is legendary and the subject of a 2010 film starring Kristen Stewart and Dakota Fanning.

## Key Looks

- Black leather biker jacket over a plain or stripy black or white logo T-shirt
- Skinny-cut, black jeans
- Biker boots
- Mohair, holey sweater over a fluorescent T-shirt
- Punk drainpipes in blue-and-black stripes or yellow-and-black checks
- String vest over a long-sleeve T-shirt
- Black leggings with an oversize men's dinner jacket
- Mini kilt worn over tight jeans or leggings
- Neckerchief or leather necktie
- Studded belts, chokers and bags
- Tightly cut men's suit jacket over skinny jeans
- Flat, black, pointy-toe pixie boots
- Heavy silver chain jewellery

## Rock Chic Lookalikes
Suzi Quatro
Heart
Girlschool
Pat Benatar
Chrissie Hynde

OPPOSITE: Note Jett's superb selection of accessories here in 1976: studded wristbands, cigarette lighter in a leather thong holder, dogtag and a tiny knife on a chain.

FAR LEFT: Chrissie Hynde rocked with her band the Pretenders, sporting a skinny frame and cut-off T-shirts and dyed black, backcombed hair with heavily lined eyes.

LEFT: Suzi Quatro in the leather catsuit that would make her famous. Quatro provided Jett with the inspiration to start her own band.

" *Aggressive, tough and defiant may describe me, but that leaves the impression I'm mean and I'm not. People expect me to have fangs.* "

— *Joan Jett*

Despite fabulous early promise, the band split in 1979, but Joan and Lita Ford carried on rocking in their own hard-edged ways.

The Runaways were groundbreakers from the start. Not only did their music sound different to every other band at the time, their pre-punk, punky look broke new ground, too. Tight, ripped T-shirts, skinny jeans, baseball boots or the occasional platform heels, leather-studded belts and jackets, or plain, Wrangler, denim bomber jackets were the foundation for the Runaways' style. A trashy, thin nylon zip-up bomber jacket or shrunken mohair sweater might occasionally creep into their wardrobes, too – these girls were anti-fashion in every way.

Pretty soon, other girls entered the rocking arena, all with their own take on Joan's Runaway style. Heart sisters, Ann and Nancy Wilson, were the next great rock girls to emerge in the US and they interpreted Joan Jett's original look into a Goth version. Sticking to the black eyeliner and backcombed hair, combined with dangerous attitude, like Joan Jett, Heart were devoted to the beat.

Throughout the 1980s, other rock girls emerged in a similar vein. Pat Benatar came onto the scene with her own increasingly outrageously camp versions of Rock Chic. By the time Cher was filmed sitting on the canons of an American naval ship for her extraordinary "If I Could Turn Back Time" video in 1989, things were out of control. The backcombed mullet, studded, ultra-revealing and skintight black leather, lace and mesh clothing, pixie boots and fierce eyeliner began to look a little clichéd. It was far removed from Joan Jett's original rocking ethic, too: Jett was eager to turn people on to music, rebellion and raw sex – in any order. She just rocked… and she still does.

Ever since the late 1980s, Rock Chick has skirted around mainstream fashion, occasionally influencing designer collections. Rock themes frequently go hand-in-glove with bondage and biker references. From the early 1980s, many British designers, including John Richmond and Pam Hogg, plus smaller collaborations such as Kahn & Bell, produced clothes based on the rock'n'roll aesthetic, featuring leatherette dresses, studded separates, biker-style jackets and bondage-inspired combats or skinny drainpipes. Roberto Cavalli's ripped-up denim, skintight leather, huge fluffy jackets and loose frilly shirts dandified Rock Chick in the 1990s, rescuing fashionistas from grunge. Gianni Versace's 1992 "Bondage" collection leant heavily on the studded leather and metal theme, albeit gold rather than steel studs. Japanese designer Michiko Koshino's 1980s and 1990s designs also relied on biker detailing, especially in the highly collectable "Motor King" collection. Today Zadig & Voltaire specialize in a high-end Rock Chick aesthetic.

# Style Guide

**The Palette:** All black with standout exceptions including denim, animal prints plus punky rock fabrics, including leatherette and Lurex, accented with fluorescent green, yellow, pink, purple and badly dyed or "off" colours.

**Key Designers:** Roberto Cavalli, Gianni Versace, John Richmond, Pam Hogg, Boy London and Sex and Seditionaries labels from Vivienne Westwood/Malcolm McLaren.

**Silhouette and Cut:** This is a feminine silhouette in boyish clothes. Despite the edgy element, the outlines are simple and unfussy.

## Tops and T-Shirts

Keep them tight and cropped or long and ragged. Adopt the punk aesthetic and take scissors to your tee – cutting a slashed neckline or slits on the sides.

*Shop vintage for:* Original concert tour T-shirts and any logo tees from the 1970s and 1980s. Pull them in and secure with safety pins for a skintight fit. Look for original 1970s Levi's or Wrangler fitted denim shirts.

## Jackets

This is the centrepiece of the Rock Chick wardrobe: a girl might sling it over her shoulder, sleep on it or shield herself from the paparazzi behind it, but the jacket is the thing. A black leather jacket, à la the Ramones, is key. A leather waistcoat worn tight with nothing underneath is another essential Joan Jett fashion feature.

*Shop vintage for:* Leather biker jackets are easy to find on the vintage market, thanks to their constant resurfacing as key fashion items through the years. Look in menswear sections for authentic, Clash-style motorcycle jackets and while you are raking through the rails, try on these gems: undersized denim jackets, black suit jackets and blue, purple or red "Teddy Boy" dinner jackets with black velvet collars. Also, hunt out men's dinner jackets (tuxedos), either snugly fitting or oversize – your jacket should make a statement. Don't forget to rock a bit of Angus Young of AC/DC and treat yourself to an undersized boy's school blazer, too.

ABOVE: Roberto Cavalli remains a master of Rock Chick. Look out for original Cavalli tailored denim with leather panels, animal-print chiffons and lace-up-sided jeans in modern vintage stores.

OPPOSITE: Joan Jett, 1978, on an interview break during a British tour: Jett's American rock look was dated by this time, as punk hairstyles and bondage gear had taken over in the UK. Jett's "mullet" hairstyle pitched her away from punk toward heavy metal.

TIP: Rock Chick is highly individualistic, so dig out your scissors, tape and maybe even a needle and thread and get busy with customizing! Chop off the sleeves of men's shirts and scrawl on them with indelible ink to make a statement or stencil images or words on with spray-paint. Hunt out fabrics that strike you, maybe purple or white chiffon shirts that you could chop into a vest top or safety-pin together for a raggedy over-top or stretch long T-shirts you can wear as a mini-dress.

## Style Tips

- Add a narrow Lurex or sparkly scarf to brighten up the black.

- Throw on a denim jacket with a spandex pencil skirt.

- Pair a men's tie with a T-shirt.

- Wear a motorcycle jacket with black leggings and chunky boots.

- Wrap a bandana around the wrist.

- Wear a black leather or denim waistcoat over bare skin.

- Try a snugly fitted denim shirt with black jeans.

- Finish off your look with a top hat like Guns N'Roses' Slash.

## Trousers

Skinny is the rule – the shape, not necessarily the wearer! Take a hint from Kate Moss, who wears husband Jamie Hince's clothes, and borrow from the men in your life. Even a pair of men's suit trousers, worn very tight, can work. You may even be able to find men's 19780s jeans that you can take in for an ultra-skinny look if you are handy with a sewing machine.

*Shop vintage for:* Hunt out 1970s and 1980s rock 'n' roll boutique labels, such as American Classics, Lloyd Johnson's "La Rocka" range, particularly for denim and leather, and anything featuring Andy Warhol prints.

## Dresses and Skirts

Skirts and dresses were not a big look for Joan Jett, but you could wear them long, like the Wilson sisters, or choose leather zipped dresses and miniskirts.

*Shop vintage for:* Long black velvet pieces to wear Goth style and leather miniskirts to wear over jeans.

## Accessories

Keep jewellery chunky and minimal, such as a skull-and-crossbones ring or a wrist weighed down with heavy silver chains. Men's identity bracelets and rings add a touch of rock 'n' roll bling. Mix up thin leather ties worn over T-shirts with studded leather belts, gloves and wristbands. Wear wispy bits of fabric as scarves or belts to add colour to a black ensemble. Don't forget black hosiery, which should be ripped on each leg for maximum effect.

*Shop vintage for:* Studded belts, biker boots and vintage Pro-Keds (Joan Jett's favourite trainer). Skinny leather or schoolboy ties. Rubber and metal jewellery by '80s-launched designers Slim Barrett and Judy Blame.

RIGHT: Biker boots, from the basic, utilitarian versions available at motorcycle outfitters to the Jimmy Choo version, remain the Rock Chick's most essential footwear.

FAR RIGHT: A narrow leather tie, worn over a white shirt or a T-shirt will always add a touch of Jett style to any outfit. Chrissie Hynde was a big fan of ties, too.

OPPOSITE: Full-on make-up in 1984, though Joan still stuck to her iconic "raccoon" eyes and spiky mullet.

# Beauty Guide

Even the grungiest girl rocker must think about how she looks, if only to maintain her image. Eye make-up is the lynchpin, adding glamour and femininity to what can be a pretty tough-girl style. However, take care when recreating Rock Chick: add some sparkle to your black and soften it up with glittery greys and silver. The only rocking lipstick colour is red, preferably a little smudged around the edges, though you can choose a nude lip to make the look more modern-day.

Hair can be any version of the original Ziggy Stardust cut. In the later 1970s, this evolved into the "Shaggy Dog", where hair was cut short on the top, sometimes spiked up, and left long beneath. Joan Jett sported a perfect example of this style, as did the Wilson sisters and all four (male) members of glam rockers the Sweet.

## Jett Black Eyes

Joan was well-known for her "raccoon" eyes. For such a smoky-eyed look a top tip is to apply eye make-up first, before foundation. This way you can clean up any smudges before finishing your make-up. Choose vixen-plum lip colour and blusher for a '70s sultry look or go androgynous with nude gloss.

1 Using your fingertips, apply a primer over the eyelid from lashline to brow to get a smooth even base.
2 Apply a flattering dark green/grey or granite-coloured sparkly eyeshadow with a flat brush, working colour into the entire lid but not up to the brow.
3 Now take the colour underneath the eye, joining to meet the colour at the outer edge. Blend outward and into the crease.
4 Line the inner waterline top and bottom with a black kohl pencil.
5 With black eyeshadow and an angle brush, line the top of the lashline, extending out to a sharp outer edge. Line underneath too, as close as possible to the bottom lashes. Add a little more black eyeshadow into the outer corner and crease to deepen the effect.
6 Finish with several coats of black mascara.

**You will need:**
Eyelid primer
Deep green-grey eyeshadow
Black eyeshadow
Black kohl pencil
Powder highlighter
Black mascara
Eyeshadow brush
Eyeshadow blending brush
Angled brush

## Spiky Hair

You don't need to have the drastic mullet or Ziggy Stardust cut to work this 'do. Annette Bening and Ellen Degeneres do cropped versions, which look less fluffy and much more modern.

1 Apply firm-hold mousse to towel-dried hair. Rough blowdry with a diffuser in all directions to make the hair stand out.
2 When dry, backcomb the top section to keep lift.
3 Rub wax (or wet-look gel) between the palms of your hands and apply to the top section to create spikes. Spritz with hairspray for staying power.

**You will need:**
Firm-hold mousse
Hair wax
Hairspray

# Debbie Harry: New Wave

When Deborah Ann "Debbie" Harry appeared on the UK chart show *Top of the Pops* for the first time in 1978, dressed in a red oversize shirt and matching thigh boots, Britain went wild. Up until this point she was considered more underground than mainstream, but it was the release of the album *Parallel Lines* that brought Debbie and her band, Blondie, international success. The tough New Yorker, with her bleached, longish hair, cut through the grungy punk scene like a cool, sharp knife – no dirty, stained T-shirts for her. Harry's look was New Wave in every way; it summed up the end of the punk era and the arrival of a new cross-cultural hybrid of fashion and music. Debbie's look was rebellious because she looked beautiful – she was pretty and made no attempt to hide it. Instead of covering herself in statement make-up, shapeless biker jackets and combats, she wore a yellow mini-dress and looked stunning. Feminism, in all its different guises, never looked like this and Debbie didn't give a damn. Journalists found it hard to get her off the topic of music and onto her looks, though. She was a natural – a bit Bombshell with a touch of the Goddess – and a total original. Debbie paved the way for other girls to look gorgeous and still be cool.

Debbie's cool style was born while she worked as a Playboy Bunny and sang in her first band, the Stilettos. In the early 1970s New York life was hard for a female rock 'n' roller. While the disco scene raged, the original punks, including the New York Dolls, Patti Smith and Lou Reed, were creating ever-more edgy sounds. Downtown, away from the bright disco lights, New Wavers pushed the boundaries ever further at clubs and bars, including CBGB's and Max's Kansas City. A young guy called Bruce Springsteen – who stood out from the post-glam rock, hard-drugs crowd with his folksy beard and checked shirts – hung around with Iggy Pop, David Bowie and Lou Reed, assisting Patti Smith on her first breakthrough UK hit, "Because the Night". After a few false starts, Debbie Harry and Chris Stein, who got together while playing together in the Stilettos, formed Blondie in 1975. They moved into a building on Manhattan's Lower East Side, where Debbie befriended their neighbour, the fashion designer Stephen Sprouse. The two got on well and soon a unique partnership was born.

OPPOSITE: Debbie Harry in 1978, the same year as the release of Blondie's *Parallel Lines*. Rock Chick-meets-New Wave, she wears her signature over-the-knee boots with gold lace-up-the-front jeans.

TOP RIGHT: Taking elements of Japanese culture and punk and mixing it up with a gothic vibe, Siouxsie Sioux was a true original.

RIGHT: Singer Wendy James of English pop group Transvision Vamp, London, 1988. Pretty Wendy was a great dancer and bubblegum, punky-pop version of Debbie Harry. Despite a short moment in the spotlight and a big fan following, Transvision Vamp never lasted the course.

***New Wave Lookalikes***
Siouxsie Sioux
Wendy O Williams of
the Plasmatics
Wendy James from
Transvision Vamp

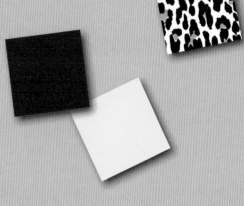

> ❝*I feel one of the things I brought to rock and roll was that sort of movie star glamour and image, and that's what always fascinated me. I always wanted to be that blonde, glowing woman on film...*❞
>
> *Debbie Harry*

Sprouse had worked for the design house of Halston for three years and then briefly for Bill Blass. He began his solo career making dresses similar to his mentors. Luxurious fabrics fashioned into simple frocks became his trademark, but the styling grew wackier and the aesthetic more offbeat for Debbie Harry. Sprouse took inspiration for his muse from Rudi Gernreich's 1960s cut-out shapes and slinky fabrics. A royal blue strapless blouson with matching tights and high-heeled shoes, a simple white shift with angled shoulders and an asymmetric gunmetal stripy number that blew about onstage were just three of the looks he created for Debbie.

Just as the press were beginning to applaud Harry as a new style icon she was to pull the rug out from beneath her glamour-girl look and take to the stage in an all-silver outfit complete with robotic walk and crazy purple wig. Her unusual approach, the constant change and Harry's ultra-modern persona – she was a revolutionary in the true sense – were all that mattered. She was eager to make music and to portray herself as a strong, independent woman: it was a potent mix and people soon became obsessed.

In the UK, Harry provided the perfect antidote to the harsh, grimy punk scene. Malcolm McLaren and Vivienne Westwood's avant-garde, art-school idea of dressing young kids up in rock'n'roll anti-fashion garb had already taken off and not since Flower Power had it been so hard to tell the boys and girls apart. Mohican haircuts, aggressive black eyeliner and facial piercings made up the unisex punk look until Debbie arrived with her New York "otherness" and heady, don't-care glamour; she left the chilly Brits reeling.

Meanwhile, other girls were breaking out of bondage, too. Siouxsie and the Banshees were a South East London band whose lead singer was a mysterious, charismatic young woman. Like Debbie Harry, Siouxsie Sioux occasionally favoured a stiletto heel or an overtly feminine take on the usual rock and bondage looks. From mesh vests and tartan mini-kilts to kimonos and Chinese-inspired headbands, she created one innovative look after another. Pale as a ghost, with blacked-up eyes and lips, Siouxsie was as quintessentially British as Debbie Harry was American: each woman reflected a moment of revolutionary change in their respective countries.

### Key Looks

- Neon pink-and-black striped sweaters or dresses
- Yellow mini shift dress
- White PVC dress
- Lime-green boiler suit and black stilettos
- Jeans and a ripped black T-shirt
- Drainpipe jeans and pixie boots
- Black patent PVC Mac
- Well-worn stilettos
- One-shoulder and asymmetrical dresses
- Over-the-knee boots
- Very short shorts or gym-style skimpy playsuits
- Animal prints
- Very thin, delicate gold jewellery and simple hoops

OPPOSITE TOP: Debbie Harry in a Stephen Sprouse design of spot-on-trend electric blue sequins, colourblocked with matching hosiery and signature delicate gold necklace.

OPPOSITE BOTTOM: Debbie in 1980: vibrant colours were part of Harry's look. Here a vivid orange sweatshirt and matching boots jazz up straight-legged '80s jeans.

# Style Guide

**The Palette:** Neons and brights, such as hot pink, purple, royal blue, yellow and red, with black, white and beige; leopard-print.

**Key Designers:** Stephen Sprouse, Betsey Johnson, Malcolm McLaren and Vivienne Westwood, Rudi Gernreich.

**Silhouette and Cut:** Feminine and boyish – leggy with slender arms but no cleavage or waist.

## Dresses and Skirts

The rules are there are no rules, as the saying goes and this applied frequently to Debbie Harry and other punk princesses of her day.

*Shop vintage for:* Black patent PVC dresses with bondage straps. Skirts in red-and-black or yellow-check tartan or neon. Slash-necked or one-shoulder dresses in jersey or Lurex, especially those by Stephen Sprouse or lookalike copies.

## Tops and T-shirts

Blousons bring this look to life. Search for 1980s styles that stop mid-thigh and wear as makeshift minis or over skinny jeans or leggings.

*Shop vintage for:* 1980s blousons and stripy tops or 1970S original rock-concert or comic T-shirts.

## Trousers and Jeans

If the fit is right, trousers and jeans can form a big part of the punkette's look; few, if any, pictures exist of Debbie Harry in a pair of flares, as they were all narrow or boyfriend cut. Wear tiny short-shorts with fishnet tights and heels. Don't forget jumpsuits, too, which came in all colours in the late 1970s and early 1980s – they look good when belted at the waist with sleeves and ankles rolled-up, high heels compulsory.

*Shop vintage for:* High-waisted jeans and shorts, or find a great-fitting pair of 1970s men's trousers then simply cut away at thigh length and roll the hems back.

## Outerwear

Debbie wasn't one for a sensible coat so trawl boys' vintage racks for bomber jackets with elasticated waists and cuffs to wear zipped up to the neck. Satin bomber jackets from the 1950s, black gabardine long coat or a gold oversized jacket with lapels are other good finds.

BELOW: Debbie in 1978 next to a photographer's camera clad in a Tulip-skirt, T-shirt and wooden-heeled sandals combo and accessorized with mirrored-lens sunglasses and thin gold bracelets. It takes a attitude to pull off a look like this.

OPPOSITE TOP: A fine gold chain adds the tiny gleam of luxury that set Debbie Harry's ultra-cool New York look apart from punk's studs and chains. Try to find a version with a personalized name plate or the word "love" or "disco" for that 1970s feel.

### Style Tips

- Add a pair of white plastic framed or mirrored-lens sunglasses.

- Mix fabrics – slinky animal prints with jeans or tartan tops with PVC.

- Colour block from head to toe in just one or two electric-bright colours.

- Cut the arms off a black fitted shirt and wear with a skinny white tie and jeans.

- Find a fabulous blonde or silver wig and channel Debbie for a mad evening out.

- Go for gold – small studs or hoops add a sexy touch to punkette style.

- Try an oversize men's jacket worn over T-shirt-come-mini-dress.

- Zip a retro tracksuit top up to the neck and wear with rolled-up drainpipe jeans or tiny gym shorts.

- Wear bright leggings or tights under minis or alone with long stretchy tops.

- Use narrow PVC belts in Dayglo colours to cinch sleeveless dresses.

- Pair tiny shorts or minis with long over-the-knee socks.

### Accessories

This is not a richly accessorized look. Debbie Harry mostly rejected the punk wristbands and chains and instead opted for a simple gold chain around her neck or fine hoops in her ears. Match shoes and tights to dresses for a fully blocked-out one-colour look. Though she often went for baseball boots off-duty, onstage Debbie was always a sexy-heels girl. One thing worth remembering is that during the late 1970s stilettos were still largely unavailable on the high street. Punkettes such as Siouxsie Sioux and Debbie Harry shopped vintage for 1950s and 1960s cast-offs, and it wasn't until toward the end of the decade that retailers on both sides of the Atlantic caught up with the trend.

*Shop vintage for:* Shoe-wise, seek out 1950s or late 1970s kitten-heel courts in bright colours (especially red) or thigh-high boots. For jewellery, look for 1970s-style gold-plate chains or thin gold bangles for an inexpensive touch of Debbie Harry-style glam. Check out secondhand jewellers or pawn shops for pure gold chains and hoops.

LEFT: Red stilettos are a fashion classic, adding Debbie Harry-heat to everything from skinny black jeans to a matching colour-blocked mini-dress. Wear them with matching red tights or bare, tanned legs in summer.

## Beauty Guide

Debbie Harry's made-up face was always ultra-glamorous with metallic eyeshadows, liners and fully drawn around, coloured-in lips. Full-on make-up was essential to the look and her immaculately made-up eyes fought with a perfect red lip for attention. Great skin and bone structure meant she could break all the beauty rules with lots of outrageous eye colour, plus heavily made-up lips and cheeks. Keeping her face a pale canvas heightened the impact of the eyes, cheekbones and lips.

As for her hair, Harry, of course, was not a natural blonde. A fantastic colourist worked to give her the perfect, bright blonde locks she required to be "Blondie" – not too white or yellow. Stylewise, her hair was usually full and chopped into. She sometimes wore it in a super-flattering chin-length bob with a messed-up fringe and a dark "V" dyed into the back of her head. Debbie brought roots-on-purpose into the spotlight and recreated the notion of the sexy blonde for a new generation. One of the best pictures ever taken of her was captured by über-cool Brit photographer Roberta Bayley: post-gig, Harry and boyfriend Chris Stein share the backseat of a limo. She's wearing a Blondie tour tracksuit top and big, black mirror shades. Her bleached'n'roots bob is all over the place but looks effortlessly fabulous.

**Beauty Tips**

- Wear messy, tousled hair

- Sport grown-out blonde highlights with dark roots.

- Choose a fire-engine red for lips and layer on super-shine gloss.

- Contour sharp-as-glass cheekbones with deep pink blusher in the hollow and shimmer highlighter.

- Add punky colour with bright pink or black clip-in hair pieces.

- Cut hair in a layered long bob with an over-the-eye fringe.

## Smoky Smudged Eye

1 Line the upper lashline with black eyeliner pencil or liquid liner – the line should become thick toward the outer edge of the eye – and extend the upper line out beyond the corner of the eye to form a flicked cat's-eye shape.

2 Line the bottom of the eye under the eyelashes with the black liner.

3 With a small eyeshadow brush apply charcoal shadow to the eye crease, blending into the socket of the eye and outer corner.

4 Fill in the eyelid with silver shadow, and take the silver under the lower lashes, just beneath the black liner.

5 Using an angled brush, add black eyeshadow on top of the eyeliner to soften and smudge, then extend the colour into the outer corner, toward the brow. Blend well with the blending brush.

6 Finish by curling the eyelashes with an eyelash curler and adding two to three coats of mascara.

> **You will need:**
> Black pencil or liquid eyeliner
> Eyeliner brush
> Eyeshadow brush
> Angled brush
> Crease blending brush
> Silver metallic eyeshadow
> Charcoal eyeshadow
> Black glitter eyeshadow
> Eyelash curler
> Black volumizing mascara

## Perfect Red Lip

1 Line the upper lip, creating a rounded heart-like shape at the cupid's bow and drawing the line slightly outside your natural lip line to create fullness.

2 Line the bottom lip slightly below your natural lip line. Fill in the entire lips with colour, right up to the line.

3 Finish by applying a super-slick glossy red lipstick on top with a brush. Don't blot!

> **You will need:**
> Pure red lip pencil
> High-shine red lipstick
> Lip brush

RIGHT: Debbie Harry in 1978. Near-perfect features made making-up easy for Debbie Harry. Copy her punkette look with lots of highlighter on the brow and cheekbones to add extra, glamorous gleam. Try a touch above the centre of the lips to enhance the cupid's bow.

# Lauren Hutton: Simply '70s

American model and actress Lauren Hutton represents the breezy feeling of 1970s high-end fashion. Classic 1970s styling remains one of the most perennial looks, returning repeatedly to the fashion top five. Minus the crazier elements of glam rock and punk that arrived later on, this look is cool, relaxed and extremely flattering to the female form. Every woman looks good in a long fluid pair of fitted, flared trousers worn over heels or wedge shoes. Chocolate brown, the key colour of the decade for sophisticated daywear, is fashion's best-kept secret. It beats black as a wardrobe staple any day and here's why: the warm tones suit almost every woman's colouring, plus you will never be mistaken for a waitress.

Revlon-sponsored cover girl Lauren Hutton was born in Charleston, South Carolina, in 1943 and moved to New York in the 1960s. She worked as a Playboy Bunny before being model-scouted. Although advised to have her famous tooth-gap filled, she resisted and her unique look took off. A slightly off-kilter face on top of an all-American healthy body proved the perfect antidote to tawdry tales of European models dabbling in drugs or transgenderism. American designers and cosmetic houses were looking for fresh-faced home-grown beauties to represent their businesses: Lauren Hutton, Jerry Hall, Rene Russo, Roseanne Vela and Beverly Johnson all epitomized the new, athletic-looking, gorgeous American model.

OPPOSITE: Lauren Hutton 1976: Natural beauty came with flaws and personality in America's new, 1970s models. While new models including Hutton, Jerry Hall and Beverly Johnson were honing their craft, young designers such as Donna Karan, Calvin Klein and Ralph Lauren were embarking on world domination.

BELOW LEFT: Cameron Diaz started out modelling and has always kept a toe in the fashion pool with her cool combination of laid-back Californian meets knock-out red carpet style. A free fashion spirit, she proves that the simple American, blue-eyed, blonde look can work with the haute couture. Here she wears a Hutton-style linen jacket.

## Key Looks

- Culottes and a matching wide-sleeved jacket
- High-waisted "baggies" trousers, fitted at the waist, flaring straight down from the curve of the buttocks
- Snugly fitted V-neck sweater, worn over a pointy-collared shirt
- Double-breasted Mackintosh-style trench coats
- Midi-length tweed A-line skirt with contrasting polo neck
- Knee-length, zip-up suede boots
- Short-sleeve sweater worn over a puffed, long-sleeve blouse
- Safari details – patch pockets, belts and epaulettes
- Clean, light neutral colours
- Bush and safari jackets, including sleeveless versions
- Square-shouldered jackets with small shoulder pads, stand-up gathered sleeves in a narrow fitted shape
- Crocodile-skin shoulder bags

LEFT: Rene Russo in 1995, after moving on from modelling to star alongside Mel Gibson in her breakthrough role in *Lethal Weapon 3*. Russo's stunning looks, based on strong features and naturally coloured hair, have stayed the fashion course.

## Simply '70s Lookalikes

Jerry Hall
Rene Russo
Margaux Hemingway
Patti Hansen
Cameron Diaz

The 1970s was a time of celebration for women when the hard-won freedom of previous decades was starting to bear fruit and fashion stepped in to support increasing numbers of busy working women. This was the decade that gave birth to Diane von Fürstenberg's famous wrap-dress. "Feel like a woman, wear a dress!" was the designer's mantra and this appealed to professional women looking for a change from business suits and separates.

Jean Muir, perhaps the most under-rated British designer of the twentieth century, created much of what we now consider the key styling of that era, including knitted jersey separates, matching waistcoat and skirt suits, slinky sweaters and culottes. She liked the versatility of a wide skirt divided into two and showed several versions of woollen jersey and woven suiting fabrics.

Culottes were the perfect example of a high-fashion 1970s look filtering down to the high street: women loved their practical styling and comfort. However, Muir understood how they needed to be cut cleverly to work, resembling a skirt in repose and only just visible as divided during motion. Cheaper versions resembled wide safari shorts, never a flattering look!

TOP LEFT: Jean Muir culottes make a return to fashion in 2006. Yves Saint Laurent and Muir pioneered culottes in the 1970s. Look for designer versions, which will be more skirt-like in appearance; cheaper copies tend to be cut like wide, unflattering shorts.

TOP RIGHT: A 1972 corduroy trench coat from Mainstreet by Tom Fallon worn with a long white pleated skirt and large pearl bracelets.

LEFT: Fashion Designer Diane von Fürstenberg (centre) with models showing her catsuit and sundress from 1976. DVF, of course, wears her iconic wrap-dress; her own stunning looks helped promote her easy-to-wear designs and no one else has ever captured the spirit of New York glamour quite like her.

OPPOSITE: Safari-inspired, white belted shirt and trousers by Geoffrey Beene for his summer 1973 cruisewear collection. This practical shape will add an authentic '70s look to any outfit. Beene, along with Perry Ellis and Bill Blass, was part of an American revolution in "sportswear". Hunt out originals for a touch of American style.

### Style Tips

• Wind a narrow silky scarf around your neck and wear with a V-neck sweater.

• Tuck a shirt into hipster flares.

• Belt a short, flared trench over skinny bell-bottom jeans.

• Hunt out ribbed, skinny polo-neck sweaters in camel colours to wear under jackets.

• Keep jewellery simple: a fine gold chain, thin gold hoops or a men's brown leather watch.

• Wear a men's shirt beneath a sweater and turn the cuffs back over your wrists.

# Style Guide

**The Palette:** Shades of chocolate, bottle green, buttery cream, taupe, tan and rust.

**Key Designers:** Jean Muir, Ted Lapidus, Missoni, Gucci, Yves Saint Laurent, Diane von Fürstenberg.

**Silhouette and Cut:** A 1940s-inspired fluid silhouette with square shoulders, narrow waist and long legs. This is a tidy, gently feminine outline that's easy to achieve, no matter what your natural shape.

## Separates

The 1970s hailed the arrival of separates. Working women bought four-piece suits complete with waistcoat, jacket, trousers and skirt, and mixed different combinations for a great-value ensemble.

*Shop vintage for:* Original 1970s office clothes. Hunt for midi-skirts in wool, tweed or thick jersey in an A-line, flared shape, V-neck sweaters to wear over a slim-fitting silk shirt and long wrap-around cardigans with belted waists. Labels to look out for knitwear include Woolmark, Jaeger and Sonia Rykiel.

## Outerwear

Key shapes for coats and jackets were wide-lapelled, Mackintosh-style or flared and slightly smocked. Safari-style – fitted, belted jackets with patch pockets – stemmed from Yves Saint Laurent's introduction of the look in 1968. Fitted jackets in heavy fabrics such as corduroy, wool and dark denim anchored the look.

*Shop vintage for:* Fitted jackets, either designer originals from YSL, Janice Wainwright, Geoffrey Beene and Bill Blass, or high-quality store labels, such as Bonwit Teller, Peck & Peck, Dobbs, House of Fraser and Simpsons of Piccadilly.

## Handbags

Shoulder bags, created for busy girls on the go, played a key part in the 1970s look.

*Shop vintage for:* Satchel styles with long straps and flap-over closures from Gucci and Ted Lapidus; canvas-and-leather-trim bags by Gucci and Louis Vuitton.

## Shoes

Platform shoes only enjoyed the briefest moment in the fashion spotlight, but can be sophisticated worn beneath flared trousers. Skirts that are knee-length or longer work best with platform heels. For a leg-lengthener, choose sandals or all-black tights and shoes.

*Shop vintage for:* Source vintage clogs for a downbeat, casual version of this look to wear with jeans. You'll also find smart 1970s slip-on shoes in patent leather with block heels and buckle- or tassel-tops, as well as preppy loafers.

## Other Accessories

Hessian, rope, wicker, cork, canvas, leather and exotic skins in natural hues fit with this look. leatherwear created by Moroccan, Mexican and Mediterranean craftsmen was sold in tourist bazaars at the time. Plaited leather belts with oversize brass buckles can be worn over long cardigans or looped through hipster jeans.

*Shop vintage for:* Seek out period leather belts and waistcoats, safari-style canvas hats, as well as berets and crochet styles. Root through the belt and bag shelves in any vintage store to unearth woven, tooled chocolate or tan leather holiday souvenirs. Reptile skins added upmarket gloss but never, ever buy these materials new.

# Beauty Guide

"She is scrubbed, sexy, intelligent, real," was how photographer Francesco Scavullo described Lauren Hutton. The key to getting her look begins with a clean, "natural" face – relying on cosmetics for gleam and accentuation of facial feature only. Many top 1970s models had quirky features– for example, Hutton's tooth-gap, Jerry Hall's large-for-a-model's nose – and it was fashionable to flaunt such perceived "flaws". Eyebrows were natural and only slightly groomed. By the way, beware of the threaders and pluckers in the beauty business. To avoid small, skinny arches and keep a simple 1970s look, tell the technician that you want your eyebrows to remain where they are with just a bit of tidying or shaping. Lips were naturally outlined and shaded in shades of sheer plum, coral pink and off-brown while nails were in the classic "American" manicure: similar to a French manicure but with creamier-coloured tips and a more neutral, beige base.

Hair was carefully coiffed into long, wavy styles or variations on Joanna Lumley's "Purdey" cut – a bowl-shaped mop-top style. Hutton herself sported a soft and wavy, just-above-the-shoulders style that was versatile enough to be pinned up or left loose and shiny. To get this look, hair needs to be clean with very little styling product to ensure it bounces.

*"That's the mistake women make – you shouldn't see your make-up. We don't want to look like we've made an effort."*

Lauren Hutton

# Barely There Make-up

This is a clean daytime look that provides a fresh, natural base. Avoid volumizing mascara, as you will want to keep the look very girl-next-door rather than vamp; add taupe eyeshadow and a tiny bit of brown eyeliner to define the eyes further if you like.

1 For a radiant, healthy glow, use a tinted moisturizer. Starting from the centre of the face and using light feathery touches, blend the tinted moisturizer outward. Use your fingers to get into all the bony areas and blend over the eyelids and the jawline.

2 Next apply concealer – you may find blending two tones of concealer gives the best results. Dot concealer around the eye area and the shady area of the bridge of the nose. Blend in gently, using your third finger. Repeat around the shadows at the base of the nose.

3 Using your fingers, apply a cream blush into the apples of your cheeks, blending toward the hairline.

4 Apply mascara to the top lashes from the roots to tips. With the bottom lashes, hold the wand horizontally and stroke the mascara brush across the bottom lashes in a see-saw motion. It often looks better to just cover the root and middle area of the bottom lashes if they're very long.

5 Using a clear mascara wand, brush the brows up and outward for an instantly groomed finish.

6 Finally, apply lip moisturizer or sheer lipstick to hydrate and give sheen.

**You will need:**
Tinted moisturizer
Concealer
Cream blusher in tawny pink
Dark brown defining mascara
Clear mascara
Nude or pinky-beige lip
moisturizer or sheer lipstick

## Beauty Tips

• Centre-part your hair for an Ali McGraw in *Love Story* look.

• Hair should be loosely wavy; if you don't have this look naturally, create it by plaiting (braiding) damp hair in two sections from the ear down, and leaving it to dry naturally, then removing the plaits (braids).

• Never choose red, plum or raisin shades of lipstick; 1970s colours are beige-pink, coral, peach or nude colours.

• Use bronzer to attain a healthy tanned glow.

• Avoid foundation and powder – women of the 1970s used a lot of moisturizer to get glowing skin with a sheen.

• Ditch the eyeliner, black mascara and fake lashes.

OPPOSITE: Lauren Hutton in 1974: the model has retained her youthful looks and is still fabulous today thanks to a healthy awareness of the importance of physical, nutritional and spiritual wellbeing – all the foundations for wholesome American beauty.

# Diana Ross: Diva

No one does Diva better than the divine Miss Ross! For the ultimate party night, simply channel your own inner Diana. This is a look for lovers of pure glamour. Form-fitting, flattering, colourful and feminine, Diva style is well constructed from beautiful fabrics. Good taste is simply a must for this look to work but you can never have too many feather boas, turbans, fishtail trains or sequins.

From an early age, Diana Ross was fascinated with fashion. Even as a young girl at school she would style herself in the latest looks, always having exactly the right skirt length or hairstyle of the moment. Her family wanted her to follow in her siblings' academic footsteps but Diana was eager to work in fashion. She took design and millinery classes while at school, and in her late teens worked as a salesgirl at Hudson's, Detroit's most exclusive department store, as the shop's only black employee.

With every fabulous step of her life, Diana Ross has broken new ground. Joining the Primettes, which became the Supremes in 1959, aged just sixteen, much of what made the Motown trio brilliant came from how fabulous they looked together. Sure, their records were amazing, but the singers' glittering dresses, matching shoes and hairstyles became legendary. Ross's personal style and star quality continued to blossom and eventually she stepped out into the spotlight alone. It was not all plain sailing, though, for she was heavily criticized by the bitterly jealous ex-Supremes and even other black singers, such as Nina Simone, bemoaned the fact that Diana had "white" features and mass appeal. Instead of trying to appease her critics, Miss Ross just shone brighter.

Starring in the movies *Lady Sings the Blues* (1972) and *Mahogany* (1975) established Ross as a star in her own right. She won a Golden Globe and an Oscar nomination for her unique portrayal of Billie Holiday in *Lady Sings the Blues* and sported a succession of gorgeously pretty 1930s-inspired outfits perfectly suited to her slender, model's frame. It was only a matter of time before she came home to a role perfectly suited to her: that of the fashion model in the film *Mahogany*. Diana was deeply involved in the costumes and styling for both films and designer Bob Mackie helped her to create the Diva style for which she has since become famous. He dressed the Supremes in pared-down, groovy ankle-length sequinned numbers and then created huge, voluminous gowns for the solo Ross. Even if she was performing alone, Mackie's outfits – combined with her powerful singing voice and confident personality – ensured she would always fill the stage.

> ### Diva Lookalikes
> Cher
> Jennifer Lopez
> Mariah Carey
> Beyoncé

OPPOSITE: Singer Diana Ross poses in 1975 in a gold lamé dress, edged with elaborate beading and embellished with a chain belt is a classic Bob Mackie design. Miss Ross's glossy beauty came alive in shades of white, silver and gold.

TOP RIGHT: Beyoncé in 2009: Diva looks conceal a seriously practical personality. Beyonce has achieved independence, success and happiness in love while following her own version of the American dream. Her ultra-glam style has also made her a fashion icon.

ABOVE: Singer and actress Cher poses in a Bob Mackie creation in 1978. Throughout the late 1960s and early '70s, Cher performed in showgirl outfits and heart-stopping, barely there costumes. One of Rock's most powerful voices, Cher's diva-glamour is totally unique.

The *Mahogany* costumes reflect a moment in fashion time. Clad in a mulberry-coloured, jersey floor-length dress with matching scarf and turban by Bob Mackie, Diana Ross is the diva in repose, relaxing at home in a simple but stunning and totally matching ensemble. Mackie also created the now-iconic dress with tassels on the sleeves worn on the cover of the album *The Best of Diana Ross*. Although off-duty Ross favoured other American designers including Halston, she always returned to Mackie for her stage costumes and key outfits. The good news is that both designers were copied and versions of their gowns are available on the vintage market.

Bob Mackie was a natural choice to work with the diva-in-the-making. Classically trained as an artist, he began his career sketching designs for the legendary Columbia Pictures costume director Jean Louis before going on to work for Edith Head, who was responsible for some of the best-known Hollywood images ever. Trained in the starriest environment, Mackie's fine craftsmanship and careful design removes any element of tackiness. "Fashion and fantasy" are his themes and as well as Diana Ross, he also dressed Barbra Streisand for *Funny Lady* (1975) and makes stage costumes for Cher and Pink, among many others.

Diana Ross's other favourite look for album covers, including her debut solo album *Diana Ross* (1970) and her 1980 *Diana*, is a pared-down pair of denim shorts and a white T-shirt. Naturally beautiful, with enormous cat-like eyes and a svelte frame, she has always looked stunning without elaborate make-up or costume. Diva-style comes from within: Ross is just as regal sitting cross-legged in denim shorts as she is sweeping down a spangled staircase in a Mackie.

### Key Looks

- Sparkling sequins
- Fitted body with a fishtail skirt
- Enormous batwing sleeves
- Bustles and shaped bottoms
- Plunging V-necks
- Off-the-shoulder, but not strapless, numbers
- Dresses long enough to cover the shoes – all the way *is* all the way!
- Diamonds or good-quality diamanté jewellery
- Oversized cocktail rings, necklaces and collars
- Bejewelled evening sandals
- Turbans
- Fur stole

*"You can't just sit there and wait for people to give you that golden dream. You've got to get out there and make it happen for yourself."*

Diana Ross

# Style Guide

**The Palette:** White, white and more white, mixed with sparking silver or gold. Colours should be pretty or jewel-like: try deep purple, crimson red or jade green for a truly dramatic effect.

**Key Designers:** Bob Mackie, Halston, Louis Féraud, Bruce Oldfield, Giorgio di Sant'Angelo, Valentino, Judith Leiber, Kenneth Jay Lane, Butler & Wilson, Jimmy Choo, Manolo Blahnik.

**Silhouette and Cut:** Silhouette is crucial to this look – it's hourglass to the max. Add height to volume with long skirts and high heels. Bodyshaping underwear will ensure you achieve the full Diva effect.

## Evening Gowns

This look relies on texture and form. Choose evening gowns with sequins, netting, beading and frills in appropriate places such as sleeves, necklines and the base of skirts. The central hourglass body shape must remain intact but any amount of decorous detail is permitted to draw attention inward. Sequins add the requisite shimmer to the look – seek out discarded prom or party dresses from the late 1970s, '80s and '90s. Sequins discolour and fall off a garment with age, and while the shabby look works for a 1930s or '40s-inspired look, it doesn't work for the Diva.

*Shop vintage for:* British designer Bruce Oldfield makes gorgeous Diva-style dresses. Because of his connection to Princess Diana, they are immensely collectable, but he has created the occasional diffusion line and it's still possible to track down originals if you are very lucky, particularly in nearly-new designer stores. Other international labels to seek out include Louis Féraud, Giorgio di Sant'Angelo and Valentino. Wildly different, they are united in an appreciation for the Diva. Féraud's classically constructed 1980s evening dresses in ruched satin with frilled, layered skirts and off-the-shoulder, puffed sleeves are dramatic and may be less highly priced than others because they were originally sold in department stores. Sant'Angelo combines drama with a more pared-down, less feather-bedecked aesthetic, and Valentino's gowns are simply gorgeous classics. Look for feather boas, fake fur wraps or elbow-length satin gloves to match your gown.

## Style Tips

- Throw a fur stole over one shoulder for a night out.

- Smile a lot and call everyone "darling!"

- Off-duty, go without make-up and wear big sunglasses.

- Wear oversized earrings or a huge necklace, not both.

- Ensure you have the perfect pedicure to do justice to those sparkly shoes.

- If in doubt, leave hair to dry naturally – remember, Divas can be a little bit wild.

- A light-coloured, fake-fur jacket will take you from cab to concert.

- Always your best accessory: a man with an umbrella!

- Finish off with a huge, bejewelled cocktail ring.

OPPOSITE: Diana Ross in the Supremes' days, 1960. She helped to build the group from its early incarnation into the girl-phenomenon it became thanks to grit, determination and talent, not to mention her innate fashion sense and style.

LEFT: This Bob Mackie gown with a butterfly motif design was owned by Cher and auctioned at Sotheby's in 2006.

## Shoes

Of course, for a truly Diva look you will need glamorous shoes. Recent designer cast-offs might prove easier to find than 1970s vintage.

*Shop vintage for:* Try Charles Jourdan if you can't find Manolo Blahnik or Roland Cartier if Jimmy Choo eludes you. Both are deluxe high-street names from the 1970s and 1980s.

## Handbags

Ornate 1980s evening accessories are currently hugely in demand and well worth collecting. Here is a trend you could get in on now and make money on later.

*Shop vintage for:* Look for good-quality evening clutches; although you will be hard pushed to find a Judith Leiber original (her combinations of python skin, precious stones and crystals are treasures), familiarize yourself with her style and source copies.

## Other Accessories

Diva pieces are large, dramatic and show-stopping. Finding vintage gold is nine-tenths knowing what you're looking for and one-tenth luck. American costume jewellery brands from the twentieth century including Judy Lee and Art are now catching up with Chanel, Givenchy and Dior in value.

*Shop vintage for:* Costume jewellery designs from the 1980s by Kenneth Jay Lane and Butler & Wilson are not only gorgeous to wear but also collectable. Look for oversized cocktail rings, chandelier earrings, pendant necklaces and bracelets you can stack.

### How to Wear White

Diana Ross was stunning in white, but it scares most women. Here are some tips.

- Layer textures such as knits, silk, linen and woven fabrics to add dimension.
- Wear it as a trouser suit – this looks more casual and less bridal.
- Add a pop of colour, such as coral or turquoise.
- Dilute it with black or navy stripes.
- Try white with cream and beige, keeping the whole look very tonal.
- Wear a fitted white dress – nothing with ruffles, frills or flounces!

# Beauty Guide

Naturally gorgeous Diana Ross was lucky enough to have the kind of face that can work almost any make-up look. She made her eyes the focal point of the face and a feline element is crucial. Eyeliner should curve upward and outward, and eyelashes must work even harder – false lashes will boost the look.

Wigs were a big part of Diana's 1970s look but she now wears her long hair in a naturally loose, curly style. This works surprisingly well and maintains her light, youthful glow. Long, painted nails are a must: for a super-glam look, try extensions with embedded diamanté studs. A late 1970s trend was for two-coloured nails. Experiment with a dark maroon base and painted-on half-moons or nail tips in bright, pearly white.

OPPOSITE TOP: Diva accessories include bronze leather peep-toes from Séducta, circa 1980s, and white leather strappy slingbacks from Charles Jourdan, circa 1980. Try out a cabouchon cocktail ring – it doesn't have to be real to be Diva.

OPPOSITE BOTTOM: Diana Ross poses at home in 1974 in a white summer dress with ethnic turquoise accessories. Look for similar, Navaho-inspired beads, bangles and rings in costume jewellery boutiques and markets.

ABOVE: This elegant portrait reveals the natural, unusual beauty of Diana Ross. Her tiny, chiselled facial structure gives way to enormous eyes and lips, the perfect canvas for silvery eyeshadows, glossy plum-coloured lips and a matching cheek sheen.

# Kate Bush: Free Spirit

This is an ethereal and romantic look that really comes out at night but works for daydreamers, too. Whimsical layers, maxi-dresses, shawls, long hair with statement adornments, dancewear and 1970s folklore sums up the Free Spirit of Kate Bush.

When 18-year-old Kate hit the pop charts of 1978 with her song "Wuthering Heights", no one considered the talented songstress a fashion icon. Instead she was dubbed an eccentric, musical genius. However, as time has moved on, Kate's signature dancewear-inspired video outfits and folksy beauty have captured a feminine spirit and style that feels totally contemporary. Her look was considered hippie-like compared to her contemporaries with their more mainstream punk or disco looks, yet her agile figure looked amazing in Lycra dancewear. Pearlized Lycra with a jewel-like sheen had only been around for a few years when Bush began wearing it for photos and videos. She was the first star to be pictured in such ballet- and dance-inspired versions of what would emerge as the fitness trend. Wrapover cardigans, legwarmers, wristbands and headbands also played a part in her dance-school ethos, sending high-street buyers running for their nearest local ballet outfitters to stock up on supplies.

Kate Bush created two videos for her debut of "Wuthering Heights". In one she can be seen wearing what looks like a white Victorian nightgown with full sheer sleeves, a lace-up back and a long, floaty skirt. Beneath this she wears a dance leotard, visible through the sheer fabric. The outfit represents a fascination with Victoriana; from the late 1960s and into the '70s rock stars, fashion models and vintage fans all began wearing secondhand clothing from that era. High lace collars, stiffened black net petticoats and black and purple ensembles in satin, velvet and lace were all Victorian elements that began to merge into and influence mainstream style. Victorian lingerie and lace were particularly popular.

Fashion designer Laura Ashley interpreted these trends into a style of clothing that she sold from her first shops in the late 1960s. Pretty soon, the Laura Ashley look became so popular that more branches opened and it remained a bastion of late-Victorian-influenced outfitting until the brand modernized its look after the demise of the Sloane Ranger's favourite, the pie-crust collar shirt, in the mid 1980s. As a young girl, Kate Bush may well have been influenced by Laura Ashley's style but she was also drawn to

OPPOSITE: Kate Bush in 1980: Deep red, embroidered satin is the glossy focal point of this Japanese-inspired ensemble. Red dance leggings and a two-tone manicure adds that all-important Kate Bush eclecticism, not to mention the stunning, strong make-up and sheer, creative force oozing from the photo.

TOP RIGHT: Icelandic chanteuse Björk wearing a kimono-style dress; although most probably not in homage to Kate Bush, the two women share an artistic, individualistic approach to style. Grab some inspiration and seek out your own inner Björk at Oriental import shops and vintage stores.

ABOVE: *Leather and Lace* is more than just an album title for the divine talent that is Stevie Nicks, it is a way of life. No other songstress has inspired fashion stylists and designers to quite the same extent as Stevie. Her timeless, flowing fabrics, platform boots, big hair and ethereal look mean she is still the quintessential Free Spirit goddess today.

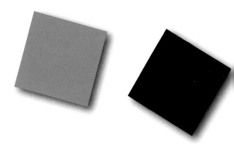

the darker side of Victoriana, hence her imaginings of herself as Cathy Earnshaw, the lonely ghost of Emily Brontë's classic novel, *Wuthering Heights*. Incidentally, Bush shares her birthday, July 30, with Brontë.

Bush's influence on vintage fashion fans has filtered down through another key aspect of her style: folklore. Owing more to Romanian gypsies than the English countryside, Kate Bush danced her way through a forest in a red, knee-length chiffon and cotton handkerchief-hemmed dress with matching red tights for her second "Wuthering Heights" video. Adorned with red blooms in her hair, on a choker round her neck and attached to her belt, she was a veritable folksy fairy queen. The look is reminiscent of late 1970s designs by Zandra Rhodes and goes back slightly further to Thea Porter and Bill Gibb. Both were purveyors of high-end designer versions of the Russian peasant and folky styles so popular in the early 1970s.

Zandra Rhodes' creativity was born of a love of fabric and colour combined with an exploratory spirit that brought butterflies, flowers and even Native American imagery into her designs. Fuchsia pink, red and purple were key mid-to-late 1970s colours for her work. Collections featured off-the-shoulder lacy gypsy dresses in beautiful light and shimmering fabrics, which were copied everywhere. Yves Saint Laurent's "Russian Peasant" collection of 1976 epitomized the luxurious direction of ethnic-style clothing, too. Featuring richly embroidered pinafore dresses and full skirts in bright hues, accessorized with turbans, scarves, gilt-edged coats and shawls, the look owes more to Russian wealth than poverty. Japanese influences also permeated high fashion design, with kimono-style padded jackets and skirts in rich colours from Kansai Yamamoto. Kate Bush incorporated the colours and ideas of these collections into her photography and videos yet she also had an ordinary girl's approach to fashion and was sometimes photographed in what were obvious high-street purchases, such as a boiler suit with heels, tight jeans, red suede boots and an oversize shirt.

LEFT: A Zandra Rhodes dress from 2007, which echoes her earlier work from the 1970s. Rhodes travelled the world seeking out ethnic inspiration for her original designs, including Navajo and Japanese cultures in her cornucopia. Although synonymous with the age of punk, Rhodes's adventurous spirit has been far more influential on fashion print and textiles than styling.

### Key Looks

- Gypsy-style dresses with brocade or fringe edging
- Pin-tuck or lace-insert bodices
- Layered peasant skirts
- Asymmetric dance leotards with matching footless tights and chiffon skirts
- Very low-cut, wrap-around stretch tops or bodysuits
- White lace or broderie anglaise Victorian-style nightdresses for evenings or summer days
- Sheer, transparent fabrics and lots of lace and very finely worked crochet
- Fringed shawls, long scarves and capes
- Footless tights under midi-length skirts
- Same-colour tights and shoe combinations
- Wedge heels or Victorian boots
- Elbow-length, bell-shaped sleeves
- Hair accessorized with flowers and feathers
- Japanese-influence quilted satin separates
- Embroidered kimonos
- Motifs and colours from nature – butterflies, flowers, leaves and exotic birds

# Style Guide

**The Palette:** Bright crimsons, blues, greens and black.

**Key Designers:** Zandra Rhodes, Thea Porter, Yves Saint Laurent, Laura Ashley, Anna Sui, Betsey Johnson

**Silhouette and Cut:** A lean dancer's physique is ideal for this look; the silhouette is very slim, narrow, small-boned and delicate.

## Dancewear

Lycra doesn't age well, and most of these elements that underpin the Free Spirit look can be bought new very easily and relatively cheaply. American Apparel is a high-street shop that stocks the perfect basics to wear under dresses and delicate pieces, but also look in sportswear and dance suppliers.

## Lingerie and Victoriana Styles

Victorian and Edwardian lingerie, slips, nightgowns and chemises feature the delicate detailing that works for the Free Spirit look – such as pintucks, lace inserts and white-on-white embroidery. Laura Ashley's 1970s designs also feature this rural romantic look, often referred to as "milkmaid".

*Shop vintage for:* Laura Ashley 1970s white cotton and lace dresses and smocked tops, Victorian and Edwardian lingerie and bridalwear and Gina Fratini 1970s floaty chiffon and lace dresses.

## Gypsy and Asian Styles

The highly stylized Japanese Kabuki theatre inspired designers such as Zandra Rhodes until well into the 1980s, and with the increase in Asian imports available in boutiques and thrift stores, mandarin-collar dresses in richly embroidered silks, kimonos and pyjamas came into alternative fashion.

*Shop vintage for:* Eveningwear from the 1990s and 2000s by Anna Sui or Betsey Johnson feature gypsy-style detailing or colourful prints on black fabric backgrounds in some of their quirky designs. Look for printed sheer silk and chiffon gowns with handkerchief hems from Zandra Rhodes, Russian peasant styling such as embroidered necklines and full skirts and Chinese silk dresses or Geisha-style kimonos. Thea Porter's dresses and jackets from the 1960s and 1970s (see page 116) will also fit the bill.

TOP RIGHT: Kate Bush in a still from the video for hit single "Babooshka". During the verses Kate looks grim and scarily beautiful in black dancewear and a veil, only to reveal this warrior-priestess ensemble for the chorus. All that is brilliant about Bush is here.

ABOVE: A blue-and-white pleated cape over a blue-and-white embroidered chiffon dress from Thea Porter in 1972. Porter's exotic designs made ethnic fabrics mainstream, and fans included Barbra Streisand and Charlotte Rampling – they are ideal for the Free Spirit.

## Trousers

Tight jeans, harem pants and knickerbockers… Kate wore them all! Designer Thea Porter filled her London boutique with loose gorgeously embroidered imports from the Indian subcontinent in the early 1970s. A harem pant with a high-heeled wedge is a classic late 1970s, early 1980s Porter-inspired look, still cool today. Alongside the eclectic designs of Porter, Bill Gibb and Zandra Rhodes, Janice Wainwright created harem pants, flares and kaftan-style dresses in sumptuous Eastern fabrics including velvets and embroidered or embellished silks.

*Shop vintage for:* Thea Porter knickerbockers and 1970s and 1980s harem trousers by Janice Wainwright or the wearable high-street versions she created for the Simon Massey label. Otherwise, buy ethnic harem pants or baggy cotton, drawstring-waisted trousers from Indian stores or markets.

## Beauty Guide

Kate Bush-a-likes stand out from their tanned sisters thanks to pale skin and contrasting hair that is often either blood red, burnished copper or black. Kate's own coiffure was famously big and shaggy – naturally curly, but brushed out, with a lot of volume at the sides. She was sometimes photographed with crimped hair, a look that can now be achieved with crimping tongs, but for a low-maintenance method, simply weave wet hair into a series of tiny plaits and then brush out when dry.

Although Bush was a natural beauty, she was always fully made up in her music videos in a theatrical style that enhanced her atmospheric performances and elaborate costumes. Coloured shadow, liner and mascara helped bring out the drama of her eyes, lips were almost always red or coral and cheeks rosy but not contoured – all against a very pale, porcelain canvas. There was never a "lips or eyes, never both" rule for her.

Bush sported long, lacquered nails in her videos, too. The shape is a bit old-fashioned looking – long ovals rather than the square shapes that are popular today, and she wore them in shades of deep vermilion red or burgundy.

ABOVE: A Chinese silk coat of Mandarin design: hunt out similar versions and wear it with black leggings and over-the-knee boots or tailored, black trousers and heels for a Kate Bush-inspired evening out.

OPPOSITE: LEFT: This portrait of Kate was photographed by Patrick Lichfield in 1980. While this headpiece may look out of place for daywear, a jauntily placed orchid or bejewelled hair clasp above the ear could channel just enough Kate Bush beauty to enhance your own look.

### Style Tips

- Tie a lightweight or mesh scarf around your waist, over a leotard and tights.

- Source hair accessories such as fake flowers, feathers and leaves to pick up a colour in your outfit.

- Wear a gypsy shirt belted at the waist over a full skirt.

- Try an all-in-one jumpsuit and high heels for a night out.

- Make your own velvet choker using ribbon and a corsage.

- Eschew footwear and go barefoot.

- Substitute a shawl for a cardigan over dresses.

## Theatrical Make-up

This technique, which is modelled on her look for the *Babooshka* video, creates a butterfly eye effect, but you can follow the basic shading techniques to create any other adaptation you like. Brighter colours are great for fancy dress, especially if you use specially made professional body paints from Mehron or Kryolan or glitter shadows. Alternatively, for a dramatic evening look, tone down using a neutral palette of powder eyeshadows in greys or browns.

1 You need a clean, smooth base before applying pale make-up. Choose a luminous foundation just a shade lighter than your natural skin tone and blend well into the hairline and over the jaw. Set with loose translucent powder. The skin should look translucent rather than matte.

2 Apply a silver-grey eyeshadow all over the eyelids up to the browbone, and into the inner corner of the eye.

3 Using an angled brush and slate-blue eyeshadow, draw in a soft outline from the inner corner of the eye below the tear duct under the eye to the outer brow. The curve is wide and rounded, rather than cat-eye. Blend the outer edge under the browbone.

4 Next apply the midnight-blue shadow into the crease and outer corner of the eye, taking the colour under the eye, close to the lashline.

5 Using the eyeliner pencil, line the eyes top and bottom close to the lashline, flicking slightly at the outer corner. Then line the waterline, top and bottom.

6 Add several coats of black mascara – you want a delicate defined lash rather than thickness and volume.

7 Finish with coral lipstick and blush if desired.

# Molly Ringwald: Indie Girl

American actress Molly Ringwald is synonymous with a cool, eclectic style with roots in the mid 1980s. Short skirts, pastel colours, flat slouchy boots, prom dresses, bows, city shorts and lacy gloves all fall into this look, as does natural-looking hair and make-up.

The John Hughes' films *Sixteen Candles* (1984), *The Breakfast Club* (1985) and *Pretty in Pink* (1986) made Ringwald a teen style icon in the US. Although she has since become a reference point for lovers of '80s fashions, most of her on-screen looks can be attributed to the costume designers on her movies. For *Sixteen Candles*, Marla Denise Schlom took on the task of dressing Ringwald in the cool schoolgirl style for which she became known. Slouchy, layered T-shirts, pinafores and cutesy, girlie looks provided a fresh on-screen contrast to grown-up glam.

*The Breakfast Club* takes place over the period of one day, so Ringwald needed just one outfit. Costume designer Marilyn Vance purchased the entire wardrobe from a branch of Ralph Lauren in Chicago, near where the movie was being made. The loose, pink T-shirt, long brown skirt, knee-length lace-up boots and double brown leather belt are classic preppy all-American Lauren from that time. It wasn't cool, but it was fashionable among wealthier teens such as Ringwald's character Claire Standish.

Costume heavyweight Donna Roberts Orme concocted a series of legendary looks for Andie, the original "vintage girl", in *Pretty in Pink*. She dressed Ringwald in the frilly collars, baseball jackets, drop-waisted full skirts, waistcoats, long strings of pearls and fedora-style hats for which her character Andie Walsh became known. The pink dress Ringwald wears in the final scene at the prom is pure 1980s in every sense, from its puffed sleeves and cutaway shoulders to the mesh detailing and high neck. It's hard to imagine a garment with more period elements, and the dress was heavily copied by high-street retailers at the time.

The early 1980s saw the New Romantics' style inspire so many classic shapes. Asymmetric haircuts, waistcoats over frilly pirate shirts, baggy trousers, Chinese slippers and even dungaree overalls became "street" fashion. Added to this were the accessories. From tribal beads and wooden bangles to retro Victorian and Art Deco jewellery or huge diamanté rocks roughly glued together on brooch or earring bases, virtually anything big worked.

### Indie Girl Lookalikes

The Bangles
Cyndi Lauper
Kirsten Dunst
Chloë Sevigny
Zooey Deschanel

TOP: Zooey Deschanel is a pin-up for vintage fans. Her cool mixing of modern designers, fun sportswear and vintage sets her apart from the usual red carpet scrum.

RIGHT: Chloë Sevigny revived vintage as a fashion-forward phenomenon. Her stylish incorporation of 1980s shoes, shaping, fabrics and colour opened the doors to a new and exciting fashion scene.

OPPOSITE: *Pretty in Pink*, 1986, was Ringwald's third movie for director John Hughes. This outfit features keynote elements of the Ringwald 1980s look: Homburg hat with scarf, men's dinner shirt with neck brooch, waistcoat, customized tuxedo and homemade-looking earrings.

For a decade or more, Ringwald's look remained firmly routed in the mid 1980s, along with Madonna and Rosanna Arquette's outfits in *Desperately Seeking Susan* (1985). The styling in these movies is wedged in our consciousness as classic, quirky '80s, until stylish young celebrities (in particular Chloë Sevigny) began buying and re-creating elements of Molly Ringwald's wardrobe in the late 1990s, making it popular again. Sevigny's high-fashion touch has made eclectic, vintage-style dressing ultra-cool. The re-emergence of the short, evening-style prom dress – now a universal fashion favourite – is definitely down to Sevigny and her trademark long legs. Ankle socks with high-heeled sandals, an ultra-short dress with a men's jacket or city shorts with a shirt and tie also typify the look. Indie Girl is all about adding an '80s touch to funk up your usual style. Instead of following traditional fashion rules, such as a fitted top with a full skirt or a baggy upper silhouette over long, lean legs, this style mixes both, allowing you to form your own shapes and looks.

# Style Guide

**The Palette:** The colour palette is bright or slightly "off" shades of rust, chocolate brown, cream, beige and off-whites. Pastel pinks, royal blue and jade green were also big fashion shades.

**Key Designers:** Chloé, Ralph Lauren, Max Mara, Escada, Issey Miyake, Yohji Yamamoto, Katharine Hamnett, PX, Bodymap, Betty Jackson, Wendy Dagworthy.

**Silhouette and Cut:** Although the 1980s inverted-triangle shape dominated fashion, this look adds variations with puffball skirts, full shorts, knickerbockers and mini-crinis. Shirts are billowing but belted on the hip; coats are full, long and sweeping.

## Dresses and Skirts

The dress comes in a range of styles and is a key component of this look. Dresses were prom dress and pinafore. For skirts, the style was preppy mid-length, mini ra-ra or puffball and stretchy or lace minis.

*Shop vintage for:* The mini-crini by Vivienne Westwood enjoyed a brief moment in the fashion spotlight, along with the puffball created by Christian Lacroix. Hunt for original Christian Lacroix, Jean-Louis Scherrer and Moschino mini prom-style dresses in ruched silk or heavy satin, or familiarize yourself with the look and hunt out copies. For pinafores, designers Sheridan Barnett, Betty Jackson and Wendy Dagworthy all featured several versions in their collections from this era.

### Key Looks

- Padded-shouldered, loose jackets
- Short, full skirts
- Flat-heeled slouchy leather boots, platforms or very high heels
- City shorts
- Peep-through-to-lingerie cardigans in pastel shades
- Mini prom dresses
- Lace –in tights, collars, camisoles and miniskirts
- Animal prints and paisley
- Bows at the neck
- Pushed-back, *Miami Vice*-style cuffs on jackets
- Rolled-up "boyfriend" jeans
- Bolero jackets
- 1970s-style blouse with long cuffs and collar
- Midi-length full skirts
- Lace-up knee boots
- Layered jackets and coats
- Ankle socks and brogues

## Jackets

Boxy but soft, double-breasted and layered one on top of the other – this was the *Miami Vice* jacket style of the time. Look for three-quarter sleeves, collarless necklines or big lapels and lengths finishing just above the hips. Denim jackets were big news, particularly longer, bigger-shouldered versions of the Wrangler classic and, later, sculpted hourglass shapes from Jean Paul Gaultier.

*Shop vintage for:* During the early 1980s there was a renewed interest in Japanese designers, including Yohji Yamamoto and Issey Miyake. For autumn/winter of 1983, both produced boxy jackets, tunics and sweaters large enough to wear as coats; the collections were styled with lots of layering over longer skirts, leggings and cropped trousers.

## Coats

The fashion for big shoulders and 1940s influences was apparent in coat designs during the mid 1980s. Calvin Klein, Donna Karan, Betty Jackson, Sheridan Barnett and Wendy Dagworthy all created heavy, brightly coloured coats in Prince of Wales check and tweed. Betty Jackson's duster coats – long, swirly, all-covering Macs – popped up everywhere.

*Shop vintage for:* The big overcoat was a staple piece, easy to pair with ankle socks and brogues or an old pair of riding boots and a bowler hat. Look for original designers or hunt out cheaper men's tweed or wool classics in vintage stores or markets.

### Style Tips

- Top off any look with a fedora hat.

- Combine unexpected mixings of evening clothes with day shoes, baggy dungarees with high heels, shorts with a suit jacket or blouson tops with short, full skirts.

- Wear dangly or chandelier-style earrings.

- Try double-wound-around leather belts.

- Go geeky glam in large, slightly rounded glasses with plastic frames.

- Carry a small purse bag on a chain, slung diagonally across the body.

- Overload the jewellery – combine multiple ropes of beads, stacks of bangles, brooches and dangly earrings all in one look.

- Layer a printed blouse and waistcoat under a slouchy jacket or wear leggings under print dresses with cardigans and scarves.

## Tops and Blouses

Blouson shapes, silk prints, puffed sleeves and outsize detailing feature on tops from this era; also look for oversized *Flashdance*-style slashed tops and sweatshirts.

*Shop vintage for:*
Gianfranco Ferré, Escada, Sportmax, Dior and Yves Saint Laurent for strong colouring and prints.

## Knitwear

Oversized slouchy jumpers, beaded cardigans and sleeveless polo necks were all Molly-style looks.

*Shop vintage for:* Beaded and cashmere cardigans, circa 1950, in pretty pastel shades

## Trousers

Cropped mid-calf trousers and men's-style Oxford "baggies" made a return. Modern ultra-skinny jeans are useful to wear with oversized knitwear and tops, as they help keep the "inverted triangle" silhouette of the period.

*Shop vintage for:* Peg or cropped 1980s styles from Norma Kamali, Chantal Thomass, Claude Montana and Calvin Klein.

## Footwear

Low-heeled court shoes and slouchy pixie or lace-up boots, as well as knee-high leather boots work well with this look. Dr Martens boots were essential for all Indie Girls by the end of the 1980s and trainers (sneakers) by Keds, Reebok and Adidas were hot.

*Shop vintage for:* High, slim but not stiletto-heeled sandals and court shoes from Maud Frizon, Russell & Bromley, Rayne and Roland Cartier; preppy Bass Weejun loafers, Dr Marten boots and Reebok Freestyles.

## Jewellery

"Alternative" designers began selling their wares to big stores. Slim Barrett, a diminutive young Irishman living in London, fashioned the coolest earrings, brooches, belts and neckpieces from black tyre rubber and other industrial fall-out. Judy Blame created similar styles and market stalls popped up selling homemade, chunky glitz. Silver and gold putty, set with fake stones and fashioned into brooches and earrings, plus chunky beads and pearls became unisex fashion accessories.

*Shop vintage for:* Slim Barrett's "Ethnic Punk" collection or Maripol crucifixes and rubber bangles. Crystal earrings and bracelets by Butler & Wilson. Original 1920s and 1930s Art Deco brooches, earrings and rings or '80s Deco Revival versions from Yves Saint Laurent and Chanel. Long ropes of beads and pearls.

## Other Accessories

Hats made a comeback and UK design colleges produced bright young accessory designers, including milliners Stephen Jones and Philip Treacy. Big and square, or skinny and silk, the scarf also was big news, particularly in exotic patterns, rich paisleys, checks and animal prints. The fringed shawl was the 1980s version of the pashmina and finished the eclectic, romantic look.

*Shop vintage for:* Ray-Ban Wayfarers, small-print long scarves in paisley and floral prints, fringed shawls and fedora, derby or small-brimmed hats.

LEFT: Molly in 1986, from *Pretty in Pink*: Layer scarves, bangles, beads and earrings in contrasting or clashing colours over basic garments like the polo neck (turtleneck) and bleached denim jacket shown here. Less is less here, so pile it on. Add a touch of lip gloss and blusher and mimic the peachy beauty of Molly Ringwald at her peak.

## Beauty Guide

Redhead beauty relies on natural-looking glowing skin, allowing the freckles to come through; model Lily Cole and actress Nicole Kidman are great examples of how to work this naturally given look. Brows in the 1980s were natural and straight, without plucking into arches, eyes are simply made up, cheeks were rosy and lips full and sensual. For a touch of 1980s quirkiness, add some bright green or blue eyeliner or frosty pink eyeshadow.

Hair-styling products and tools burst onto the scene in the 1980s like never before, allowing women to style their hair in voluminous "big hair" curls, gelled spikes and wet looks or frizzy, fluffy diffuser-dried manes. Molly's short, chunky layered bob, however, was gentler and more natural and effortless-looking. Short crops or kooky, pageboy styles straight out of the 1980s suit the slightly boyish look and can be dressed up beautifully with hair accessories for parties and special occasions. If a Ringwald style isn't you, you can still rock the '80s with side ponytails and messy bobs.

OPPOSITE: Victorian-inspired pearl pieces, such as this heart brooch, and black DMs were the height of fashion in the Ringwald era.

### Beauty Tips

- Avoid over-tweezing the brows – skinny arches are too high maintenance for the naturally groomed Indie Girl look.

- Choose lip balms, stains and glosses rather than heavy-weight lipsticks.

- Keep skin protected with sunscreen and cultivate skin health rather than relying on foundation and concealer to mask problems.

- Use concealer where needed and skip the foundation entirely.

- Avoid bronzer which can look harsh on delicate skin tones and substitute pale pink or peach blusher instead.

- Natural colours work well on the eyes, but liven the look up with gold eyeliner or a bright green.

- Use brown mascara, never black.

- Wear a bob or cropped hair cut boyishly tousled and messy.

- For long hair, sweep your hair into a smooth, low side ponytail (much chicer than the 1980s high, backcombed side ponytail)

# Cindy Crawford: Glamazon

For a retro early 1990s look featuring boyfriend jeans, a midriff-baring white T-shirt, Chanel jacket and lots of bling, look no further than the original supermodel, Cindy Crawford and her Glamazon friends.

Cindy Crawford was an Illinois girl who moved to New York after the pull of modelling contracts became too lucrative to ignore, despite a promising start studying chemical engineering. With her voluminous chestnut-coloured hair, amazing eyebrows, signature beauty spot and curves, she was more movie star than model, yet fashion and cosmetic houses adored her and she became one of the world's biggest modelling stars with everyone clamouring to copy her easy, breezy American style. Along with Christy Turlington, Linda Evangelista and Tatjana Patitz, she shared a strong, healthy and versatile glamour. These girls were as much at home running along the beach in denim shorts as they were strutting their stuff on the red carpet in stunning gowns or leaping out from the pages of the top fashion magazines – in fact, they seemed to leap around a lot in photos! Cindy Crawford was rarely photographed in stationary positions, for much of what made her image so hot came from the vibrancy and energy she emanated. These girls smiled, ran, punched the air, hugged each other and conveyed the sheer joy they must have experienced to be living in their own fabulous bodies.

Evangelista's celebrated quote to American *Vogue* that she didn't "get out of bed for less than $10,000 a day" was said in humour, but in reality this was no joke. Featured on the magazine's cover in wrap-around Lycra tops, T-shirts and jeans, Evangelista, Crawford, Patitz, Turlington and Naomi Campbell, with their big hair, curves and natural beauty, signalled the end of the recession-wracked '80s. As economies improved after the 1987 Wall Street Crash, the world needed something good to look at and the Glamazons were manna from heaven for fashion. Youthful enough

### Glamazon Lookalikes
Heidi Klum
Stephanie Seymour
Linda Evangelista
Liz Hurley
Gisele Bündchen

OPPOSITE: With breasts, muscle definition and shamelessly gorgeous hair and make-up on show, Cindy Crawford looks effortlessly glam in a body-con Azzedine Alaïa dress.

ABOVE: Heidi Klum's multitalented and cheerful approach to life, not to mention her leggy looks, embodies the spirit of the Supers.

FAR LEFT: Gisele Bündchen sums up the next generation of Glamazons, adding fashion designing to her list of accomplishments.

LEFT: With her toned body and long hair and legs, Liz Hurley fits into the Glamazon camp.

to attract the attention of pop stars, trendy enough to feature in all the top magazines, everything about the Glamazon girls was highly covetable. Claudia Schiffer in a Chanel jacket and Linda Evangelista swinging a Prada bag brought fashion back to the masses: these models had a girl-next-door-makes-good quality about them – it was okay to want what they had. And what they wanted was Versace or Chanel.

Sashaying down catwalks for Donna Karan or Calvin Klein in New York, Dolce & Gabbana in Milan or Chanel in Paris, these women breathed new life into fashion with every step. Off-camera, they wore the clothes they modelled and were showered with gifts from designers and big global corporations alike in the hope that they might be caught on-camera. Azzedine Alaïa, quiet after an early 1980s surge, returned with stunning collections – dresses of body-hugging Lycra that became his trademark. His 1991 autumn/winter collection provided inspiration for career girls everywhere. Smart and sexy, featuring black and chocolate brown stretchy dresses, pinafores and skirts, it remains a fabulously workable look. Designer Hervé Léger also contributed to the trend in the 1980s and 1990s with his strappy "bandage dresses".

Late 1980s to early 1990s style is enjoying a return to the fashion spotlight. Recently, dresses from Versace's 1992 fetish-inspired collection, as modelled by Cindy, her super-sisters and Liz Hurley at the *Four Weddings and a Funeral* premiere of 1994, were the vintage world's hottest ticket. The collection was the pinnacle of a moment in time brought about by a return to glamour.

## Style Guide

**The Palette:** Strong, simple colours and modern neutrals underlie this look: saturated black, chocolate brown and beige, as well as black-and-white or red-and-black checks, and black worn with gold.

**Key Designers:** Gianni Versace, Giorgio Armani, Dolce & Gabbana, Azzedine Alaïa, Chanel, Hervé Léger, Calvin Klein, Christian Lacroix, Donna Karan, Chantal Thomass and Sonia Rykiel.

**Silhouette and Cut:** A structured inverted triangle: broad-shouldered, fitted waist, feminine physique with curves in all the right places and an emphasis on long, strong legs. Shoulders are balanced out by the hips.

### Dresses

Although this is a short, fitted, sexy look, it requires great-quality garments: subtle colours and designer names in heavy jersey fabrics or Lycra that has retained its colour. Also look for eveningwear and cocktail dresses with short hemlines, or versions that are mini-length in front and longer behind.

### Key Looks

- Fitted jacket or blazer over straight-leg jeans
- Plain white T-shirt and black leather jacket
- Soft grey fleecy tracksuit pants, rolled down at the waist, worn with a cut-off vest
- Bandage-style, body-fitting dress
- Chanel jewellery
- Gold big hoop earrings
- Designer watch, bag and accessories
- High heels or bare feet
- Expensive matching lingerie sets
- Long, loose hair
- Over-the-knee, flat-heeled leather boots
- Body-hugging Lycra in any form

OPPOSITE LEFT: Azzedine Alaïa 1980s jersey dress with contrast topstitching. Alaia is back in the fashion spotlight with his wearable, body-contouring and elegant designs and a super-luxe accessories collection.

OPPOSITE RIGHT: Hervé Léger bandage dress, circa 1980s. Many mimic the master of the bandage frock but financial fallout meant Hervé had to sell his valuable brand in the 1990s. It's still available but without the master behind the look.

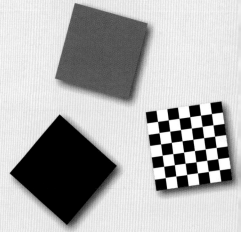

*Shop vintage for:* High-quality vintage from this era is hard to find because it was heavily worn, but designer nearly-new shops may stock body-con dresses by Alaïa, Léger, Chantal Thomass, Sonia Rykiel and Donna Karan. Also hunt for bright metal-mesh dresses from Versace's 1982 "Oraton" collection and floral prints from Christian Lacroix.

## Tops

In April 1992 for *Vogue*'s 100th Anniversary Special, Herb Ritts shot Cindy and a ladder-full of other models for the cover, all wearing the white Gap shirt that became a classic. Perfect to pair casually with jeans or a suit for work, the crisp, structured white shirt is always a winner. Casual faded blue denim shirt and quality cotton T-shirts in neutrals also formed basics for the Glamazon look. Wrap-around ballerina styles, cropped and tied-at-the-waist, were other pieces that underpinned the body-con silhouette. Donna Karan created a series of easy-to-wear Lycra tops, including the infamous "body", which fastened with poppers (snaps). Not the easiest garment in the world to manage but useful for staying tucked into your business suit!

*Shop vintage for:* Wrap-around Lycra tops with long ties and shirts and blouses with waist ties by Donna Karan, Armani, Calvin Klein, Norma Kamali and good-quality high street brands including Wallis, Way In at Harrods and Neiman Marcus.

## Jackets and Suits

Key to the Glamazon look, the smartly fitting, snazzy jacket was worn with jeans, skirts and trousers. Shiny black leather jackets and coats were also popular. "Designer" leather jackets from the era were hot and still look slick combined with a pencil skirt.

*Shop vintage for:* Original Chanel or Chanel-style (there were lots of imitators) jackets in bouclé fabric with ribbon braiding, gold buttons and detailing. Bolero jackets by Lacroix and Armani, which offer waist-accentuating glamour; also fitted leather blazers by Alaïa and super-structured suits by Thierry Mugler.

ABOVE: Fashion model Helena Christensen modelling Versace in 1991 and demonstrating her own supermodel status. Glam up your own version of this look with a vintage-bought military jacket over a gold brocade mini-dress. Accessorize with as much bling as you like, but keep hair, body and make-up simple, gleaming and clean.

RIGHT: Thanks to the Glamazons and their anti-recession glamour, luxury brands including Gina shoes, are back in expensive style. This 1980s Gina shoe features decorous details typical of the decade – diamanté and silver ribbon on red suede.

## Jewellery

The real key to this look is serious jewellery, which relies on a "pile it all on" aesthetic. Costume jewellery, particularly with brand logos, became very popular as the fad for oversize shapes grew. By 1981 huge, thick gold hoops had come into style, thanks to the singer Sade. Her simple style, featuring a lean silhouette and huge accessories, crossed the Atlantic and preempted the 1980s primary fashion obsession. Sade wore her earrings and hats large, adding waspy leather belts or leather gloves to complete the look. The effect was pulled together and accessorized, with statement items doing all the talking.

*Shop vintage for:* Costume gold jewellery by Chanel, Yves Saint Laurent, Bulgari and Paloma Picasso, particularly thick, short gold ropes and chains, gold and bronze cuff bracelets and big button-style earrings with pearls.

## Shoes and Bags

This was the dawning of the age of the designer handbag, watch, sunglasses and fragrance. Shoes (invariably stiletto) and bags (the clutch being the favourite style) were matching. Both appeared in super-luxury materials and exotic skins, with lots of hardware detailing and decoration.

*Shop vintage for:* Prada's black nylon totes with chain handles, Hermès Kelly and Birkin bags, the Miss Dior by Christian Dior, or anything by Gucci, Louis Vuitton or Chanel. Stilettos and ankle boots by Gucci and Chanel, plus Ferragamo, Manolo Blahnik, Gina, Sergio Rossi (for Dolce & Gabbana and Azzedine Alaïa) and early 1990s Sigerson Morrison.

## Sunglasses

Improved economies and the prevalence of luxury goods meant classic Ray-Ban "Wayfarers" gave way to designer names who licensed their brand to accessory manufacturers to create a lucrative designer sunglasses business. Versions from the 1980s were big and blingy. Early 1990s accessory houses, including Gucci and Loewe, produced highly desirable simple, square metal-framed sunglasses, still covetable today.

*Shop vintage for:* Wrap sunglasses from Versace, Gucci and Dior as well as Carrera aviators and square-framed Cazal 670s or 633s, Revo mirrored glasses and Oakley Eyeshades.

### Style Tips

- Knot a men's shirt at the waist and wear with jeans.

- Chop a T-shirt halfway for a midriff-baring summer look with jeans or cut-off shorts.

- Wear a Lycra skirt as a mini-dress. "Micro" minis were the new skirt length.

- Keep dresses and coats extremely short or long and very fitted.

- Push your sunglasses up on top of your head.

- Carry a statement designer bag with casual clothes.

- Keep heels slim with "bandage" dresses for sophistication. No wedges or clunky shoes.

- Colours should be kept subtle and neutral for tight-fitting clothes.

ABOVE: Chanel vintage jewellery, circa mid 1980s. Karl Lagerfeld is rightfully credited with re-vamping the famous CC logo and making it as covetable for the young and fabulous as for the traditional middle-aged-lady market. Pre-1990s Chanel jewellery is immensely collectable for it's solid, French-made detailing and durable quality. Today stylists beg and borrow pieces for films and TV, including the hugely successful New York socialites-saga, *Gossip Girl.*

# *Beauty Guide*

Be prepared to reveal a flash of shoulder, a hint of thigh and a glimpse of cleavage. Cindy's was a "body beautiful" look, so ensure your skin is gleaming and polished. A great body moisturizer is essential, as is a bit of a tan. While a total "faked bake" is unnecessary, this look smacks of the healthy outdoors and a fabulous, glam glow is a definite plus – whether achieved via St Tropez or spray-on fake tan, or just tinted moisturizer.

The naturally gorgeous Glamazon look appears make-up-free but on closer inspection, the truth is revealed. Highlighter for cheek- and browbones, warm blusher or bronzer, lip gloss, dark brown mascara and neutral eyeshadow and liners are the tools of the Glamazon beauty kit: ditto a good blowdryer. The volume blowdry (or "blowout") is key to this look and even if your hair is short, wavy or curly, it still requires an element of full-on swish. Cindy's hair was big, bouncy and wavy, often lightly backcombed for extra volume.

### Beauty Tips

- For a gentle and natural tanned look, apply a moisturizer with a gradual self-tan included to your skin, rather than a full-strength spray-booth tan.

- Toned muscles are essential – this is a gym body.

- Exfoliate the body regularly with a sugar-scrub mixture, concentrating on your elbows and knees.

- It's claimed Cindy uses a milk-and-water mixture to mist her face and keep her skin smooth; if this doesn't appeal, try a balancing rosewater facial mist.

- Cindy's make-up look is warm: choose a cosmetic palette with bone, cream, beige, copper, chocolate and gold for the eyes and burgundy for the lips and cheeks.

- For super-high hair, backcomb the top section, then smooth down and comb to unify the style.

**"** *The thing I like about my body is that it's strong. I can move furniture around my apartment. I can ride my horse... I can play basketball. It's a well-functioning machine.* **"**

*Cindy Crawford*

OPPOSITE: Cindy Crawford in a dressfrom Versace's Harlequin-inspired 1991 collection. Elaborate detailing negated the need for accessories and adornment. Simple pearl ear studs do nicely here. Her make-up is clean and understated, but her hair is high-wattage blowdry. Glamazon chic is all about the girl!

## The Volume Blowdry

Thick, long-layered, voluminous and wavy, Cindy's hair hasn't changed dramatically since her peak modelling days – it's full of bounce and volume, though not quite as big-haired as in the 1980s. With a deep side part, her long side fringe brings out the cheekbones and eyes.

1 Apply volumizing mousse or spray to the roots of clean, towel-dried hair.
2 Part and section off the hair with clips into three back sections, two side sections and a top "fringe" section.
3 Blowdry the bottom layer at the nape of the neck first, using a large round bristle brush. Lift the hair at the roots with the brush and pull away to dry the length, before returning to the roots. Finish with a blast of cold air directed down the length of the hair before moving to the next section.
4 Continue with the next two back section in the same way, and then blowdry the sides.
5 Finish with the top section, blowdrying away from the face and keeping the brush as high as you can to create volume.
6 Run your fingers through the sections to combine, then mist with a volumizing hairspray.

**You will need:**
Volumizing spray or mousse
Large, round, vented
bristle brush
Blowdryer
Volumizing hairspray

TIP: Angle the blowdryer up at the roots using a hot setting to create volume and set the product, then point the blowdryer down the length of the hair using a cool setting to smooth the cuticle.

# DIRECTORY

## HAIR AND MAKE-UP SERVICES

### UK

**Beehive Brides**
Tel: 07710 415365
Website: www.beehivebrides.co.uk
From classic glamour to full-on retro styling, professional hair and make-up artist Fiona Maynard has worked on numerous film and TV productions. She now specializes in bespoke bridal hair and make-up.

**Burlesque Baby**
Tel: 020 3287 5164
Email: contact@burlesquebaby.com
Website: www.burlesquebaby.com
England's first school of Burlesque offers pin-up makeovers, Burlesque and retro photo parties.

**Cherry Pop Pictures**
Website: www.cherrypoppictures.com/vintagepinupmakeover.htm
Be a pin-up girl for the day! Vintage hair and make-up pampering, plus a glamorous half-day's photo-shoot.

**Flamingo Amy**
Website: www.flamingoamy.co.uk
Based in Norwich, Norfolk, Flamingo Amy is a hairstylist who loves to recreate looks inspired by our glamorous past, the 1940s and 50s being particular favourites with clients. View hair galleries and book an appointment online.

**Lisa George**
Email: info@lisageorge.co.uk
Website: www.lisageorge.co.uk
Professional hair and make-up artist/designer whose clients include Vintage at Goodwood Festival.

**Olivia Howarth**
Tel: 07738 172 102
Email: 0215044@yahoo.co.uk
Website: www.vintage-styling.com
Hairstylist specializing in vintage services, who also offers a make-up service. Will travel throughout the UK.

**It's Something Hells**
2.16 Kingly Court (just off Carnaby Street)
London W1B 5PW
Tel: 07896 153491
Email: misterducktail@yahoo.fr
Website: www.myspace.com/something_hells
Run by Miss Betty and Mr Ducktail, this French retro hair salon is worth visiting for 1940s/50s Hollywood coiffures and rockabilly styling.

**LeKeux Events**
2 Acacia Grove
Rugby
Warwickshire CV21 2QT
Email: info@lekeuxevents.co.uk
Website: www.lekeuxevents.co.uk
Private hair and make-up parties, online tutorials, styling (including bridal), learn burlesque and various ticketed events. Also, Birmingham-based salon and pop-up mobile hair and beauty salon travels nationally to events and vintage fairs, offering open appointments. To book hair, make-up or manicures, email: vintagehair@leukeuxevents.co.uk.

**Lauren Luke**
Website: www.bylaurenluke.com/looks.aspx
Watch online and then purchase the renowned make-up artist's "Vintage Glams" tutorials.

**Miss Dixiebelle**
19 Bruntfield Place
Edinburgh EH10 4HN
Tel: 0131 6297783
Email: info@missdixiebelle.co.uk
Website: www.missdixiebelle.co.uk
Expert hairstylist and make-up artists recreate 40s- and 50s-inspired looks (bookings for groups, hen parties and individuals) alongside boutique stocking vintage clothing, accessories, lingerie and corsetry.

**Nina's Hair Parlour**
1st Floor
Alfie's Antique Market
13 Church Street
Marylebone
London NW8 8DT
Tel: 020 7723 1911
Website: www.ninasvintageandretrohair.com
The first UK specialist in retro hair and beauty: unique, one-of-a-kind salon plus classes; handpicked original and rare hats and snoods for sale and hire within the parlour.

**Pin Curls and Pompadours**
Tel: 07866 428769
Facebook page: www.facebook.com/pages/Pin-Curls-and-Pompadours/112489328777132?ref=search
Email: pincurlsandpompadours@googlemail.com
Leicester-based vintage stylist specializing in authentic hair and make-up looks from the 1920s to the 1970s.

**The Powderpuff Girls**
136 Columbia Road
London E2 7RG
Tel: 0844 879 4928
Email: dolls@thepowderpuffgirls.com
Website: www.thepowderpuffgirls.com
Immaculate make-up artists, manicurists and hairstylists poised and ready to pamper at any sophisticated event.

**Lauren Rennells**
Email: lrennells@yahoo.com
Website: http://lrennells.com
Period and vintage hairstyles; make-up, wardrobe and fashion styling.

**Rouge Makeovers**
Tel: 078 17520696
Email: info@rougemakeovers.co.uk
Website: www.rougemakeovers.co.uk
Leading vintage make-up artist (Portsmouth area), who has worked with Kate Moss and Naomi Campbell.

**Sam Roberts Wedding Hair Specialist Ltd**
60 Beverstone
Orton Brimbles
Peterborough
Cambridgeshire PE2 5YN
Tel: 07976 378 095
Email: enquiries@samrobertsweddinghairjewellery.co.uk
Website: http://samrobertsweddinghairjewellery.co.uk
Handcrafted vintage hair cages and other elegant hairpieces custom-made and featuring Swarovski crystals and pearls.

**Tanya Skinner**
Website: www.tanyamakeupnorwich.co.uk
Norwich-based make-up artist who enjoys interpreting influences from different eras.

**Vintage Hair Lounge**
Kimber House
118 High Street
Southampton SO14 2AA
Tel: 023 8033 7109
Website: http://vintagehairlounge.com
Expert advice on authentic vintage looks; salon also stocks international vintage make-up range Bésame.

**Lesley Vye**
Tel: 079 73880478
Email: Lesley@lesleyvye.com
Website: www.lesleyvye.com
Freelance make-up artist trained in fashion editorial, with experience in film and commercial work. Clients include Vintage at Goodwood Festival and The Powderpuff Girls.

**What Katie Did**
26 Portobello Green
281 Portobello Road
London W10 5TZ
Tel: 0845 430 8943
Website: www.whatkatiedid.com
This vintage lingerie boutique also stocks Bésame and T Le Clerk cosmetics and offers expert advice on retro-style make-up.

### Australia

**Tony at Sterling Hairdressing Parlour & Barber Shop**
Shop 3
29 Brisbane Street
Surrey Hills, NSW
Website: www.facebook.com/sterlinghair
Recreates vintage styles for men and women and has a big following among the vintage aficionados and rockabillies in town.

### US

**Artistic Impressions by Riviera Salon**
7228 Taft Street
Hollywood FL 33024
Tel: 954 632 1942

Email: Riviera@rivieraweddings.net
From decadent 1920s fingerwaves to the bedroom curls of the 1950s, stylist Riviera Decordova will bring out the pin-up girl in you.

**Ashley Parrino at Nicholas Cruz & Co. Salon**
1902 E. Prien Lake Road
Lake Charles LA 70605
Tel: 337 478 1722
Email: ashleyparrino@yahoo.com
Vintage and retro-inspired styles for men and women; specializes in colour and cuts.

**Bésame Cosmetics Inc**
Website: www.besamecosmetics.com
Renowned retro cosmetics range. Go online to request a catalogue, place an order or locate your nearest salon for products.

**Brittany Castaneda with Clive and Co.**
5301 Alpha Rd. 46
Dallas TX 75240
Tel: 972 934 0500
Email: Brittany@cliveandco.com
Website: www.thegalbehindthechair.com
Work ranges from classic vintage hairstyling to avante garde, with a strong emphasis on precision haircuts and blending techniques to create structured looks that are still soft.

**Cha Cha Beauty & Barber**
912 Williamson St.
Madison, WI
Tel: 608 204 3988
Email: chachahair@yahoo.com
Website: www.chachahair.com

**Eleanor Jean Haute Beauty**
13812 Ventura Blvd.
Sherman Oaks, CA
Tel: 818 788 1546
Email: jacey@eleanorjeanboutique.com
Website: www.eleanorjeanboutique.com
Celebrity make-up artist: among other looks, choose from "Gone With The Wind" to "The Marilyn" lashes, "Jetsetter" nails, "Elizabeth Tayor" eyes to "Grace Kelly" bridal make-up. Haute Beauty Party Menu offered too.

**Rebecca Gohl**
Tel: 616 776 7050 (salon) / 616 802 4399 (cell)
Email: vintagelook3@yahoo.com
Vintage hairstylist and make-up artist based in Grand Rapids, Michigan and specializing in 1800s hairstyles (Marie Antoinette); also period correct hair from the 1920s–60s.

**Hair Comes the Bride**
Website: www.haircomesthebride.com
Bridal beauty agency offering hair and make-up services in Los Angeles, San Diego, New York, New Jersey and Connecticut.

**Los Angeles Make-up School**
1624 Wilcox Ave
Los Angeles
Ca 90028
Tel: 888 816 0548 / 818 288 6919
Email: info@lamuschool.com

Website: www.losangelesmakeupschool.com
Offers a range of professional beauty make-up courses, including period make-up application and retro looks.

**Makeup & Hair by Vivian**
Tel: 650 329 9397
Website: http://makeupandhairbyvivian.webs.com
Vintage hair, make-up and styling artist located in the San Francisco Bay area.

**Maria B Makeup & Hair**
Tel: 714 848 5705
Email: Mariabmuah@gmail.com
Website: http://mariabmuah.blogspot.com
This retro hair and make-up artist will travel throughout the US.

**Moxie Beauty and Hair Parlor**
4329 Kalamazoo Ave SE
Grand Rapids, MI
Tel: 616 281 8699
Achieve the look of a more glamorous time. Moxie hair designers and make-up artists are also available for photoshoots, fashion shows, weddings and other events.

**New Vintage Beauty Lounge**
3864 N Mississippi Ave
Portland OR 97227
Tel: 503 327 8442
Email: info@newvintagebeautylounge.com
Website: www.newvintagebeautylounge.com
High-end salon and cosmetic boutique.

**Pimps & Pinups**
101 Stanton Street
New York NY 10002
Tel: 646 861 3766
Website: www.pimpsandpinups.com
Black-walled elegance meets 1950s glamour in this Big Apple boutique hair salon.

**Retro Beauty Bar**
10781 Los Alamitos Bld
Los Alamitos CA 90720
Tel: 562 596 9151
Website: www.retrobeautybar.com
1950s-inspired cocktail themed nail and waxing salon.

**reVamp**
Platt Building
834 South Broadway Suite 1200
Los Angeles CA 90014
Tel: 213 488 3387
Website: www.revampvintage.com
Salon offers period appropriate hair styling and make-up application workshops.

**Michelle St Darling**
Tel: 586 350 4492
Email: michellestdarling@gmail.com
Website: www.michellestdarling.blogspot.com
Freelance stylist specializing in vintage hair art, from the Victorian era through to modern-day hair art; also writes a blog about the science of hair.

**The Makeup Artist Workshop**
Website: www.themakeupartistworkshop.com
Offers hair and make-up tuition, including vintage hair classes, in this Los Angeles-based school.

**Ultra Lux Salon and Lounge**
1312 Aviation Bld Suite 101
Redondo Beach
California 90278
Tel: 310 372 3332 / 310 372 1371
Website: www.ultraluxsalon.com
This beautiful, vintage-inspired salon (hair and make-up services) opened in 2002 and is now established as one of the top-rated establishments in Los Angeles.

**Vintage Vamp**
Email: vintagevampinc@yahoo.com
Professional make-up artist (located San Diego, California), who works with MAC cosmetics.

## Canada

**Cherry Bomb Kustoms**
Email: kristadee@cherrybombkustoms.com
Website: www.cherrybombkustoms.com
Professional make-up artist and hairstylist whose passion lies in recreating the styles of the 1920s–50s.

**Shimona Henry**
Website: www.shimonahenry.com
Vancouver Film School Make-up Artistry graduate specializing in vintage make-up and hairstyles of the twentieth century and photographer with a love of retro glamour.

## VINTAGE BOUTIQUES

### UK
**Asos Marketplace**
Website: https://marketplaceasos.com
Where anyone who loves fashion, anywhere in the world, can sell fashion to anyone who loves fashion, anywhere in the world. Online boutiques made up of indie labels, emerging designers and vintage sellers.

**Barnardo's**
7 George Street
London W1U 3QH
Tel: 020 7935 2946
Website: www.barnardos.org.uk
Flagship store with a good range of vintage and designer clothes, sometimes featuring celebrity volunteers.

116 West Bow
Grassmarket
Edinburgh
Midlothian
EH1 2HH
Tel: 0131 225 4751
Website: www.barnardos.org.uk
Wide range of vintage, retro and designer clothes for men and women, as well as accessories and jewellery, all handpicked by staff from other

Barnardos branches.
54 Wilson Street
Merchant City
Glasgow
Lanarkshire
G1 1HD
Tel: 0131 225 4751
Website: www.barnardos.org.uk
Boutique section: vintage, retro and designer clothes.

**Beyond Retro**
Email: customercare@beyondretro.com
Website: www.beyondretro.com
Men's and women's vintage clothing: London (Brick Lane and Soho), Brighton, Sweden and online.

**British Red Cross**
69–71 Old Church Street
Chelsea
London SW3 5BS
Tel: 0845 054 7101

85 Ebury Street
Westminster
London SW1W 9QU
Tel: 020 7730 2235

10 Chaloner Street
Guisborough
Cleveland TS14 6QD
Tel: 01287 630 029
17–19 Nun Street
Newcastle
Newcastle-upon-Tyne NE1 5AG
Tel: 0191 222 1815

92 High Street
Poole
Dorset BH15 9DB
Tel: 0120 268 2211

10 Drummond Street
Inverness
IV1 1QD
Tel: 01463 232 729
Website: www.redcross.org.uk/Get-involved/Our-shops/Our-specialist-shops
Pick up some bargain vintage, retro and designer clothes from Barnardo's.

**Cloud Cuckoo Land**
6 Charlton Place
Camden Passage
Islington
London N1 8AJ
Tel: 020 7354 3141
Small boutique packed full of affordable garments from the 1920s to the 1980s; strong range of accessories, including exquisite 1950s floral cocktail hats.

**Etsy**
Website: www.etsy.com
Shop for, and sell vintage here. A community of artists, creators and collectors (English, Dutch, French and German), you can also join a team, share ideas, attend an event in your area, join a streaming workshop or watch an archived one.

**Heirloom Couture**
21 Lonsdale Road
Queen's Park
London NW6 6RA
Tel: 020 8969 4013
Email: enquiries@heirloomcouture.com
Website: www.heirloomcouture.com
From 1930s Schiaparelli to Ossie Clark, decades-old dresses are lovingly restored and reinvented by couture embroidery designer Rachel Spencer. She also has a collection of vintage-inspired, custom-fitted gowns.

**Off the Cuff Vintage**
Email: offthecuffvintage@gmail.com
Facebook page: www.facebook.com/pages/Off-the-Cuff-Vintage/154410191252471
Buy colourful, eclectic pieces from the 1950s to 80s at knockdown prices (as sold to Florence Welch from Florence and The Machine). Available online or visit the stall in London's Portobello Road Market (Portobello Green, Sundays and soon to be Saturdays).

**Oxfam**
Find out about Oxfam shops in your area, including events taking place at your local shop: www.oxfam.org.uk/shopfinder
Online store: www.oxfam.org.uk/shop/content/secondhandstore/fashion/vintage/default.html?ito=3614&itc=0
Affordable men's and women's vintage clothing from every era; also homewares.

**Rellik**
8 Golborne Road
North Kensington
London W10 5NW
Tel: 020 8962 0089
Website: www.relliklondon.com
Clothing and accessories from the 1920s to the mid-1980s.

**Time After Time**
30 High Street
Stroud
Gloucestershire GL5 1AJ
Tel: 07944 809 808
Website: www.stroudvintage.co.uk
Vintage fashion in the heart of the Cotswolds: designer pieces, accessories, jewellery, music, menswear, home and more.

**Traid**
61 Westbourne Grove
London W2 4UA
Tel: 020 7221 2421
Website: www.traid.org.uk
Charity shop stocking good-quality vintage and designer clothes, plus a fine range of accessories.

**V&A Enterprises Limited**
Website: www.vandashop.com
Reproduction jewellery, fashion and accessories created from original designs (men's and women's); also, home, stationery and fabrics. Every purchase supports the Victoria and Albert Museum.

**Virginia**
98 Portland Road
Notting Hill
London W11 4LQ
Tel: 020 7727 9908
Fax: 020 7229 2198
Exquisite vintage clothing and accessories, especially 1900s–30s.

**Vivien of Holloway**
294 Holloway Road
London N7 6NJ
Website: www.vivienofholloway.com
Boutique featuring authentic 1940s and 50s reproduction ready-to-wear ladies clothing – dresses, separates, accessories and hair flowers.

# Australia
**Fanantique**
282 Bay Street
Brighton
Victoria
Australia
Tel: +61 3 9596 9072
Website: www.fanantique.com.au
Vintage boutique with glamorous vintage gowns from the 1940s and 50s, as well as a unique collection of accessories; stocks Bésame Cosmetics.

**La Bella Donna**
Tel: (07) 3399 2124
Website: www.labelladonna.com.au
Vintage and pre-loved clothing specialists.

# USA
**American Vintage**
Website: www.american-vintage.net
From the 1900s to 1990s, this site offers a great selection of garments and accessories.

**American Vintage Classics**
Website: www.americanvintageclassics.com
Site catering for men and women who prefer the quality and style of vintage clothing.

**Babygirl Boutique**
Website: www.babygirlboutique.com
Retro rockabilly pin-up clothes, shoes, make-up and accessories.

**Beatnix**
3400 N Halsted St.
Chicago IL 60657
Tel: 773 281 6933
This vintage clothing store is a hidden gem.

**The Cat's Pajamas**
335 Maynard St.
Williamsport PA 17701 (by appointment only)
Tel: 570 322 5580
Email: catspajamasvintage@gmail.com
Website: www.catspajamas.com
The perfect online source for vintage clothing, accessories, jewellery and more.

**Decades**
8214½ Melrose Avenue
Los Angeles CA 90046
Tel: 323 655 0223
Website: www.decadesinc.com
Cameron Silver's fabulous twentieth-century vintage couture.

**Guvnor's**
178 Fifth Ave
Brooklyn NY 11217
Tel: 718 230 4887
Website: http://guvnorsnyc.com
Vintage men's and women's clothing including some punk-inspired pieces.

**Karma Couture**
591 Main St.
East Greenwich RI 02818
Tel: 401 398 0576
Email: karma.couture@yahoo.com
Website: www.karmacoutureri.com
One-of-a-kind vintage pieces.

**Keni Valenti Retro-Couture**
155 West 29th St.
Third floor, Room C5
New York NY10001
Tel: 212 967 7147
Website: www.kenivalenti.com
Large four-room showroom displaying Keni Valenti's collection of vintage couture clothing.

**Manhattan Vintage Clothing Show**
125 W 18th St.
New York NY 10011
Tel: 518 434 4312
Website: ww.manhattanvintage.com
Regular vintage clothing and antique textile shows and sales.

**Meow**
2210 E 4th Street
Long Beach
California 90814
Tel: 562 438 8990
Email: bigkitty@meowvintage.com
Website: http://meowvintage.com
Original apparel and accessories from the 1940s to the 1980s.

**Mister Freedom**
7161 Beverly Boulevard
Los Angeles
California 90036
Tel: 323 653 2014
Website: www.misterfreedom.com
Vintage clothing and accessories supplier.

**My Sisters' Closet**
Website: http://mysistersclosetmn.com
Consignment vintage clothing and accessories.

**New York Vintage Inc.**
117 West 25th Street
New York NY 10001
Tel: 212 647 1107
Fax: 212 647 1108
Email: info@NewYorkVintage.com

Website: http://newyorkvintage.com
Finest vintage couture, designer clothing and accessories; collection caters closely to fashion's top stylists, a host of Hollywood celebrities, film, TV and theatrical productions and can offer something unique for your red carpet event.

**The Paper Bag Princess**
8818 Olympic Boulevard
Beverly Hills CA 90211
Tel: 310 385 9036
Email: info@DoyleNewYork.com
Website: www.doylegalleries.com
Auctioneers and appraisers of haute couture and antique costume.

**Rag-O-Rama**
1111 Euclid Avenue NE
Atlanta GA 30307
Tel: 404 658 1988
Website: www.ragorama.com
One-stop vintage shopping store: men's and women's 1960s, 70s and 80s fashion.

**Retrodini Vintage**
81 A North Washington St.
Berkeley Springs WV 25411
Tel: 304 258 1580
Website: www.retrodini.com
Carries quality items spanning several decades, from the 1940s through the 1980s.

**Rockin' Betty**
The Meadows Mall
4300 Meadows Ln.
Ste 145
Las Vegas NV 89107
Tel: 702 877 3000
Website: www.facebook.com/pages/Rockin-Bettie/160516040669071?sk=info
Pin-up girl boutique.

**Tavin**
1543 Echo Park Ave.
Los Angeles 90026
Tel: 213 482 5832
Website: www.lifebytavin.com
This new concept boutique with a well-organized collection of vintage clothing and redesigned pieces also offers designer appointments, personal styling and alterations.

**Torso Vintages**
Union Square
272 Sutter Street at Grant
San Francisco CA 94108
Tel: 503 348 9195
Email: john@torsovintages.com
Website: www.torsovintages.com
Show-stopping gowns, furs, jewellery and accessories as well as in-house designs.

**Unique Vintage**
2013 W Magnolia Blvd.
Burbank CA 91506
Tel: 818 742 6210 (Burbank store); 800 721 6589 (online inquiries)
Website: www.unique-vintage.com
Vintage-inspired clothing. From 1920s flapper dresses to Mad Men-style wiggle dresses and 1960s

retro Mod go-go dresses.

**William Doyle Galleries**
175 East 87th Street
New York, NY 10128
Tel: 212 427 2730
Email: info@DoyleNewYork.com
Website: www.doylegalleries.com
Auctioneers and appraisers of haute couture and antique costume.

## Canada
**Deluxe Junk Company**
310 W Cordova Street
Vancouver, British Columbia V68 1E8
Tel: 604 685 4871
Email: dixjunk@telus.net
Website: www.deluxejunk.com
Vancouver's oldest vintage clothing store offers a great selection of vintage and contemporary clothing, accessories and costume jewellery.

**A note on buying black vintage**
When shopping for black garments, be cautious of different shades. Mixing blacks is very difficult because the actual hues can vary from blue to green to brownish-black. After a few washes, black cotton loses density of colour but you can re-dye it if you find a garment you love enough to restore. Pair like with like, so if you mix black garments, wear satin, silks and velvet together. Velvet can look good with cotton or denim, but beware of mixing black cotton fabrics.

A key part of this look is made up of long skirts and dresses, but extra care must be taken when shopping. Long clothes often get stepped on at the back and frequently lose their shape. Check among the folds for fading and staining. Contrary to popular belief, black is not an easy option for disguising dirt – in fact, it can show up every mark. In particular, study the armholes of black garments for discoloration. Due to its very nature, eveningwear doesn't always receive as many washes and can sometimes take on the previous owner's shape so badly, it can never be redeemed.

**Nearly-new, second-hand high fashion and designer retail**
Friends and family may have owned such pieces first time around, so ask if you can root through their wardrobes or hunt for garments in designer nearly new shops, a great source of designer names from recent decades. Very often the clothes haven't been worn all that much as they tend to be the "mistakes" of affluent, busy women who have shopped in a rush. If you live in a major city, such finds can be the result of a wardrobe clearout by your local fashionista so it's well worth tracking down the stores where canny designer darlings sell off their cast-offs.

# INDEX

Page numbers in **bold** refer to the main feature for each style icon. Page numbers in *italic* refer to illustration captions. Main design houses and their labels are indexed under the surname of the original designer.

Many thanks to the vintage collectors and traders of New York City who not only tolerated my BLT-ing (Bitching, Looking, Touching) but shared knowledge and inspiration. Special thanks to John Krawiec of Catwalk10021 for sharing his expertise on designer costume jewellery. Thanks also to Jacqueline Barnes, Luxor Tavella and Joanna Lombardi for conversations which proved to be important keys to enormous doors for me.

Extra Special Thanks to Lisa Dyer and the excellent team at Carlton Books.

**The publishers would like to thank the following sources for their kind permission to reproduce the pictures in this book.**

Key: t=Top, b=Bottom, c=Centre, l=Left and r=Right

**Aged and Opulent Jewelry:** /www.agedandopulentjewlry.com: 71b

**AKG Images:** /Album: 87t

**Baron Wolman Photography:** 134

**The Bridgeman Art Library:** /Private Collection: 132c

**© Carlton Books:** 36, 68, 106l, 107, 108, 116, 130, 139r, 181l, 181r, /Courtesy Gina Shoes: 102cl (Court Shoe with Cross Design), 102bl (Cream and gold court shoe), 182b

**Corbis:** /Bettmann: 4b, 20, 26, 54, 74, 76, 84, 113br, /CinemaPhoto: 65, 99r, /Condé Nast Archive: 9, 22, 32, 52-53, 61t, 61b, 77, 93, 94, 112, 115, 117, 118, 119b, 156tr, 157t, /Matt Dunham/Reuters: 13l, /Armando Gallo/Retna Ltd.: 7, /Gianni Dagli Orti: 15b, /Martyn Goddard: 150, /Stan Godlewski/Zuma Press: 83bl, /Lynn Goldsmith: 4cl, 138, 146, 153, /Rune Hellestad: 60b, 168, /Hulton-Deutsch Collection: 5cr, 17b, 25, 28, 90, 109, /LAN: 91br, /Scott McDermott: 41, /Genevieve Naylor: 40, /Norman Parkinson/Sygma: 4c (Bianca Jagger), 126, /Neil Preston: 167b, /Reuters: 92, /Steve Schapiro: 165, /Christian Simonpietri/Sygma: 120, /Sunset Boulevard: 4tr, 4c (Grace Kelly): 31, 44, 46, 57, 58, 86, 89, 111r, /Sigma: 83tr, /Underwood & Underwood: 55, /Pierre Vauthey/Sygma: 131, /Hoch Zwei/dpa: 179cb

**Salvatore Ferragamo Museum, Florence Italy, courtesy of:** 48tl, 48cl

**Getty:** 5t, 5cl, 29, 30t, 33r, 37l, 59t, 67l, 67r, 75t, 78r, 82, 98, 106r, 110l, 121br, 123, 124t, 125, 135b, 137, 141l, 142, 147b, 149t, 155r, 158, 160, 161t, 161b, 164bl, 178, /ABC: 21r, /AFP: 39t, 51l, 75b, /Bloomberg: 163, /FilmMagic: 156tl, 167t, /Gamma-Keystone: 33l, 85, /Gamma-Rapho: 121tr, /Hulton Archive: 19t, 38, 127l, /Lichfield: 171, /Michael Ochs Archives: 4cr, 127c, 140, /Redferns: 111l, 122, 141r, 145, 162, /Eugene Robert Richee/John

**Kobal Foundation:** 4tl, 12, /Time & Life Pictures: 27r, 78l, 127r, 129, 149b, /WireImage: 72, 79, 105cb, 121bl, 184

**Istockphoto.com:** /Adisa: 176t, /Aguirre_mar: 110r, /Arican: 164br, /Antagain: 157b, /Mark Fairey: 30b, /Alexandra Draghici: 132b, /Felinda: 87b, 119tr, /Floortje: 17t, /homydesign: 144br, /Inga Ivanova: 63cr, /Eduardo Jose Bernardino: 48bl, /Ulrich Knaupe: 63br, /Ian Loew: 170t, /Anna Lurye: 124br, /Milos Luzanin: 30c, /Heather McGrath: 2, 176br, /Erkki Makkonen: 151t, /penguenstok: 43, /Tomasz Pietryszek: 151b, /Sasha Radosavljevic: 144cb, /Nick Schlax: 139l, /Igor Terekhov: 119tl, /Sawayasu Tsuji: 124cb, /Camilla Wisbauer: 176bl

**The Jewelry Stylist:** /Courtesy of Melinda Lewis, The Jewelry Stylist/Photographic Editor Darrel Chua: 183

**Mary Evans Picture Library:** 16-17, 23, /Illustrated London News: 64, /Interfoto Agentur: 101tl, /National Magazines: 24, 62, /Adrian Woodhouse: 35

**Mirrorpix:** 91t, 169t,175

**Musée international de la chaussure:** /Christophe Villard: 102tl (Green Mary Jane shoe), 102cl (Black Mary Jane with multi-coloured toe detail), 102cl (Cream shoe with buckle detail), 132t, 164tr, 164cr

**Photoshot:** /LFI: 1, 166

**Picture Desk/The Kobal Collection:** /Focus Features/Bailey, Alex: 21l, /Paramount: 5b, 172, /Paramount/Fraker, Bud: 50

**Press Association Images:** /AP: 81, /PA Archive: 169b

**Rex Features:** 42, 71, 99l, 135t, 136, 154, 155l, /Action Press: 179bl, /AMC/Everett: 59b, /Ray Brigden/Associated Newspapers: 104, /Reginald Davis: 70, /Everett Collection: 6, 10, 27l, 45r, 80, 83br, 124bl, 174, 177, /David Fisher: 13r, 91bl, /Forum Press: 113tr, /John French/Daily Mail: 103, /GTV Archive: 66, /HBO/Everett: 17c, /Zdenko Hirschler: 2-3, /ITV: 27c, /Dezo Hoffmann: 105tr, /Nils Jorgensen: 38r, /Martin Karious: 105bl, /Shaan Kokin/Juliens Auctions: 47, /Henry Lamb/Photowire/BEI: 179tr, /Clifford Ling/Evening News: 156bl, /MCP: 143, /Ciaran McCrickard: 48r, /Ken McKay: 53r, /Neville Marriner/Daily Mail: 182t, /Roger-Viollet: 95, 96, /Carl Simmons: 49, /Sipa Press: 45l, 51r, 63t, 133, /SNAP: 18, 69, /Startraks Photo: 113bl, 173t, 173b, /Ray Stevenson: 147t

**Topfoto.co.uk:** /PA Photos: 34, /The Print Collector/HIP: 8

**Victoria & Albert Museum/V&A Images:** 101bl, 101r

Every effort has been made to acknowledge correctly and contact the source and/or copyright holder of each picture and Carlton Books Limited apologises for any unintentional errors or omissions, which will be corrected in future editions of this book.